Donald Campbell

A Narrative of the Extraordinary Adventures and Sufferings

By Shipwreck & Imprisonment, of Donald Campbell, esq., of Barbreck

Donald Campbell

A Narrative of the Extraordinary Adventures and Sufferings
By Shipwreck & Imprisonment, of Donald Campbell, esq., of Barbreck

ISBN/EAN: 9783744799638

Printed in Europe, USA, Canada, Australia, Japan

Cover: Foto ©Andreas Hilbeck / pixelio.de

More available books at **www.hansebooks.com**

NARRATIVE

OF THE

EXTRAORDINARY ADVENTURES,

AND

Sufferings by Shipwreck & Imprisonment,

OF

DONALD CAMPBELL, Esq.

OF BARBRECK:

WITH THE SINGULAR HUMOURS OF HIS TARTAR GUIDE,

Hassan Artaz;

COMPRISING

The Occurrences of Four Years and Five Days,

IN AN

OVERLAND JOURNEY

TO

INDIA.

IN A SERIES OF LETTERS TO HIS SON.

" What is this world ? Thy school, O misery !
" Our only lesson is, to learn to suffer ;
" And he who knows not that, was born for nothing."
           YOUNG.

SECOND AMERICAN EDITION.

NEW-YORK:
PRINTED FOR EVERT DUYCKINCK & CO.
No. 110, PEARL-STREET.
1798.

ADVERTISEMENT.

THE events related in the following pages, naturally became a frequent subject of conversation with my children and my friends. They felt so much satisfaction at the accounts which I gave them, that they repeatedly urged me to commit the whole to paper; and their affectionate partiality induced them to suppose, that the narrative would be, not only agreeable to them, but interesting to the public. In complying with their solicitations, I am far from being confident that the success of my efforts will justify their hopes: I trust, however, that too much will not be expected, in regard to literary composition, from a person whose life has been principally devoted to the duties of a soldier and the service of his country—and that a scrupulous adherence to truth will compensate for many blemishes in style and arrangement.

CONTENTS.

PART I.

LETTER I. Page 13.
Introductory.

LETTER II. Page 16.
Ridiculous Effects of Ignorance, exemplified in a whimsical Story of two Dublin Aldermen.

LETTER III. Page 21.
Author's Motives for going to India. Melancholy Presentiments. Caution against Superstition. Journey to Margate. Packet. Consoled by meeting General LOCKHART on board. Lands at Ostend.

LETTER IV. Page 24.
Short Account of the Netherlands. Conduct of the Belgians. Ostend described. Wonderful Effects of LIBERTY on the Human Mind, exemplified in the Defence of Ostend against the Spaniards.

LETTER V. Page 29.
Caution against using Houses of Entertainment on the Continent kept by Englishmen. Description of the Barques. Arrives at Bruges. Gross Act of despotism in the Emperor. Imprisonment of LA FAYETTE.

LETTER VI. Page 34.
Description of Bruges. Reflections on the Rise and Decay of Empires. Chief Grandeur of the Cities of Christendom, consisted in Buildings, the Works of Monkish Imposture and Sensuality. Superstition a powerful Engine.

LETTER VII. Page 39.
Opulence of the Bishop of Bruges. Cathedral. Church of Notre Dame. Vestments of THOMAS A BECKET. Extra-

A 2

CONTENTS.

ordinary Picture. Monastery of the Dunes. The Mortification of that Order. A curious Relic.

LETTER VIII. Page 45.
Passage to Ghent. Cheapness of Travelling. Description of Ghent. Cathedral. Monastery of St. Pierre. CHARITY of the Clergy.

LETTER IX. Page 51.
Description of two brazen Images, erected in Commemoration of an extraordinary Act of Filial Virtue. Journey from Ghent through Aloft to Bruffels.

LETTER X. Page 55.
General Review of Auftrian Flanders.

LETTER XI. Page 60.
Short description of Bruffels. Royal Library. Arsenal. Armour of Montezuma. The Enormities committed under the Pretext of Christianity, by far greater than thole committed by the French in the Frenzy of emancipation.

LETTER XII. Page 66.
Bruffels continued. Churches, Chapels, Toys, Images and Pictures. A Hoft, or Wafer, which was ftabbed by a Jew, and bled profufely. Inns excellent and cheap.

LETTER XIII. Page 71.
General Remarks on the people of the Netherlands. Account of the Emperor JOSEPH the Second. Anecdote of that Monarch His Inauguration at Bruffels. Burning of the Townhoufe. Contrafted conduct of the Belgians to JOSEPH on his Arrival, and after his Departure. The deteftable Effects of Ariftocracy.

LETTER XIV. Page 79.
Liege. Conftitution of the German Empire. Tolerant Difpofition of JOSEPH the Second, occafions a Vifit from His Holinefs the Pope, who returns to Rome in difappointment. Situation of the prefent Emperor. Reflections on the Conduct of Ruffia and Pruffia to Poland.

LETTER XV. Page 86.
Luxury of the Bifhop of Liege. Reflections on the Inconfiftency of the Profeffions and Practice of Churchmen, particularly the *Nolo Epifcopari,* which Bifhops fwear at their In-

CONTENTS. 7

ſtatement. Advantages of the ſtudy of the Law in all Countries. Liege, the Paradiſe of Prieſts. Sir JOHN MANDEVILL's Tomb.

LETTER XVI. Page 91.

Aix-la-Chapelle. A bit of Earth in a Golden Caſket. Conſecration of the Cathedral, by an Emperor, a Pope, and three hundred and ſixty-five Biſhops. Their valuable Preſents to that Church.

LETTER XVII. Page 96.

Juliers. Reflections on Religious Perſecution. Cologne. Church of St. Urſula. Bones of eleven thouſand Virgin Martyrs. Church of St. Gerion. Nine hundred Heads of Mooriſh Cavaliers. Reflections on the Eſtabliſhment of Clergy, and the Superiority of that of Scotland.

LETTER XVIII. Page 101.

Cologne continued. Strange Ambition of Families to be thought Deſcendants of the Romans. Story of Lord ANSON and a Greek Pilot. Bonne. Bridge of Cæſar. Coblentz. Mentz. Frankfort.

LETTER XIX. Page 106.

Frankfort deſcribed. Golden Bull. Augſburgh. Manufactory of Watch-Chains, &c. Happy State of Society ariſing from the tolerant Diſpoſition of the Inhabitants.

LETTER XX. Page 111.

Augſburgh continued. Adventure in the Convent of Carmelites. A good Friar.

LETTER XXI. Page 116.

Tyrol Country, Story of Genii leading the Emperor MAXIMILION aſtray. Innſpruck.

LETTER XXII. Page 121.

Tyroleſe. Innſpruck. Riches of the Franciſcan Church there. One Maſs in it ſufficient to deliver a Soul from Purgatory. Hall. Curioſities at the Royal Palace of Ombras. Briſen. Valley of Bolſano. Trent.

LETTER XXIII. Page 126.

Deſcription of the Biſhopric of Trent, Obvious Difference between Germany and Italy. Contraſt between the Characters of the Germans and Italians. Council of Trent. Tower for drowning adulterers. Baſſano. Venice.

LETTER XXIV. Page 131.
General Deſcription of Venice, and Reflections on the Venetians.

LETTER XXV. Page 137.
Concubinage more ſyſtematically countenanced in Venice than London. Trieſte. Loſs of ſervant and Interpreter, Sail for Alexandria. Zante.

LETTER XXVI. Page 143.
Adventure at the Iſland of Zante. Alexandria. The Plague, and an Incurſion of the Arabs. Pompey's Pillar, Cleopatra's Obeliſk, &c. Iſland of Cyprus, Latichea. Aleppo.

PART II.

LETTER XXVII. Page 156.
Deſcription of Aleppo.

LETTER XXVIII. Page 162.
Short Account of the Turkiſh Conſtitution and Government.

LETTER XXIX. Page 168.
Account of Turkiſh Conſtitution and Government continued, Moral Character of the Turks.

LETTER XXX. Page 174.
Prejudices of Chriſtian Writers, and their Miſrepreſentations of the Turkiſh Morals and Religion. Vindication of the latter.

LETTER XXXI. Page 180.
Vindication of the Turks continued. Deſcription of a Caravan. Account of Ceremonies uſed by Pilgrims at Mecca.

LETTER XXXII. Page 194.
Aleppo continued. Frequent Broils in the Streets.

CONTENTS.

LETTER XXXIII. Page 200.
Aleppo continued. Coffee-Houses. Story-tellers.

LETTER XXXIV. Page 206.
Aleppo continued. Puppet-shews. Rargahuze, or Punch, his Freedom of Speech and Satire.

LETTER XXXV. Page 213.
Disagreeable Adventure, which occasions a sudden Departure from Aleppo.

LETTER XXXVI. Page 220.
A plan of Travelling settled. Tartar Guide. Departure from Aleppo.

LETTER XXXVII. Page 227.
Description of Tartar Guide. His conduct. Arrival at Diarbeker. Padan Aram of Moses. Scripture Ground. Reflections. Description of the City of Diarbeker. Whimsical Incident occasioned by Laughing. Oddity of the Tartar.

LETTER XXXVIII. Page 233.
Strange Traits in the Tartar's Character. Buys Women, ties them up in Sacks, and carries them 50 miles. Reflections on the Slave Trade. Apostrophe to the Champion of the oppressed Africans.

LETTER XXXIX. Page 239.
Extravagant Conduct of the Tartar, which he afterwards explains satisfactorily. Extraordinary Incident and Address of the Tartar, in the Case of Santons.

LETTER XL. Page 245.
Explanation of the Affair by the Santons. Bigotry. Reflections.

LETTER XLI. Page 252.
Arrives at Mosul. Description thereof. A Story-teller. A Puppet-shew. The Tartar forced to yield to Laughter, which he so much condemned. Set out for Bagdad. Callenders—their artful Practises.

PART III.

LETTER XLII. Page 258.

Arrives at Bagdad. Whimfical Conduct of the Guide. Character of the Turks. Short Account of Bagdad. Effects of Opinion. Ruins of Babylon. Leaves Bagdad. Attacked by Rrobbers on the Tigris.

LETTER XLIII. Page 265.

Arrives at Baffora. Account of that City. Leaves, it, and arrives at Bufheer. More Difappointment. Bombay. Goa. Gloomy Prefentiments on leaving Goa. A ftorm.

LETTER XLIV. Page 271.
Shipwreck.

LETTER XLV. Page 278.
The fame.

LETTER, Page 283.

Made Prifoner by fome of HYDER ALLI's Troops. Humanity of a Lafcar. Hardfhips. Meets a Friend. Mr HALL.

LETTER XLVII. Page 288.

Mr. HALL's Mifery aggravated by the Lofs of a Miniature which hung at his Bofom. Sent under a guard up the Country.

LETTER XLVIII. Page 293.

Arrives at Hydernagur, the capital of the Province of Bidanore. Brought before the Jemadar. Committed to Prifon.

LETTER XLIX. Page 299.

Hiftory of HYAT SAHIB. Called upon to enter into the Service of HYDER, and offered a Command. Peremptorily refufes. Another Prifoner, a Native. Court of Juftice. Tortures and Exactions. Mr. HALL declining faft.

LETTER L. Page 307.
Mr. HALL's affecting Story.

CONTENTS.

LETTER, LI. Page 313.

Preſſed to enter into the Service of HYDER ALLI. Refuſal. Threatened, to be hanged. Actually ſuſpended, but let down again. Still perſiſts in a Refuſal, and determined to undergo any Death rather than enter. Projects a Plan to excite a Revolt, and eſcape.

LETTER LII. Page 319.

Projects to eſcape defeated. Laid in Irons. Intolerable Hardſhips. Death of Mr. HALL.

LETTER LIII. Page 324.

Melancholy Situation. Cruelty. Releaſed from Priſon. Account of HYDER, and the Eaſt India Politics in general.

LETTER LIV. Page 329.

Eaſt India Politics continued.

LETTER LV. Page 333.

Account of HYDER, and Indian Politics continued. General MATHEWS's Deſcent on the Malabar coaſt. Mounts the Ghauts. Approaches towards Hydernagur. Author's Delight at getting into the open Air. Delivered by an unexpected Encounter from his Guards.

LETTER LVI. Page 340.

Returns to the Fort, and propoſes to the Jemadar to give it up to the Engliſh. Proceeds to the Engliſh Camp.

LETTER LVII. Page 345.

Meeting with General MATHEWS. Returns to the Fort with a Cowl. Delivers it to the Jemadar. Leads General MATHEWS into the Fort, and brings him into the Preſence of the Jemadar. Engliſh Flag Hoiſted. Vindication of General MATHEWS from the Charge of Peculation.

LETTER LVIII. Page 351.

Sets off for Bengal. Cundapore. Unable to proceed. Letter from General MATHEWS. Proceeds in an open Boat for Anjengo. Stopped by Sickneſs at Mangalore. Tellicherry. Anjengo. Travancore. Dancing Girls. Palamcotah. Madura. Revolt of ISIF CAWN.

LETTER LIX. Page 357.

Trichinopoly. Tanjore. Burning of Gentoo Women with the Bodies of their Huſbands. Negapatnam.

CONTENTS.

LETTER LX. Page 369,

Leaves Negapatnam. Taken by a French Frigate, Horrible Reflections. SUFFREIN. Character of TIPPOO SAHIB. Escape. Arrives at Madras.

LETTER LXI. Page 378.

Passage to Bengal. Negociation for HYAT SAHIB. Mr. HASTINGS. Sir JOHN MACPHERSON. Hears from MACAULEY, Sir JOHN's Secretary, of the Servant I lost at Trieste. Jagranaut Pagoda. Vizagapatnam.

LETTER LXII. Page 383.

Masulipatam. Arrives at Madras. Determines to proceed on HYAT's Business to Bombay. Reaches Palamcotah. Takes sick. Recovering, crawls to Anjengo, and thence to Bombay. Resolves to return again to Madras.

LETTER LXIII. Page 397.

Adventures with a young Lady. Surat. China. Bath. Conclusion.

A JOURNEY TO INDIA, &c.

LETTER I.

My dear Frederick,

THE tenderness of a fond father's heart admonishes me, that I should but poorly requite the affectionate solicitude you have so often expressed, to become acquainted with the particulars of my journey over land to India, if I any longer with-held from you an account of that singular and eventful period of my life. I confess to you, my dear boy, that often when I have endeavoured to amuse you with the leading incidents and extraordinary vicissitudes of fortune which chequered the whole of that series of adventures, and observed the eager attention with which, young though you were, you listened to the recital, the tender sensibility you disclosed at some passages, and the earnest desire you expressed that "I should the whole relate," I have felt an almost irresistible impulse to indulge you with an accurate and faithful narrative, and have more than once sat down at my bureau for the purpose: but sober and deliberate reflection suggested that it was too soon, and that, by complying with your desire at such a very early period of your life, I should but render the great end I proposed by it abortive, fruſtrate the inſtruction which I meant to convey, and impreſs the mere incident on your memory, while the moral deducible from it muſt neceſſarily evaporate, and leave no trace, or rather excite no idea, in a mind not ſufficiently matured for the conception of abſtract principles, or prepared by practice for the deduction of moral inferences.

I am aware that there are many people, who, contemplating only the number of your days, would conſider my undertaking this arduous taſk, and offering it to your reflection, even now, premature: but this is a ſubject on which I have ſo long and ſo deliberately dwelt, which I have diſcuſſed with ſo much care, and examined with ſuch impartiality, that I think I may be acquitted of vanity, though I ſay I am competent to form a judgment on it. The reſult of that judgment is, that I am determined to indulge you without further delay; and I truſt that you will not, on your part, render it an empty indulgence, but, on the contrary, by turning every circumſtance to its beſt uſe, by converting every feeling which theſe pages may excite in your heart into matter of ſerious reflection, and by making every event (as it happens to deſerve) an example to promote either emulation on the one hand, or circumſpection and caution on the other, juſtify me in that opinion of you on which I found this determination.

I remember, that when, at an early age, I entered upon that ſtage of claſſical education at which you are now, at an earlier age, arrived—I mean the Æneid—I was not only captivated with the beautiful ſtory of the Hero, in the ſecond Book, but drew certain inferences from parts of it, which I ſhall never forget, and which afterwards ſerved to give a direction to the growth of my ſentiments on occaſions of a ſimilar nature: above all, the filial piety of Æneas made a deep impreſſion on my mind, and, by imperceptibly exciting emulation in my bosom, augmented considerably the natural warmth of my affection and respect for my father. It is under the recollection of this sensation, and a firm persuasion that your heart is fully as susceptible of every tender impression, and your understanding as fit for the reception of useful history, as mine was then, that I overlook your extreme youth, and write to you as though you were an adult. If there be a thing on earth of which I can boast a perfect knowledge, it is my FREDERICK's heart: it has been the object of my uninterrupted study almost since it was first capable of manifesting a sensation; and, if I am not very much mistaken in it indeed, the lively interest he feels in the occurrences of his father's life, is the result, not of idle curiosity, but unbounded filial affection. Such an amiable motive shall not be disappointed in its end; and while I discharge the duty of a parent in gratifying it, I shall be encouraged and sustained under my labours by the sanguine expectation, that he will derive from my exertions the most solid advantages in his future progress through life. As those advantages are expected also to extend to my dear boy JOHN, whose tender years disqualify him from making the same immediate reflections on the various subjects as they occur, my FREDERICK will perceive that it becomes his duty, not only as a good son, but as an affectionate brother, to assist and enforce them upon his mind, to explain to him the difficulties, and furnish him with his reasonings and inferences on them, so as that they may make, as nearly as possible, equal impressions on the heart and understanding of both.

"Felix quem faciunt aliena pericula cautum:"

And though few have the felicity to be warned by other men's misfortunes or faults, because they seldom make deep impressions on their feelings, I am convinced that my sufferings and errors, as they will interest my FREDERICK's heart, and gratify his curiosity, cannot fail to enlarge his understanding, and improve his conduct.

I am my dear FREDERICK, &c.

D. C.

LETTER II.

HAVING, in compliance with your reiterated solicitations, determined to give you a narrative of my journey to the East Indies, and the singular turns of fortune which befel me there, I think it necessary, on reflection, to prepare you still further for the reception of it, by proposing certain terms to be fulfilled on your part; and as, in my last, I told you that I expected you, and, with your assistance, your brother, to turn my relation to a more useful account than the gratification of mere idle curiosity, by letting the moral deducible from my errors and misfortunes strike deep and take root in your mind—so there are other things, which, though not so extremely important, are too weighty to be neglected; to which I desire to direct your attention.

I believe you must have already perceived, that the well-being of yourself and your brother is my first—I might, perhaps, without trespassing much upon truth, say, my only object in life; that, to the care of your education, and the cultivation of your mind, I exclusively devote my time and my thoughts; and that, to insure your future happiness, I would sacrifice every thing I have a right to dispose of, and risk even life itself. The time, I trust, is not far distant, when your brother will be as well qualified to understand this as you are now—when both will feel alike the important duty it enforces on you—and when your only emulation will be, who shall produce the most luxuriant harvest to reward the labours I have taken—to reward yourselves.

In order, therefore, on my part, to give every thing I do a tendency to the great object of my wishes, and induce you, on your's, to contribute your share to it, I shall give you, as I proceed in my narrative, a topographical description of the various Countries through which I shall have occasion to conduct you, and, as concisely as may be, an account of their manners, policy, and municipal institutions, so far as I have been able to collect them; which I hope will serve to awaken in you a thirst for those indispensible parts of polite education, Geography and History. I expect that you will carefully attend to those sciences, and that you will not suffer yourself, as you read my Letters, to be carried away by the rapid stream of idle curiosity from incident to incident, without time or disposition for reflection: you must take excursions, as you go along, from my Letters to your Geographical Grammar and your Maps—and, when necessary, call in the aid of your Tutor, in order to compare my observations with those of others on the same places, and by those means to acquire as determinate an idea as possible of their local situation, laws, and comparative advantages, whether of Nature or Art. You will thus enable yourself hereafter to consider how society is influenced, and why some communities are better directed than others.

Here I must observe to you, that as geography is a science to which rational conversation, as supported by gentlemen of breeding and education, most frequently refers, the least ignorance of it is continually liable to detection, and, when detected, subjects a man to the most mortifying ridicule and contempt.

The ingenious GEORGE ALEXANDER STEEVENS has, in his celebrated Lecture upon Heads, given a most ludicrous instance of this species of ignorance, in the character of a citizen, who, censuring the incapacity of ministers, proposes to carry on the war on a new plan of his own. The plan is, to put the troops in cork jackets—send them, thus equipped, to sea—and *land them in the Mediterranean ;* When his companion asks him where that place lies, he calls him *fool*, and informs him that the Mediterranean is the capital of Constantinople. Thus, my dear son, has this satirist ridiculed ignorance in pretenders to education ; and thus will every one be ridiculous who betrays a deficiency in this very indispensable ingredient in forming the character of a gentleman. But a story which I heard from a person of strict veracity, will serve more strongly to shew you the shame attendant on ignorance of those things which, from our rank, we are supposed to know ; and as the fear of shame never fails to operate powerfully on a generous mind, I am sure it will serve to alarm you into industry, and application to your studies.

During the late American war, about that period when the KING of FRANCE was, so fatally for himself, though perhaps in the end it may prove fortunate for the interests of mankind, manifesting an intention to interfere and join the Americans, a worthy alderman in Dublin, reading the newspaper, observed a paragraph, intimating, that in consequence of British cruisers having stopped some French vessels at sea, and searched them, France had taken *umbrage !* The sagacious alderman, more

EFFECTS OF IGNORANCE.

patriotic than learned, took the alarm, and proceeded, with the paper in his hand, directly to a brother of the board, and, with unfeigned sorrow, deplored the loss his country had sustained, in having a place of such consequence as UMBRAGE ravished from it!—desiring, of all things, to be informed in what part of the world *Umbrage* lay. To this the other, after a torrent of invective against ministers, and condolence with his afflicted friend, answered that he was utterly unable to tell him, but that he had often heard it mentioned, and of course conceived it to a place of great importance; at the same time proposing that they should go to a neighbouring bookseller, who, as he dealt in books, must necessarily know every thing, in order to have this gordian knot untied. They accordingly went; and having propounded the question, "what part of the globe *Umbrage* lay in?" the bookseller took a Gazetteer, and, having searched it diligently, declared that he could not find it, and said he was almost sure there was no such place in existence. To this the two aldermen, with a contemptuous sneer, answered by triumphantly reading the paragraph out of the newspaper. The bookseller, who was a shrewd fellow, and, like most of his countrymen, delighted in a jest, gravely replied, that the Gazetteer being an old edition, he could not answer for it, but that he supposed *Umbrage* lay somewhere on the coast of America. With this the wise magistrates returned home, partly satisfied: but what words can express their chagrin when they found their error—that the unlucky bookseller had spread the story over the city—that the newspapers were filled with satirical squibs upon it—nay, that a caracature print of themselves leading the city-watch to the *retaking of Umbrage*, was stuck up in every shop—and finally, that they could scarcely (albeit aldermen) walk the streets, without having the populace sneer at them about the *taking of Umbrage!*

Thus, my child, will every one be more or less ridiculous who appears obviously ignorant of those things which, from the rank he holds in life, he should be expected to know, or to the knowledge of which vanity or petulence may tempt him to pretend.

I am sure I need not say more to you on this subject; for I think you love me too well to disappoint me in the first wish of my heart, and I believe you have too much manly pride to suffer so degrading a defect as indolence to expose you hereafter to animadversion or contempt. Remember, that as nothing in this life, however trivial or worthless, is to be procured without labour—so, above all others, the weighty and invaluable treasures of erudition are only to be acquired by exertions vigorously made and unremittingly continued.

" Quid munus reipublicæ majus aut melius afferre
" possumus quam si juventutem bene erudiamus."—
Thus saith the matchless TULLY. If, then, the education of youth interests so very deeply a state, can it less powerfully interest him who stands in the twofold connection of a citizen and parent? It is the lively anxiety of my mind, on this point, that obliges me to procrastinate the commencement of my narrative to another letter, and induces me to entreat that you will, in the mean time, give this the consideration it deserves, and prepare your mind to follow its instructions.

LETTER III.

A VARIETY of unpropicious circumstances gave rise to my journey to the East Indies, while domestic calamity marked my departure, and, at the very outset, gave me a foretaste of those miseries which fate had reserved to let fall upon me in the sequel. The channels from which I drew the means of supporting my family in that style which their rank and connections obliged them to maintain, were clogged by a coincidence of events as unlucky as unexpected: the war in India had interrupted the regular remittance of my property from thence: a severe shock which unbounded generosity and beneficence had given to the affairs of my father, rendered him incapable of maintaining his usual punctuality in the payment of the income he had assigned me; and, to crown the whole, I had been deprived, by death, of two lovely children (your brother and sister), whom I loved not less than I have since loved you and your brother.

It was under the pressure of those accumulated afflictions, aggravated by the goading thought of leaving my family for such a length of time as must necessarily elapse before I could again see them, that I set out for India in the month of May, in the year 1781, with a heart overwhelmed with woe, and too surely predictive of misfortunes.

From the gloomy cave of depression in which my mind was sunk, I looked forward, to seek, in the future, a gleam of comfort—but in vain: not a ray appeared—Melancholy had thrown her sombre shadow on the whole. Even present affliction yielded up a share of my heart to an unaccountable dismal presentiment of future ill; and the disasters and disappointments I had passed, were lost and forgotten in ominous forebodings and instinctive presages of those that were to come.

Of all the weaknesses to which the human mind is subject, superstition is that against which I would have you guard with the utmost vigilance. It is the most incurable canker of the mind. Under its unrelenting dominion, happiness withers, the understanding becomes obscured, and every principle of joy is blasted. For this reason I wish to account for those presages, by referring them to their true physical causes, in order thereby to prevent your young mind from receiving, from what I have written, any injurious impression, or superstitious idea of *presentiment*, as it is fashionably denominated.

If the mind of man be examined, it will be found naturally prone to the contemplation of the future—its flights from hope to hope, or fear to fear, leading it insensibly from objects present and in possession, to those remote and in expectation—from positive good to suppositious better, or from actual melancholy to imaginary misfortune. In these cases, the mind never fails to see the prospect in colours derived from the medium through which it is viewed and exaggerated by the magnifying power of fancy. Thus my mind, labouring under all the uneasiness I have described, saw every thing through the gloomy medium of melancholy, and, looking forward, foreboded nothing but misfortune: accident afterwards fulfilled those forebodings; but accident, nay, the most trifling change of circumstances, might possibly have so totally changed the face of my subsequent progress, that good fortune, instead of misadventure, might have been my lot,

MOTIVES FOR THE JOURNEY. 23

and so all my forebodings been as illusory and fallible as all such phantoms of the imagination really are. Thus I argue now—and I am sure I argue truly; but if reason be not timely called in, and made, as it were, an habitual inmate, it avails but little against the overbearing force of superstition, who, when she once gets possession of the mind, holds her seat with unrelenting tenacity, and, calling in a whole host of horrors, with despair at their head, to her aid, entrenches herself behind their formidable powers, and bids defiance to the assaults of reason.

Thus it fared with me—Under the dominion of a gloomy presentiment, I left London; and my journey down to Margate, where I was to take shipping, was, as SHAKSPEARE emphatically says, "a phantasm, or a hideous dream—and my little "state of man suffered, as it were, the nature of "an insurrection:"—the chaos within me forbade even the approach of discriminate reflection; and I found myself on board the packet, bound to Ostend, without having a single trace left upon my mind, of the intermediate stages and incidents that happened since I had left London.

It has been observed—and I wish you always to carry it in memory, as one of the best consolations, under affliction—that human sufferings, like all other things, find their vital principle exhausted, and their extinction accelerated, by overgrowth; and that, at the moment when man thinks himself most miserable, a benignant Providence is preparing relief, in some form or other, for him. So it, in some sort, happened with me; for I was fortunate enough to find in the packet a fellow-passenger, whose valuable conversation and agreeable manners beguiled me insensibly of the gloomy contemplation in which I was absorbed, and afforded my tortured mind a temporary suspension of pain. This gentleman was General LOCKHART: he was going to Bruſſels, to pay his court to the Emperor JOSEPH the Second, who was then ſhortly expected in the Low Countries, in order to go through the ceremonies of his inauguration. As Bruſſels lay in my way, I was flattered with the hopes of having for a companion a gentleman at once ſo pleaſing in his manners and reſpectable in his character, and was much comforted when I found him as much diſpoſed as myſelf to an agreement to travel the whole of the way thither together. Thus, though far, very far from a ſtate of eaſe, I was, when landing at Oſtend, at leaſt leſs miſerable than at my coming on board the packet.

As this letter is already ſpun to a length too great to admit of any material part of the deſcription I am now to give you of Oſtend, and the country to which it belongs, I think it better to poſtpone it, to my next, which I mean to devote entirely to that ſubject, and thereby avoid the confuſion that ariſes from mixing two ſubjects in the ſame letter, or breaking off the thread of one in order to make way for the other.

Adieu, my dear boy!—Forget not your brother JOHN. That you may both be good and happy, is all the wiſh now left to, &c.

LETTER IV.

THAT country to which I am now to call your attention—I mean, the Netherlands—is marked by a greater number of political changes, and haraſſed by a more continued train of military operations, than perhaps any country in the records of modern history. It may truly be called the Cockpit Royal of Europe, on which tyrants, as ambition, avarice, pride, caprice, or malignity, prompted them, pitted thousands, and hundreds of thousands, of their fellow-creatures, to cut each other's throats about some point frivolous as regarding themselves, unimportant to mankind, and only tending to gratify a diabolical lust for dominion; Yet, under all these disadvantages, (such are the natural qualities of this country), it has, till lately, been in a tolerably flourishing state; and would, under a good government and proper protection, equal any part of Europe for richness.

Flanders, Brabant, and the country now called the United Netherlands, were in general known by the name of Netherlands, Low Countries, or Pais-bas, from their situation, as it is supposed, in respect of Germany. Anciently, they formed a part of Belgic Gaul, of which you may remember to have read an account in the Commentaries of JULIUS CÆSAR, who describes the inhabitants as the most valiant of all the Gallic Nations—"Horum "omnium Belgæ sunt fortissmi." They afterwards were subject to petty princes, and made part of the German Empire; and, in the sixteenth century, became subject to CHARLES the Fifth of the House of Austria; but, being oppressed beyond endurance by his son, PHILIP the Second of Spain, (that blind and furious bigot), they openly revolted —flew to arms to assert their freedom; and, after a struggle as glorious in effect as virtuous in principle—after performing prodigies of valour, and exhibiting examples of fortitude, to which none but men fighting in the godlike cause of LIBERTY are competent—led on by the wisdom and valour of the PRINCE of ORANGE, and assisted by the SOVEREIGN of GREAT BRITAIN—they at length so

C

far succeeded, that those now called the United Netherlands, entered into a solemn league, and forced the gloomy tyrant to acknowledge their independence. But that part to which I am now particularly to allude, continued annexed to the House of Austria. In 1787, they revolted, and made a temporary struggle to disengage themselves from the dominion of the Emperor; but, owing to some cabals among themselves, and the temperate conduct of that prince, they again returned to their allegiance, and were rewarded with a general amnesty. In 1792, they were over-run by the French army under General Dumourier—opened their arms to those republicans, and were rewarded for it by oppression, tyranny, and injustice. The French, however, were driven back out of the country; and, wonderful to relate, they again received their old master, the Emperor, with strong demonstrations of joy; and manifested their loyalty and attachment to him by every expression that abject hypocrisy could suggest.

"O! how unlike their Belgic sires of old!"

Here, could I stop with strict justice, I would— But, behold! the French again came; again they opened their gates to receive them; and again they were, with tenfold fury and rapacity, pillaged, oppressed and insulted; and at the very time I am writing this, the guillotine is doing its office—enforcing the payment of the most exorbitant and enormous contributions, and compelling, it is said, one hundred thousand of the ill-fated inhabitants to take the field, as soldiers of the republic.

Human opinion is so chequered and uncertain, that two very honest men may, in certain cases act in direct contradiction and hostility to each other, with the very best intentions—He, therefore, must have but a cold heart, and a contracted understand-

ing, who cannot forgive the man that acts in such
cases erroneously, when he acts from the exact dictates of his opinion, and upon the principle which
he has conscientiously adopted: but when a whole
people are seen whisking about with every gust of
fortune, and making a new principle for every new
point of convenience, we must despise them even
when they happen to act right, and can scarcely afford them so much as pity in their calamities. The
Austrian Netherlands are now in that state; and,
without presuming to say in which of their tergiversations they were right, I will venture to pronounce
that they deserve punishment, and I believe they
are in hands very likely to give them their due.

To return—Ostend is a sea-port of Austrian
Flanders, and is situated in the Liberty of Bruges.
It was, at one time, the strongest town in Flanders; but a double ditch and ramparts, which constituted its strength, are now destroyed; and in
the place where the former stood, docks, or rather
basons, extremely capacious and commodious, are
formed, for the reception of shipping. The ground
about the town is very low and marshy, and cut into
a number of fine canals—into some of which, ships
of the largest size may enter—and in one of which,
vessels of great burthen may ride, even close to
Bruges. The harbour here is so fortunately circumstanced, that it was once thought, by engineers,
entirely secure from a blockade; and its pristine
strength can in no way be so well described, as by
a relation of the defence it made in the four first
years of the seventeenth century—though, near the
close of the sixteenth, it was no better than an insignificant fishing town. It held out against the
Spaniards for three years, two months, and sixteen
days. Eighty thousand men lost their lives before
it, while fifty thousand were killed or died within.
It at last surrendered, but on good terms; and not

for want of men or provisions, but for want of ground to stand on, which the enemy took from them, at an amazing loss, step by step, till they had not room left for men to defend it. Three hundred thousand cannon-balls, of thirty pounds weight each, were fired against it; and the besieged often filled up the breaches made in their ramparts with heaps of dead bodies.

Such, my dear boy, are the miracles that men, animated with the all-subduing spirit of Liberty, can perform—Liberty! that immediate jewel of the soul—that first moving principle of all the animal creation—which, with equal power, influences the bird to beat the cage with its wings, and the lion to tear the bars of his imprisonment—the infant to spring from the tender confinement of its nurse, and the lean and shrivelled pantaloon, to crawl abroad, and fly the warmth and repose of his wholesome chamber—Liberty! which, for centuries enthralled by artifice and fraud, or lulled into a slumber by the witching spirit of priestcraft, now rises like a giant refreshed with wine—in its great efforts for emancipation, destroys and overturns systems—but, when finding no resistance, and matured by time, will, I sincerely hope, sink appeased into a generous calm, and become the blessing, the guardian and protector of mankind!

It is your good fortune, my dear children, to be born at a time when Liberty seems to be well understood in your own country, and is universally the prevalent passion of men. It is almost needless, therefore, for me to exhort you to make it the groundwork of your political morality: but let me remind you to guard, above all, against the despotism of certain tyrants, to whom many of the greatest advocates for liberty are strangely apt to submit.—I mean, your passions. Of all other tyrants, they are the most subtle, the most bewitching, the most overbearing, and, what is worse, the most cruel. Beneath the dominion of other despots, tranquility may alleviate the weight of your chains, and soften oppression; but when once you become the slave of your passions, your peace is for ever fled, and you live and die in unabating misery.

LETTER V.

THE pride of the English is remarked all over the globe, even to a proverb! But pride is a word of such dubious meaning, so undefined in its sense, and strained to such various imports, that you shall hear it violently execrated by one, and warmly applauded by another—this denouncing it as a sin of the first magnitude, and that maintaining it to be the most vigilant guardian of human virtue. Those differences in opinion arise not from any defect in the intellects of either, but from each viewing the subject in that one point in which it first strikes his eye, or best suits his taste, his feeling, or his prejudices. I have no doubt, however, but a full consideration of the subject would shew, that pride, as it is called, is only good or bad as the object from which it arises is mean or magnificent, culpable or meritorious. That noble pride which stimulates to extraordinary acts of generosity and magnanimity, such as, in many instances, has distinguished, above all others, the nobility of Spain, exacts the homage and admiration of mankind; But I fear very much that our English pride is of another growth, and smells too rankly of that overstrained commercial spirit which makes the basis of the present grandeur of Great Britain, but which, in my humble judgment, raises only to debase her

—by slow, subtle degrees, poisons the national principle, enslaves the once bold spirit of the people, detracts from their real solid felicity, and, by confounding the idea of national wealth with that of national prosperity, leads it in rapid strides to its downfall. In short, we are approaching, I fear, with daily accelerated steps, to the disposition and sordid habits of the Dutch, of whom Doctor GOLDSMITH so very pertinently and truly speaks, when he says,

" Ev'n Liberty itself is barter'd here !"

Without leading your mind through a maze of disquisition, on this subject, which might fatigue with abstruseness and prolixity, I will bring you back to the point from which the matter started, and content myself with remarking, that the pride of the English, speaking of it as a part of the national character, is the meanest of all pride. The inflation of bloated, overgrown wealth, an overweening affection for money, an idolatrous worship of gain, have absolutely confounded the general intellect, and warped the judgment of the many to that excess, that, in estimating men or things, they always refer to " what is he worth ?" or, " what will it fetch ?" This sordid habit of thinking was finely hit off by a keen fellow, the native of a neighbouring kingdom, who, for many years, carried on business in London, and failed :—Sitting one day in a coffee-house in the city, where some wealthy citizens were discussing a subject not entirely unconnected with cash concerns, one of them observing him rather attentive to their conversation, turned to him, and said, " What is your opinion, Sir, of the matter ?"—" 's blood, Sir !" returned he, peevishly, " what opinion can a man have in this country, who has not a guinea in his pocket ?"

Under the influence of all the various caprices inspired by this unhappy purse-pride, I am sorry to say our countrymen do, when they go abroad, so play the fool, that they are universally flattered and despised, pillaged and laughed at, by all persons with whom they have any dealing. In France, Mi Lor Anglois is, or at least was, to have six times as great a profusion of every thing as any other person, and pay three hundred per cent* more for it; and the worst of it was, that a Mi Lor was found so conducive to their interest, that they would not, if they could help it, suffer any Englishman to go without a title—nay, would sometimes, with kindly compulsion, force him to accept of it, whether he would or not: but if an Englishman be, above all others, the object of imposition in foreign countries, certainly none pillage him so unmercifully as his own countrymen who are settled there. In all the places through which I have travelled, I have had occasion to remark (and the remark has been amply verified by every gentleman I have ever conversed with on the subject), and the most extravagant houses of entertainment are those kept by Englishmen. At Ostend, as well as other places, it was so; therefore, as economy, when it does not trespass upon the bounds of genteel liberality, is the best security for happiness and respect, I advise you, whenever you shall have occasion to visit the Continent, in the first place to avoid all appearance of the purse-proud ostentation of John Bull; and, in the next place, to avoid all English houses of entertainment.

It is a singular circumstance, and belongs, I should suppose, peculiarly to Ostend, that the charity-children of the town are permitted to come on board the vessels arrived, to beg of the passengers, one day in the week.

Before I bid adieu to Oftend, I muft remark one heavy difadvantage under which it labours—the want of fresh water; all they use being brought from Bruges. In going from Oftend to Bruges, a traveller has it in his choice to go by land, or water —If by land, he gets a good voiture for about ten shillings of our money; the road is about fourteen or fifteen miles—If by water (the mode which I adopted, as by far the cheapeft and pleafanteft), he travels in a veffel pretty much refembling our Lord Mayor's barge, fometimes called a trackfchuyt, but often la barque, or barke: it is, in truth, fitted up in a ftyle of great neatnefs, if not elegance; ftored with a large ftock of provifions and refrefhments of all kinds, and of fuperior quality, for the accommodation of the paffengers; and has, particularly, a very handfome private room between decks, for the company to retire to, in order to drink tea, coffee, &c. &c. or play at cards. In this comfortable, I might fay, delightful vehicle, as perfectly at eafe as lying on a couch in the beft room in London, are paffengers drawn by two horfes, at the rate of about four miles an hour, for about ten pence, the fame length of way that it would coft ten shillings to be jumbled in a voiture over a rough paved road.

The country between Oftend and Bruges is very level, and of courfe deftitute of thofe charms to a mind of tafte, which abound in countries toffed by the hand of Nature into hill, dale, mountain, and valley: the whole face of it, however, is, or at leaft then was, in fo high a ftate of cultivation, and fo deeply enriched by the hands of art and induftry, aided by the natural fertility of the foil, that its appearance, though far from ftriking or delightful, was by no means unpleafant; and on approaching the town of Bruges, we paffed between two rows of trees, beautiful, fhady, and of lofty fize—forming, with the surrounding objects, a scene, which, if not romantic, was at least picturesque.

In passing through countries groaning beneath the despotic scourge of unlimited monarchy, where subsidies are raised, and taxes laid on *ad libitum*— where guilty distrust and suspicion, with the eyes of a lynx and the fangs of a harpy, stand sentinels at every gate, to scrutinize the harmless passenger, awake him to the clanks of his fetters, and awe him into compliance, a free-born Briton feels a cold horror creep through his whole frame : his soul recoils at the gloomy ferocious and insolently strict examination, with which a centinel, at the entry of a town, stops, investigates, demands a passport ; and, in short, puts him, *pro tempore*, in a state of durance, with all its hideous formalities and appendages, its gates, its bars, its armed ruffians, its formal professions of laws, and its utter violation of reason and of justice. Entering the town of Bruges, we were stopped by a centinel, who, with all the saucy, swaggering air of authority, of a slave in office, demanded to know, whether we had any contraband goods ? whether we were in any military capacity ? whence we came ? and whither we were going ? with a variety of other interrogatories, to my mind equally impertinent and detestable, but which seemed to make no greater impression on the good Flemings themselves, than demanding the toll at a turnpike-gate would make on an English waggoner.

Talking over this subject, since that time, with a gentleman who is well acquainted with all those places, he informed me, that in the war between the Emperor and the States General, some French officers, travelling through Flanders to join Count MAILLEBOIS, were stopped at the gate of Bruges, and, by order of the Emperor, sent to his army, turned into the ranks, and obliged to do duty as common soldiers.—Here, my dear FREDERICK, was an act, not only despotic in itself, but aggravated by circumstances of collateral profligacy, of such enormous magnitude, as bids defiance to all power of amplification, and leave eloquence hopeless of describing it with greater force than it derives from a simple narration of the fact: on the one hand, the inroad upon the just personal rights of the individual; on the other, the rights of a nation violated. Some men in England, judging from their own constitutional security, may disbelieve the fact: but let them consider, that the Marquis de la FAYETTE, an alien, taken upon neutral ground, is now, even now, held in illegal, unjust thraldom and persecution—let them, I say, remember this, and let their incredulity cease.

Bless your stars, my dear boy, that you were born in a country where such outrages as these can never be perpetrated by any, and will never be approved of *but by a few*.

LETTER VI.

IN my last, I carried you past a ferocious, impertinent sentinel, into the town of Bruges; and now, having got you there, I must endeavour, from the loose materials I have been able to collect, to give you a short description of it.

I had heard much of Bruges, its grandeur, and its opulence; you will guess my surprise then, when, on entering it, I found nothing but an old-fashioned, ill-built, irregular town; the streets, in general, narrow and dirty, and most of the houses strongly expressive of poverty and squalid wretchedness: yet this was anciently a most flourishing city. Did the difference between the town at this time, and its state as it is represented of old, consist only in its external appearance, we might readily account for that, in the great improvements made by the moderns in the art of house-building; but its present inferiority goes deeper, and is the result of departed commerce—commerce, that fluctuating will-with-a-wisp, that leads states in hot pursuit after it, to entrap them ultimately into mires and precipices, and which, when caught, stays till it extinguishes the spirit of freedom in a nation, refines its people into feeble slaves, and there leaves them to poverty and contempt.

Perhaps there is no subject that affords an ampler field for a speculative mind to expatiate upon, than the various, and, I may say, incongruous revolutions which have chequered the progress of human society from the first records of history down to the present time. It is indeed a speculation which not only tends to improve the understanding, by calling in experience to correct the illusions of theory, but is highly instructive in a moral point of view, by pointing out the instability of the very best structures of human wisdom, and teaching us how little reliance is to be placed upon human casualties, or earthly contingencies. Look to Greece, once the fountain-head of arts, eloquence, and learning, and the mother of freedom—her poets, her legislators, her soldiers, and her patriots, even to this day considered the brightest examples of earthly glory!—see her now sunk in slavery, ignorance, sloth, and imbecility, below any petty nation of Europe. Look to Rome—in her turn, the queen of arms and arts, the land of liberty, the nurse of heroes—the stage on which inflexible patriots, accomplished philosophers, and a free people, acted for centuries a drama that elevated man almost above his nature!---fee her now reduced to the laſt ſtage of contemptibility---even below it, to ridicule and laughter---ſwayed by the moſt contemptible impoſture, and ſunk into the moſt deſpicable enſlavement, both of perſon and opinion---the offices of her glorious ſenate performed by a kind of heteroclite being, an hermaphroditical impoſture, who, deducing his right from the very dregs and offſcourings of ſuperſtition and fanaticiſm, and aided by a ſet of diſciples worthy of ſuch a maſter, rules the people, not with the terrors of the Tarpeian rock, nor yet with that which to a Roman boſom was more terrible, baniſhment---but with the horrors of *eternal damnation!*---ſee her valiant, vigorous ſoldiery converted into a band of feeble fidlers and muſic-maſters, and the clangor of her arms into ſhrill concerts of ſqueaking caſtratoes; thoſe places where her CICERO poured forth eloquence divine, and pointed out the paths that led to true morality---where her BRUTUS and her CATO marſhalled the forces of freedom, and raiſed the arm of juſtice againſt tyrants, over-run by a knaviſh hoſt of ignorant, beggarly, bald-pated friars, vomiting, to a crowd of gaping bigots, torrents of fanatical bombaſt, of miracles never performed, of gods made of wood or copper, and of ſaints, that, like themſelves, lived by impoſture and deception!----ſee her triumphs and military trophies changed into proceſſions of prieſts ſinging pſalms round wafers and wooden crucifixes; and the code of Philoſophy and religion, which operated ſo effectually upon the morals of her people that there was none among them found ſo deſperate or ſo baſe as to break an oath, exchanged for the Roman Catholic branch of the Chriſtian Faith----for diſpenſations for inceſt, indulgences for murder, fines for fornication, and an excluſive patent for adultery in their prieſthood. Then look to England!---ſee her, who once stooped beneath the yoke of Rome, whose chief, CARACTACUS, was carried there in chains to grace his conqueror's triumphs, while herself was made the meanest of the Roman provinces, now holding the balance of the world, the unrivalled mistress of arms, arts, commerce—every thing.

It was in this irresistible mutation of things, that Bruges sunk from the high state of a most flourishing city, where there are still (unless the French have destroyed them) to be seen the remains of seventeen palaces, anciently the residences of consuls of different nations, each of which had distinct houses, magnificently built and furnished, with warehouses for their merchandises: and such was the power and wealth of the citizens in those days, that it is an indubitable fact, they kept their sovereign, the Archduke MAXIMILIAN, prisoner, affronted his servants, and abused his officers; nor would they release him until he took an oath to preserve inviolate the laws of the state. Even so late as the time I was there, Bruges had some trade —indeed as good a foreign trade as most cities in Flanders. The people seemed cheerful and happy, and the markets were tolerably supplied.

Several fine canals run in a variety of directions from Bruges: by one of them, boats can go, in the course of a summer's day, to Ostend, Nieuport, Furnes, and Dunkirk; and vessels of four hundred tuns can float in the bason of this town. Another canal leads to Ghent, another to Damme, and another to Sluys. The water of those canals is stagnant, without the least motion; yet they can, in half an hour, be all emptied, and fresh water brought in, by means of their well-contrived sluices. This water, however, is never used for drinking, or even for culinary purposes; a better sort being conveyed through the town by pipes from the

D

two rivers Lys and Scheldt, as in London; for which, as there, every house pays a certain tax.

Although the trade of this city has, like that of all the Low Countries, been gradually declining, and daily sucked into the vortices of British and Dutch commerce, there were, till the French entered it, many rich merchants there, who met every day at noon in the great market-place, to communicate and transact business, which was chiefly done in the Flemish language, hardly any one in it speaking French; a circumstance that by this time, is much altered—for they have been already made, if not to speak French, at least to sing *Ca-ira*, and dance to the tune of it too, to some purpose.

The once-famed grandeur of this city consisted chiefly, like that of all grand places in the dark periods of Popery, of the gloomy piles, the ostentatious frippery, and unwieldy masses of wealth, accumulated by a long series of monkish imposture—of Gothic structures, of enormous size and sable aspect, filled with dreary cells, calculated to strike the souls of the ignorant and enthusiastic with holy horror, to inspire awe of the places, and veneration for the persons who dared to inhabit them, and, by enfeebling the reason with the mixed operations of horror, wonder, and reverence, to fit the credulous for the reception of every imposition, however gross in conception, or bungled in execution. Those are the things which constituted the greatness and splendor of the cities of ancient Christendom; to those has the sturdiest human vigour and intellect been forced to bend the knees: they were built to endure the outrages of time; and will stand, I am sure, long, long after their power shall have been annihilated.

What a powerful engine has superstition been, in the cunning management of priests! How lamentable it is to think, that not only all who believed,

but all who had good fenfe enough not to believe
fhould, for fo many centuries, have been kept in
proftrate fubmiffion to the will and dominion of an
old man in Rome!—My blufhes for the folly and
fupineneſs of mankind, however, are loft in a warm
glow of tranfport at the prefent irradiation of the
human mind; and though I can fcarcely think with
patience of that glorious, godlike being, HENRY
the Second of England, being obliged by the Pope
to lafh himfelf naked at the tomb of that faucy,
wicked prieft, THOMAS A BECKET, I felicitate
myfelf with the reflection, that the Pope is now
the moſt contemptible fovereign in Europe, and
that the Papal authority, which was once the terror and the fcourge of the earth, is now not only
not recognifed, but feldom thought of, and, when
thought of, only ferves to excite laughter or
difguft.

LETTER VII.

THE town of Bruges, although the
ftreets be, as I have already defcribed them, fo
mean, narrow, dirty, and irregular in general, contains, neverthelefs, fome few ftreets that are tolerable, and a few fquares alfo that are far from contemptible.—I fhould think it, neverthelefs, not
worth another letter of defcription, were it not
that the churches, and church-curiofities, demand
our attention; for you will obferve, that in all rich
Popifh countries, every church is a holy toy-fhop,
or rather a mufeum, where pictures, ftatues, gold
cups, filver candlefticks, diamond crucifixes, and
gods, of various forts and dimenfions, are hoarded

up, in honour of the Supreme Being. This city having been for centuries the see of a bishop, who is suffragan to the archbishop of Mecklin, and at the same time hereditary chancellor of Flanders, it is not to be wondered at, if ecclesiastical industry should have amassed some of those little trinkets which constitute the chief or only value of their church. The mitre of this place conveys to the head that wears it a diocese containing six cities, from the names of which you will be able to form some small judgment of the opulence of one poor son of abstinence and mortification.—Those cities are, in the first place, Bruges itself, then Ostend, Sluys, Damme, Middleburgh in Flanders, and Oudenberch—not to mention one hundred and thirty-three boroughs and villages; and if you could compute the number of inferior clergy with which the streets and highways are filled, you would be thunderstruck. There, and in all those Popish countries, they may be seen, with grotesque habits and bald pates, buzzing up and down like bees, in swarms, (a precious hive!)—and, with the most vehement protestations of voluntary poverty in their mouths, and eyes uplifted to Heaven, scrambling for the good things of the earth with the eagerness of a pack of hounds, and the rapacity of a whole roll of lawyers! With loaded thighs (I might say, loaded arms too, for they have large pockets even in their sleeves, for the concealment of moveables), they return to the great hive, where, contrary to the law of bees, the drone lives in idle state, and he plunders them: contrary, too, to the habits of those useful insects, they banish the queen-bee, and suffer no female to approach their cells, but keep them in contiguous hives, where, under cover of the night, they visit them, and fulfil in private that which they deny in public—the great command of Providence.

The firſt building in nominal rank, though by no means the firſt in value, is the great cathedral, which has at leaſt bulk, antiquity, and gloomineſs enough to recommend it to the faithful. It is by no means unfurniſhed within, though not in ſo remarkable a manner as to induce me to fill a letter with it. In a word, it is an old Popiſh cathedral, and cannot be ſuppoſed wanting in wealth : at the time I write, it has been ſtanding no leſs a time than nine hundred and twenty-nine years, having been built in the year 865.

The next that occurs to me, as worthy of notice, is the church of Notre Dame, or that dedicated to *our Lady* the Virgin MARY. This is really a beautiful ſtructure of the kind—indeed magnificent. Its ſteeple is beyond conception ſtupendous, being ſo very high as to be ſeen at ſea off Oſtend, although it is not elevated in the ſmalleſt degree by any riſe in the ground ; for, ſo very flat is the whole intermediate country, that I believe it would puzzle a ſkilful leveller to find two feet elevation from high-water-mark at Oſtend up to this city. The contents of this church are correſpondent to its external appearance—being enriched and beautified with a vaſt variety of ſacerdotal trinkets, and fine tombs and monuments. As to the former, the veſtments of that ſame THOMAS A BECKET whom I mentioned in my laſt, make a part of the curioſities depoſited in this church : this furious and inflexible impoſtor was archbiſhop of Canterbury ; and his ſtruggles to enſlave both the king and people of England, and make them tributary to the Pope, have canonized him, and obtained the very honourable depot I mention for his veſtments. To do juſtice, however, to the ſpirit and ſagacity of the holy fathers who have ſo long taken the pains to preſerve them, it muſt be commemorated, that they are, or at leaſt were ſet with diamonds, and other precious stones! Probably, among the many priests who have, in so many centuries, had the custody of those divine relics, some one, more sagacious than the rest, might conceive, that, to lie in a church, and be seen by the all-believing eyes of the faithful, a little coloured glass was just as good as any precious stone, and wisely have converted the originals to some better purpose. If so, it will be some consolation to Holy Mother Church to reflect, that she has bilked the *Sans-culottes*, who certainly have got possession of Saint THOMAS A BECKET's sacerdotal petticoats; and, if they have been found enough to stand the cutting, have, by this time, converted them into comfortable campaigning breeches. O monstrous! wicked! abominable!—that the Royal MARY, sister to the great Emperor CHARLES the Fifth, should, so long ago as the Reformation, have bought at an immense price, and deposited in the treasury of the church of *our Lady* the blessed Virgin MARY, the vestments of a saint, only to make breeches, in the year 1794, for a French soldier! The time has been, when the bare suggestion of such sacrilege would have turned the brain of half the people of Christendom: but those things are now better managed.

Of the tombs in this church, I shall only mention two, as distinguished from the rest by their costliness, magnificence, and antiquity. They are made of copper, well gilt. One of them is the tomb of MARY, heiress to the Ducal House of Burgundy; and the other, that of CHARLES (commonly called *the Hardy*), Duke of Burgundy, her father.

In Bruges there were four great abbeys, and an amazing number of convents and nunneries. The buildings, I presume, yet stand; but there is little doubt that their contents, of every kind, have been, before this, put *in requisition*, and each part of them, of course, applied to its natural use.

The church once belonging to the Jesuits, is built in a noble style of architecture: and that of the Dominicans has not only its external merits, but its internal value; for, besides the usual superabundance of rich chalices, &c. it possesses some very great curiosities—

As, first, a very curious, highly wrought pulpit—beautiful in itself, but remarkable for the top being supported by wood, cut out, in the most natural, deceptive manner, in the form of ropes, and which beguile the spectator the more into a belief of its reality, because it answers the purposes of ropes.

Secondly, a picture—and so extraordinary a picture! Before I describe it, I must apprise you that your faith must be almost as great as that of a Spanish Christian to believe me—to believe that the human intellect ever sunk so low as, in the first instance, to conceive, and, in the next, to harbour and admire, such a piece. But I mistake—it has its merit; it is a curiosity---the demon of satire himself could not wish for a greater.

This picture, then, is the representation of a marriage!--but of whom? why, truly, of JESUS CHRIST with Saint CATHARINE of Sienna. Observe the congruity—Saint CATHARINE of Sienna lived many centuries after the translation of JESUS CHRIST to Heaven, where he is to sit, you know, till he comes to judge the quick and the dead!—But who marries them? In truth, Saint DOMINIC, the patron of this church! The Virgin MARY joins their hands—that is not amiss—But, to crown the whole, King DAVID himself, who died so long before CHRIST was born, plays the harp at the wedding!

My dear FREDERICK, I shall take it as no small instance of your dutiful opinion of me to believe, that such a picture existed, and made part of the holy paraphernalia of a temple consecrated to the worship of the Divinity: but I assure you it is a fact; and as I have never given you reason to suspect my veracity, I expect you to believe me in this instance, improbable though it seems: for such a farrago of absurdities, such a jumble of incongruities, impossibilities, bulls, and anachronisms, never yet were compressed, by the human imagination, into the same narrow compass.

I protract this letter beyond my usual length, on purpose to conclude my account of Bruges, and get once more upon the road.

The monastery of the Carthusians, another order of friars, is of amazing size, covering an extent of ground not much less than a mile in circumference. The Carmelites, another order, have a church here, in which there is raised a beautiful monument, to the memory of HENRY JERMYN, Lord Dover, a peer of England—But the monastery called the Dunes, a sect of the order of Saint BERNARD, is by far the noblest in the whole city: the cloisters and gardens are capacious and handsome; the apartment of the abbot is magnificent and stately, and those of the monks themselves unusually neat. Those poor mortified penitents, secluded from the pomps, the vanities, and enjoyments of life, and their thoughts no doubt resting alone on hereafter, keep, nevertheless, a sumptuous table, spread with every luxury of the season—have their country-seats, where they go a hunting, or to refresh themselves, and actually keep their own coaches.

Among the nunneries there are two English: one of Augustinian nuns, who are all ladies of quality, and who entertain strangers at the grate with sweet-meats and wine; the other, called the Pelicans, is of a very strict order, and wear a coarse dress.

To conclude—In the chapel of Saint BASIL is said to be kept, in perfect preservation, the blood which JOSEPH of Arimathea wiped off with a sponge from the dead body of CHRIST. *Finis coronat opus.*

I fancy you have, by this time, had as much of miracles as you can well digest: I therefore leave you to reflect upon them and improve.

LETTER VIII.

AS I was going to the barque, at Bruges, to take my departure for Ghent, the next town in my route, I was surprised to see a number of officious, busy, poor fellows, crowding round my effects, and seizing them—some my trunk, some my portmanteau, &c. I believe two or three to each: but my astonishment partly subsided when I was told that they were porters, who plied on the canal, and about the city, for subsistence, and only came to have the *honour* of carraying my baggage down to the vessel. Noting their eagerness, I could not help smiling. I know there are those, and I have heard of such, who would bluster at them: but my mirth at the bustling importance which the poor fellows affected, soon sunk into serious concern; I said within myself, "Alas, how hard must be your lot indeed!" and my imagination was in an instant back again in London, where a porter often makes you pay for a job, not in money only, but in patience also, and where the surliness of independence scowls upon his brow as he does your work. Every one of my men demanded a remuneration for his labour: one man could have eafily done the work of five---but I refolved not to fend them away difcontented: he is but a fordid churl that would; and I paid them to their full fatisfaction. Here, my dear FREDERICK, let me offer you (fince it occurs) my parental advice on this point---from the practice of which you will gain more folid felicity than you can poffibly be aware of now: never weigh fcrupuloufly the value of the work of the poor; rather exceed than fall fhort of rewarding it: it is a very, very fmall thing, that will put them in good humour with you and with themfelves, and relax the hard furrows of labour into the foft fmile of gratitude---a fmile which, to a heart of fenfibility fuch as yours, will, of itfelf, ten-thoufand-fold repay you, even though the frequent practice of it fhould abridge you of a few of thofe things called pleafures, or detract a little from the weight of your purfe.

Being again feated in my barque, I fet off for Ghent, a city lying at a diftance of twenty-four miles from Bruges. I muft here remark to you, that the company one meets in thofe veffels is not always of the firft rank; it is generally of a mixed, motley kind: but to a man who carries along with him, through his travels, a love for his fellow-creatures, and a defire to fee men, and their cuftoms and manners, it is both pleafant and eligible---at leaft I thought it fo, and enjoyed it. There were thofe amongft us who fpoke rather loftily on that fubject: I faid nothing; but it brought to my mind a reflection I have often had occafion to concur in, viz. that a faftidious ufurpation of dignity (happily denominated *ftatelinefs*) is the never-failing mark of an upftart or a blockhead. The man of true dignity, felf-erect and ftrong, needs not have recourfe, for fupport, to the comparative wretchednefs of his fellow-creature, or plume himself upon spurious superiority. You will understand me, however! When I say, "the man of true dignity," I am far, very far, from meaning a lord, a squire, a banker, or a general officer---I mean a man of intrinsic worth---homo emunctæ naris---one who, in every station into which chance may throw him, feels firm in the consciousness of right---who can see and cherish merit, though enveloped and concealed behind a shabby suit of clothes---and who scorns the blown-up fool of fortune, that without sense or sentiment, without virtue, wisdom, or courage, presumes to call himself great, merely because he possesses a few acres of earth which he had neither the industry nor merit to earn, or because his great-great-great-grandfather purchased a title by perfidy to his country, the plunder of his fellow-citizens, or the slaughter of mankind.

Although the face of that part of the country through which we are now passing, like that of the preceding stage from Ostend to Bruges, wants diversity, it has its charms, and would be particularly delightful in the eye of an English farmer; for it is covered with the thickest verdure on each side of the canal, and the banks are decorated all along by rows of stately trees, while the fields in the back ground are cultivated to the highest degree of perfection, and bear the aspect of producing the most abundant harvest.

You will be able to form a judgment of the trifling expence of travelling in this country, from my expences in this stage of twenty-four miles. I had an excellent dinner for about fifteen pence of our money; my passage cost me but sixteen more, amounting in all to two shillings and seven pence: compare that with travelling in England, where one cannot rise up from an indifferent dinner, in an inn, under five shillings at the least, and you must be astonished at the disproportion.

Ghent is the capital of Flanders, and is to be reckoned among the largest cities of Europe, as it covers a space of ground of not less than seven miles in circumference; but there is not above one half of that occupied with buildings, the greater part being thrown into fields, gardens, orchards, and pleasure-grounds. Situated on four navigable rivers, and intersected into no fewer than twenty-six islands by a number of canals, which afford an easy, cheap, and expeditious carriage for weighty merchandize, it may be considered, in point of local advantages for commerce, superior to most cities in Europe; while those islands are again united by about a hundred bridges, some great and some small, which contribute much to the beauty of the city.

To a man accustomed to mould his thoughts by what he sees in Great Britain, the strong fortifications that surround almost all towns on the Continent convey the most disagreeable sensations---reminding him of the first misery of mankind, War!---denoting, alas! too truly, the disposition of man to violate the rights of his fellow-creatures, and manifesting the tyrannous abuse of power. On me, though trained and accustomed to military habits, this "dreadful note of preparation" had an unpleasing effect; for, though born, bred, and habituated to the life of a soldier, I find the feelings of the citizen and the man claim a paramount right to my heart.

Ghent was once extremely well fortified, and calculated, by nature as well as by art, to repel encroachment. It had a very strong castle, walls, and ditches; and now, though not otherwise strong, the country may, by shutting up the sluices, be, for above a mile round, laid in a very short time under water. It was formerly so populous and powerful, that it declared war more than once against its sovereign, and raised amazing armies. In the year 1587, it suffered dreadfully from all the ravages of famine, under which a number not less than three thousand of its inhabitants perished in one week.

This town is distinguished by the nativity of two celebrated characters: one was the famous JOHN of Gaunt, son of King EDWARD the third of England; the other, the Emperor CHARLES the Fifth, who was born there in the year 1500.

It was in this city that the Confederation of the States, well known under the title of the Pacification of Ghent, which united the Provinces in the most lasting union of interest and laws, was held: this union was chiefly owing to the vigorous, unremitted efforts of WILLIAM the First, Prince of Orange, to whose valour and virtue may be attributed the independence of the United States.

In this city there were computed to be fifty companies of tradesmen, among whom were manufactured a variety of very curious and rich cloths, stuffs, and silks: it is certain, that the woollen manufacture flourished here before it had made the smallest progress in England, whose wool they then bought. There was also a good branch of linen manufacture here, and a pretty brisk corn trade, for which it was locally well calculated. You will observe, once for all, that in speaking of this country, I generally use the past tense; for, at present, they are utterly undone.

Ghent was the see of a bishop, who, like the bishop of Bruges, was suffragan to the archbishop of Mechlin. Thus, in most Christian countries, are the intellects, the consciences, and the cash too, of the people, shut up and hid from the light, by priest within dean, and dean within bishop—like

E

a ring in the hand of a conjurer, box within box —till at laſt they are enveloped in the great receptacle of all deception, the capacious pocket of the archbiſhop. Let not ſceptered tyrants, their legions, their ſcaffolds, and their ſwords, bear all the infamy of the ſlavery of mankind! Opinion, opinion, under the management of fraud and impoſture, is the engine that forges their fetters!!— JANSENIUS, from whom the Janſeniſts took their name, was the firſt biſhop of this place; and the late biſhop, I think, may be reckoned the laſt.

The municipal government of this city is correct, and well calculated to ſecure internal peace and order. The chief magiſtrate is the high bailiff; ſubordinate to whom are burgomaſters, echivins, and counſellors.

Ghent is not deficient in ſtately edifices; and, true to their ſyſtem, the holy fathers of the church have their ſhare, which, in old Popiſh countries, is at leaſt nineteen twentieths. In the middle of the town is a high tower, called Belfort tower: from whence there is a delightful proſpect over the whole city and its environs. Monaſteries and churches, there, are without number; beſides hoſpitals and market-places: that called Friday's market, is the largeſt of all, and is adorned with a ſtatue of CHARLES the Fifth, in his imperial robes. The ſtadthouſe is a magnificent ſtructure—So is the cathedral, under which the reverend fathers have built a ſubterraneous church. What deeds are thoſe which ſhun the light! Why thoſe holy patriarchs have ſuch a deſire for burying themſelves, and working like moles under ground, they themſelves beſt know, and I think it is not difficult for others to conjecture.

This cathedral, however, is well worth attention, on account of ſome capital pictures it contains. The marble of the church is remarkably fine, and the altar-piece splendid beyond all possible description; and, indeed, in all the others, there are paintings, eminent for their own excellence, and for the celebrity of the masters who painted them.

In the monastery of St. PIERRE, there is a grand library, filled with books in all languages; but it is chiefly remarkable for the superlative beauty of its ceiling, one half of which was painted by RUBENS.

Thus you may perceive, my dear FREDERICK, the charity of the clergy!—how, in pure pity for the sins of mankind, and in paternal care of their souls, they exact from the laity some atonement for their crimes, and constrain them at least to repent—and, with unparalleled magnanimity, take upon themselves the vices, the gluttony, the avarice, and the sensuality, of which they are so careful to purge their fellow-creatures.

LETTER IX.

HAVING given you a general outline of the city of Ghent, I shall now proceed to give you an account of one of the most excellent, and certainly the most interesting, of all the curiosities in that place. It is indeed of a sort so immediately correspondent to the most exalted sensations of humanity, and so perfectly in unison with the most exquisitely sensible chords of the feeling heart, that I resolved to rescue it from the common lumber of the place, and give it to you in a fresh letter, when the ideas excited by my former might have faded away, and left your mind more clear for the reception of such refined impressions.

On one of the many bridges in Ghent stand two large brazen images of a father and son, who obtained this distinguished mark of the admiration of their fellow-citizens by the following incidents:

Both the father and the son were, for some offence against the state, condemned to die. Some favourable circumstances appearing on the side of the son, he was granted a remission of his share of the sentence, upon certain provisions—in short, he was offered a pardon, on the most cruel and barbarous condition that ever entered into the mind of even monkish barbarity, namely, that he would become the executioner of his father! He at first resolutely refused to preserve his life by means so fatal and detestable: This is not to be wondered at; for I hope, for the honour of our nature, that there are but few, very few sons, who would not have spurned, with abhorrence, life sustained on conditions so horrid, so unnatural. The son, though long inflexible, was at length overcome by the tears and entreaties of a fond father, who represented to him, at all events, his (the father's) life was forfeited, and that it would be the greatest pathos consolation to him, at his last moments, to think that in his death he was the instrument of his son's preservation. The youth consented to adopt the horrible means of recovering his life and liberty: he lifted the axe; but, as it was about to fall, his arm sunk nerveless, and the axe dropped from his hand! Had he as many lives as hairs, he would have yielded them all, one after the other, rather than again even conceive, much less perpetrate, such an act. Life, liberty, every thing, vanished before the dearer interests of filial affection: he fell upon his father's neck, and, embracing him, triumphantly exclaimed, "My father, my father! we will die together!" and then called for another executioner to fulfil the sentence of the law.

Hard muſt be their hearts indeed, bereft of every ſentiment of virtue, every ſenſation of humanity, who could ſtand inſenſible ſpectators of ſuch a ſcene—A ſudden peal of involuntary applauſes, mixed with groans and ſighs, rent the air. The execution was ſuſpended; and on a ſimple repreſentation of the tranſaction, both were pardoned: high rewards and honours were conferred on the ſon; and finally, thoſe two admirable brazen images were raiſed, to commemorate a tranſaction ſo honourable to human nature, and tranſmit it for the inſtruction and emulation of poſterity. The ſtatue repreſents the ſon in the very act of letting fall the axe.

Lay this to your mind, my dear FREDERICK: talk over it to your brother; indulge all the charming ſympathetic ſenſations it communicates; never let a miſtaken ſhame, or a falſe idea (which ſome endeavour to impreſs) that it is unmanly to melt at the tale of woe, and ſympathize with our fellow-creatures, ſtop the current of your ſenſibility—no! Be aſſured, that, on the contrary, it is the true criterion of manhood and valour to feel; and that the more ſympathetic and ſenſible the heart is, the more nearly it is allied to the Divinity.

I AM now on the point of conducting you out of Auſtrian Flanders—One town only, and that comparatively a ſmall one, lying between Us and Brabant: the name of this town is Aloſt, or, as the Flemings ſpell it, Aelſt.

From Ghent to Bruſſels (the next great ſtage in my way), I found, to my regret, that there was no conveyance by water: I therefore was obliged to go in a voiture, and ſtopt at Aloſt, as an intermediate ſtage; and mathematically intermediate it is—for it lies at equal diſtance from Ghent and Bruſſels, being exactly fifteen miles from each.

This is a small, but exceeding neat town, situated on the river Dender; and being a remarkably great thoroughfare accommodations of every kind are tolerably good in it. It would be idle to suppose, that Catholic zeal had left so many souls unprotected and undisciplined, where there were so many bodies capable of drudgery to pay for it. In truth, there has been as ample provision made for the town of Aloft in the way of sacerdotal business, as for any other town in the Netherlands—regard being had to its bulk; for there were several convents of friars, and of course several of nuns: besides, there was a Jesuit's college of some note. How they all fare by this time, it is difficult for me to determine.

The church of Saint MARTIN could boast of some excellent pictures, particularly a most capital piece, "*La Peste,*" by RUBENS.

In a convent inhabited by a set of monks, denominated Gulielmite, I saw the tomb of THIERRY MARTIN, who first brought the art of printing from Germany to that place. His name and fame are transmitted to us by an epitaph upon his tomb, written by his friend, the ingenious Erasmus.

This tomb of THIERRY MARTIN stands a monument, not only of his merit, but of the shortsightedness and folly even of monks. Alas, silly men! they little knew, that when they granted THIERRY MARTIN the honours of the convent, they were harbouring, in their hallowed ground, one of their greatest enemies, and commemorating the man who was contributing to the overthrow of their sacred order: for the art of printing, wherever it reached, illuminated the human mind, and first kindled up that light, before which priestcraft, and all its pious impostures, like evil spectres, have vanished. To the art of printing is human society indebted for many of the advantages which it possesses beyond the brute or savage tribes—for the perfection of arts, the extension of science, the general enlargement of the mind, and, above all, for the emancipation of person and property from the shackles of despotism, and of the human intellect from the fetters of blindness and ignorance with which sacerdotal fraud had chained it for centuries to the earth.

The territory of this city is of pretty large extent, and is called a county, having, in ancient times, had counts of its own; and the whole of it is extremely fruitful in pasture, corn, hops, flax, and most other productions of those climes.

I made but a very short stay at Aloft, when I proceeded on to Brussels; and, having thus brought you through that part of the Netherlands called Austrian Flanders, I think I ought to give you a general account of the country at large, as I have hitherto confined myself merely to the cities and towns of it; but as this letter is already of a length that will not allow of any great addition, I shall postpone my intended description to my next.

LETTER X.

WERE mankind to be guided by moderation, reason, and justice—were there no lust for territory in particular states—no ambition or desire in kings for an undue enlargement of their power—no unjustifiable infractions attempted by one state or potentate upon the peace and possession of another—no armies to carry desolation and plunder through the world, nor churchmen more mild, but not more moderate, to drain them with their subtile deceptions—were the husbandman, the fisherman, the manufacturer, and the labourer, permitted to make, by their industry, the best use of the soil on which chance or nature had planted them, and to lift the fruits of their labour to their own lips—no people were more happy than the inhabitants of Austrian Flanders.

This country is bounded, to the north, by the Scheldt; to the north-west, by the Northern Sea: to the south, and south-west, by Artois, one of the finest Provinces of France; and to the east, by Brabant. Its greatest length is seventy-five miles; and its greatest breadth, fifty-five. The air is good; but it is said to be better in proportion as it recedes from the sea. The winters are sometimes long and severe, and the summers sometimes wet and sultry; yet, in general, the climate is agreeable. The soil is in most parts fertile, and in some to a degree equal to that of any part of Europe. It is chiefly famous for its pasturage; in consequence of which, great numbers of black cattle, horses and sheep, are bred in it, and immense quantities of butter and cheese made. It is, besides, abundantly productive of all sorts of culinary vegetables—fruit in great quantities—corn and flax, which last is not only raised in great plenty, but is celebrated for the fineness and strength of its staple. It is true, that in some parts they have not corn sufficient for the inhabitants; but this is well recompensed by other productions, with the redundance of which they purchase the superfluous grain of their neighbours—for, where the inhabitants do follow tillage, the produce is unequalled, and the superfluity must of course be great.

The superior fecundity of the sheep of this country is very remarkable, and difficult, perhaps, to be accounted for—a ewe here bringing forth constantly three lambs at a birth, sometimes four, sometimes five, and some have been known to produce as many as six and seven—no small instance of the prodigality of nature in providing for this spot.

At some distance from the sea-coast, the face of the country is decorated with a profusion of wood, fitted either for timber or for fuel; and towards the coast, where nature has been rather niggard of that blessing, the inhabitants substitute, in its stead, for fuel, a kind of turf, which they find at the depth of four or five feet from the surface of the earth, and which makes a fire, not only cheerful, pleasant, and hot, but remarkably wholesome, being free from the destructive sulphurious and bituminous vapour attendant upon coal.

Perhaps no part of the world is better supplied than this province with all sorts of fish, as well those of sea as fresh water: fowl and venison were extremely plenty and reasonable; and a great deal of excellent beer was brewed in it. It is washed by several rivers, four of which are noble streams, namely, the Scheldt, the Lys, the Scarpe, and the Dender; and there are several canals, the chief of which is that between Bruges and Ghent.

Thus in whatever way it be considered, nature seems to have made ample provision for the happiness of the people: how far they are so, you shall hear when I come to give a general view of the Netherlands—that which is applicable to Austrian Flanders being equally so to all the other parts of the Netherlands, excepting those under the dominion of the Republic of the United States.

The States of this country, according to the constitution it once possessed, consisted of clergy, the nobility, and the commoners. The clergy were the bishops and abbots: the nobility was composed of certain families holding hereditary offices or baronies, to which that privilege was annexed; and the commoners were made up of the burgomasters, pensioners and deputies of the cities and districts. But the only religion professed or tolerated in this country, was the Roman Catholic.

Of the people of Austrian Flanders a celebrated Author gives the following account, which I transcribe for your use, the rather as my stay there was too short to enable me to make any material observations on them, or their manners.—

" With respect to the persons and characters of the inhabitants," says he, " they are, generally speaking, lusty, fat, and clumsy—very industrious, both in cultivating their lands, and in their trades and manufactures—lovers of liberty, and enemies to slavery—and not defective in good sense or judgment, though they have not so lively an imagination as some other nations. Their women are fair, handsome enough, and honest by their natural constitution, as well as from a principle of virtue: as they cannot pretend to wit and repartee, they do not make themselves ridiculous by the nauseous affectation of them. Both sexes are great lovers of public diversions; and every city, town, and village, have their kermisses, or fairs, in which all sorts of shews are exhibited."

Many arts which now enrich other nations, and the importance of which has excited contests and struggles of the most serious kind in the political world, were invented or improved in that country. Weaving, in general, though not invented, was greatly improved; and the art of forming figures of all sorts in linen was first invented there. To the Flemings we are also indebted for the arts of curing herrings, dyeing cloths and stuffs, and oil-colours. But those arts, and the manufactures, have gradually slid away from them, and left but a small share behind, when compared with their former flourishing state: they have flown to a land of liberty and security, where hostile feet never tread, where slavery corrupteth not, where war devoureth not, nor Priests nor Despots break in and steal. Nevertheless, silk, cotton and woollen stuffs, brocades, camblets, tapestry, linen, and lace, are still manufactured here to some small extent.

This province had counts of its own, from the ninth century up to the year 1369, when it was made over, by marriage, (like a farm of cattle) to the dukes of Burgundy; and afterwards, again, was by them made over, in like way of marriage, to the House of Austria. In 1667 France seized the southern part; and the States General obtained the northern, partly by the treaty of Munster, and partly by the Barrier treaty of 1715.

To reckon upon the natural endowments of this country, one would suppose that it should be a terrestrial paradise: yet such is the wickedness of man, and the outrageous spirit of power, that it is almost the last country in Europe in which I would have property, and fix a permanent residence. Just now, while I am writing, I have before me an account, that the French, to whom they have opened their gates, have plundered them to the last atom of their moveable possessions; and that the property of the unfortunate people is now in waggons, on its way to Paris.

Once more, my boy, I say, bless your God, that planted you in a country cheered by the voice of freedom, defended by British valour, and, what is of more consequence, surrounded by the Ocean.

LETTER XI.

Having conducted you through that part of the Netherlands called Austrian Flanders, we are now to direct our attention to that called Austrian Brabant, of which part, as well as of the Netherlands in general, Brussels, where I arrived the same day I left Ghent, is the capital, giving its name to a quarter or territory that surrounds it.

In all parts of the Netherlands through which I travelled, I could not help admiring the uniform decorations of the roads, rivers, and canals, with rows of lofty trees, which form a most agreeable shade from the summer's burning sun, and yet do not obstruct any great extent of prospect, the country is so extremely flat. And one thing I remarked, and which certainly seems at first view, extraordinary, is, that in the great extent of country through which we have hitherto passed, from Ostend to Brussels, being sixty-eight miles, I scarce saw one nobleman or gentleman's seat---nothing above the house of a husbandman, a curate, or some person of small fortune: and yet the country is extremely rich; and I saw many spots, as I went along, charming beyond description, and such as would tempt, I should think, a man of taste and opulence to settle in them. This must appear unaccountable to those who do not recollect, that in a country subject like this to the ravaging incursions of contending armies, fortified towns are considered as the most pleasing, because the most secure retreats of opulence.

DESCRIPTION OF BRUSSELS.

As I approached the city of Bruſſels, I was ſtruck with a mixed ſenſation of ſurpriſe and delight at the appearance it made—none that I had ever ſeen being comparable to it, and not one in Europe, by the account of travellers, being in that reſpect ſuperior to it, Naples and Genoa only excepted: like them, however, it, when entered, falls far ſhort of the expectation raiſed by its external appearance, being all compoſed of hills and hollows, which not only fatigue, but render the appearance of the ſtreets, though well built, contemptible and mean.

Bruſſels ſtands on the beautiful little river Senne, on the brow of a hill. The city is about ſeven miles in circumference, has ſeven gates, with extenſive ſuburbs, and is encompaſſed with a double wall made of brick, and ditches; but its ſize is too great for ſtrength, as a face of defence of ſuch extent could not poſſibly hold out a long ſiege—a great and inſuperable defect in ſuch a country as I have deſcribed.

Great as is the extent of ground on which this city ſtands, it is neverthelefs very well built, and extremely populous. It is ornamented with no fewer than ſeven ſquares, all of them remarkably fine, particularly the great ſquare or market place, which is reckoned to be perhaps the fineſt in Europe. Around it are the halls of the different trades, the fronts of which are adorned, in a ſuperb manner, with emblematical ſculpture, with gilding, and a variety of Latin inſcriptions. One quarter of this ſquare is entirely occupied by the town-houſes, a noble pile of building, in which there were apartments where the States of Brabant met, finely adorned with tapeſtry in gilt frames, and ſome admirable original paintings. At the time I was there, the whole city was in motion, preparing for the Inauguration of the Emperor, who was then impatiently expected, and whoſe ap-

F .

proach made such a bustle, and promised such a spectacle, as made me regret the necessity I lay under of proceeding on my journey. The town-house was put into the highest order, and subsequently fell a sacrifice to the great and important event for which it was prepared.

The steeple of this building is of a most stupendous height—three hundred and sixty-four feet; and on the top of it is erected a statue of Saint MICHAEL killing the Dragon, of the enormous height of seventeen feet: this colossal statue is so constructed as to serve for a weather-cock; and being made of copper, well gilt, is at once conspicuous, magnificent, and ornamental.

The public buildings of Brussels, particularly the palaces and courts of the several princes, counts, and other persons of distinction, (and, you may be sure, the churches and cloisters too), are spacious, expensive, and magnificent. Behind the imperial palace, which stood in the highest part of the city, but was burnt down many years ago, is a park, well stocked with deer, and planted with trees, like St. James's-park at London, for the inhabitants to walk in. At the farther end of it is a fine pleasure-house, built by the Emperor CHARLES the fifth, after his abdication.

The palace is a magnificent structure: the rooms of it are finished in a style far superior to those of any palace in England, and enriched with many fine paintings: that of the family of HECTOR, in the council chamber, lays claim to the first rank of eminence. Of the other buildings (the grandeur of which entitle them to the names of palaces), those of the Prince de la Tour and Taxis, and the British Earl of Aylesbury, are distinguished by great beauty and magnificence. Indeed, in all the palaces, there are collections of original paintings, by the most eminent masters, both Italian and Flemish.

The royal library of Bruffels claims particular attention, for the magnitude and liberality of its eftablifhment, containing a grand collection of the moft excellent books in all languages, and being open all the year on Tuefdays, Thurfdays, and Saturdays, to public accefs.

The arfenal of Bruffels is extremely well worth going to fee, on account of the very curious antique arms it contains—of which it is, at this diftance of time, impoffible for me to give you any account worth attention. The armour of the Emperor CHARLES the Fifth, together with the furniture of his horfe, and ftate fword, are fhewn: I could fee nothing either novel or interefting in them—a ftrong mark I prefume, of my want of tafte; but I confefs my organs are not fo refined as to feel any extraordinary emotions at the fight of a heap of inert matter, mearly becaufe it once enveloped the carcafe of a tyrant: neither were they fo very coarfe or dull as not to undergo very pointed fenfations at the fight of the armour of MONTEZUMA, the injured Emperor of Mexico, the victim of avarice and rapine, under their ufual mafk, religion. Why MONTEZUMA's armour fhould make a part of the trophies of a Popifh ftate, and be triumphantly exhibited, is hard to account for in human folly: why that fhould be exhibited which is a ftain of the deepeft-damned black, in their black code of faith, is aftonifhing, unlefs we allow the truth of the old faying, " Quos DEUS vult perdere, prius dementat;" and that, after having violated every principle of virtue, morality, and human feeling—after having furpaffed in cruelty all that we know of the worft monfters of the earth, or of the deep, the fell hyena, or the ravening fhark—after having fuccefsfully emulated the worft efforts of the moft malignant fpirits that are faid to hold counfel for the ruin of mankind in hell—they were defirous to tranfmit the fpoils of their ravages to pofterity, to tell them what glorious things have been atchieved in days of yore, for the love of CHRIST—to demonstrate what benefits are to be derived from a religion which has, for so many hundred years, given sanction to every enormity that strikes the soul of man with horror, and thereby to make converts to their principles. Monsters! fools! Away with your idle cants, ye hypocrites, who would brand the cruelties of the present days, the massacres of the Jacobins, with the crime of infidelity, and attribute those much lamented defections from humanity to a falling off from the Christian faith. Look to Mexico!—see a monster, a high priest of your religion, collecting, by fair promises and sweet pursuasion, a people round him; and, when a plain was filled, commanding his bloodhounds, armed with sword and crucifix, to fall upon and murder them—because one poor creature, who knew not what a book meant, had accidentally dropped a bible from his hands!—see him not sparing age or sex, but butchering all, for the love of CHRIST!—When have the deluded and enfrenzied mob of France perpetrated, in the full torrent of popular frenzy, such atrocities as this cruel priest committed in cold blood? when have they hunted down their fellow creatures, massacred children, and given their yet panting members to their dogs for food, as pious Christians, headed by a pious priest, have done in Mexico? Never! never!—Learn wisdom, then, ye hypocrites! and if you cannot convince your enemies by reason, or conquer them by force, and if their predatory and wicked progress is not to be stopped, do not sanctify their enormities, or palliate their crimes, in the eye of reason, by a comparison with those of a deeper dye: remember, that "not to be the worst stands in some rank of praise," and that the Jacobin cruelties of Paris, horrible though they were, were pity and tender mercy, compared with the

Christian butchery in Mexico, in Europe, in Asia, in every place where Popery ever set its bloody hoof.

You are not, from what I say, to infer that I entertain any illiberal animosity to Popery, as many men, and more women, do, merely because its articles of faith differ from those in which I was bred; I trust my heart and understanding are above such very degrading prejudices: but I abhor every thing that militates against human happiness—every thing that crushes the operations of intellect—every thing that stops the current of opinion, and prevents its course from enlarging and meliorating our condition: I abhor the impertinent and hypocritical intrusion of all churchmen upon national or domestic concerns; the more, when that intrusion is mischievous; and more still, when it assumes the mask of piety—for that is at once a fraud upon man and an abuse of GOD. All those causes of abhorrence attach, more or less, to all sects of the Christian religion, the Quakers only excepted—but to Popery rather more than to any of the others; for it is observed, that while the very first principles of Christianity, as originally laid down in theory, are peace and good-will towards men, warfare, persecution, and bloodshed, have practically marked its footsteps wherever it has trod, and its very essence been perverted by its own ministers, who, entrusted with the key of the temple, steal the vestments from the alter, to cover the deformed, crooked back of vice. But the rays of dawning reason now break with fuller light upon mankind; and it hastens to meridian resplendence, before which those phantoms raised by pious jugglers will vanish, and, "like the baseless fabric of a vision, leave not a wreck behind."

LETTER XII.

IN the arsenal of Brussels was another curiosity, which I overlooked in my last—a model of a cannon, constructed so as to throw seven balls at once. It is some consolation to philanthropy to reflect, that of all the abominable engines and instruments which the inventive faculties of man have discovered to increase the cruelty and carnage of war, not one has been of late times adopted. This model lies here, therefore, only as a memorial of the diabolical genius of the inventor.

The opera-house of Brussels, accounted the noblest and largest in Europe, is built after the Italian manner, with rows of lodges or closets, in most of which are chimneys. One of those, which belonged to a prince, whose title I now forget, was hung with looking-glasses, in which, while he sat by the fire, took refreshments, or reclined on his couch, he could see the whole representation, without being exposed to the view of either the actors or the audience.

The markets of Brussels are very remarkable. The dukes of St. Pierre paid no less than forty thousand florins, or upwards of three thousand pounds Sterling, for four pictures of them, painted by RUBENS and SYNDER—LEWIS the Fourteenth of France offered an immense sum of money for them; but they found their way at last into the collection of the British Earl of Orford. The value of them is said, by connoisseurs, to be beyond computation.

Brussels is extremely well supplied with water: for, besides the river, it has twenty public foun-

DESCRIPTION OF BRUSSELS.

tains, adorned with statues, at the corners of the most public streets; and the lower part of the city is cut into canals, which communicate with the great one, extending from Bruffels to the Scheldt, fifteen miles: by means of this canal, which was finished in 1561, and cost the city eight hundred thousand florins, a person may sail from Bruffels to the North Sea; and barques do actually go twice a-day to Antwerp, and back again.

This city is full of churches, of which the most remarkable is that of Saint MICHAEL and Saint GUDULA, commonly called the cathedral. It is a superb, old Gothic structure, and, from its celebrated situation, a most beautiful ornament to the city. It is not only grand in its external appearance, but finely adorned within. The pillars which support the roof are lofty and elegant: and against each is a statue of ten feet in height. There are no less than sixteen chapels in it; and each chapel is enriched with abundance of splendid ornaments, altar finery, candle-sticks, crucifixes, &c. and with some excellent pictures too: a picture of JESUS CHRIST presenting the keys of Paradise to Saint PETER, which is reckoned among the chef-d'œuvres of RUBENS, hangs in one of those chapels. There are some monuments, also, of very great merit, in the choir of this church. But that which I think by far the greatest and most admirable curiosity (I mean of human workmanship) in the church, is a pulpit—one of the richest and most exquisitely wrought pieces I have ever seen: at the bottom are seen ADAM and EVE as large as life, represented as at the moment when the angel drove them out of Paradise: in both of their faces are deeply and expressively marked the traits of a mind agonised with anguish and remorse: behind EVE is a figure of Death, which follows them; and on the top of the pulpit are seen the figures of JESUS CHRIST and the Virgin MARY crushing the head of the

Serpent. The strong expressions in the faces of all those figures, and the exquisite turn of the workmanship, is the more remarkable, as it is all cut out of oak wood.

Of supernatural curiosities, one of the chapels in this cathedral contains some, that, for miracle, yield to none in the long catalogue of monkish devices. Three hosts or wafers are daily worshipped by the people; which hosts or wafers, the priests firmly assert, and the people as firmly believe, were, so long ago as the year 1369, stabbed by a Jew, and bled profusely. They are exposed on every festival, in a chalice richly set with diamonds; and on the first Sunday after every thirteenth of July, there is a yearly procession in memory of this stabbing and bleeding, when the hosts are carried in great state round the city, embellished with all manner of precious stones, and attended by all the clergy, secular and regular, the magistrates, the courts of justice, and even by the governor of the province: the chapel where they are kept is of marble, and the altar of solid silver.

Great GOD! what an opprobrium to the human understanding, that, at the time when the mind of man is sufficiently enlightened to avoid the weakness of shameful credulity, a whole people should stoop to such extravagant imposition! what a shame to justice and honesty, that those who are trusted to guard the rights of a people, and who certainly are too well informed to yield their belief to such trash, should yet join in, and give the weight of their authority to so gross, so wicked a deception on a community! The magistrates, the courts of justice, and the governor—they walk, too, in company with the bald-pated impostors—Good GOD! can more be said? volumes of comment could not elucidate or render it more conspicuously absurd than the bare recital of the fact itself.

DESCRIPTION OF BRUSSELS.

It is impossible for me to recount to you the number of nunneries, of various orders, in which unfortunate women were cloistered up, some from bigotry, and others by force, in this city. There were, however, two of them English—one of Dominican ladies, founded by Cardinal HOWARD, in the reign of CHARLES the Second, of which a lady of the noble House of Norfolk was always abbess: the other is of Benedictine nuns; the Beguinage of the latter is like a little town, surrounded with a wall and ditch, and divided into pretty little streets, where every Beguine has her apartment; the number of them amounts in general to seven or eight hundred, sometimes more.

If population be the true strength of a nation, this part of Popery is very impolitic. The succession of women in this one convent since the reign of CHARLES the Second, must amount to many thousands. Had those been married, and, on an average, had only two children each, with the children, grandchildren, and great-grandchildren, down to the present day, in all the ramifications of descent, there is no doubt but their number would equal that of the whole people of some extensive provinces. What, then, must be the loss to the population of the earth, arising from the celibacy of so many millions of males and females as have been consigned to sterility in the catholic countries, ever since that extraordinary doctrine came first into fashion? It is out of the reach of calculation: not but, now and then, they may have children—indeed they certainly have but those are generally disposed of in a way not to bring shame on the frail Sisterhood, or their Confessors.

In wading through such a torrent of offensive ideas as the innumerable absurdities and deceptions of Popish countries continually raise in the mind, it is a pleasing circumstance to be relieved by the contemplation of some really useful, humane institution; and such a one presents itself now to my recollection: At Brussels, and, I am told, at all great towns of the Netherlands, there is a public office for lending money at a very moderate interest upon pledges: it is called the Mount of Piety; and was established nearly 108 years ago by the Archduke, ALBERT, and ISABELLA, his wife. By this institution, the poor are saved from the fleecings and frauds of pawn-brokers: and to render it still more perfect in accommodation, there are private passages for entrance; so that those who would wish to conceal their necessities, are exempted from the mortification of being seen publicly going in, or coming out.

You have read, I presume, that in the days of Heathenism, the Deities of that curious Mythology were supposed to rejoice in the number Three. The Popish Code has fixed upon Seven as the lucky number. Thus they have seven sacraments, seven deadly sins, &c. &c. Brussels has improved upon that; and, taking the hint from their blessed liturgy, has seven grand streets; seven parish-churches; seven Patrician families, out of which the Magistrates are or were elected; seven large squares; seven midwives, licensed and sworn by the Senate; and seven gates, leading to seven places of recreations and exercise, one to a place proper for fowling, a second to a place for fishing, a third to one for hunting, a fourth to pleasant fields, a fifth to pastime grounds, a sixth to springs and vineyards, and a seventh to gardens. Besides all which sevens, they boast of having once had the great good fortune of entertaining, at one time, seven crowned heads, with seven thousand horse belonging to their retinue. If there were any spell in the number Seven, the people of Brussels surely must have been secure from all mischief; but the *Sans-culottes* have broken the charm, dispersed the necromancers, and lowered poor number Seven to its mere arithmetical value.

The inns, or eating houses, in this city, were equal to any in the world: a stranger might dine there better and cheaper than in any place perhaps, on earth. The wines, also, were excellent and cheap; and coach-hire beyond expectation reasonable—And here I recollect to remark to you, that, all the way from Ostend to Brussels, one is obliged to sit, dine, &c. in bed-chambers; a circumstance which is extremely discordant to the feelings of those who have been used to British inns, although the bed-chambers are, to say the truth, large and commodious. At the very walls of Brussels begins the famous wood of Sogne, from which the inhabitants were allowed to cut wood for fuel: as fast as the trees were cut down, fresh ones were planted in their stead; by which means the wood was preserved, and it afforded a continual supply to the poor.

Brussels is so very remarkable a place, that I have taken more than my usual scope of description of it. Just as I had finished it, I read a paragraph in the public papers, stating that it is likely to be annexed to the territories of the French Republic.

LETTER XIII.

HITHERTO, as I have proceeded on my travels, I have been purposely very particular in my descriptions of the towns through which I passed on my way to India, in order to give your mind a disposition to inquiry, and point out to you an overflowing source of improvement and delight. Having so far shewn you how amply you will be rewarded, even in amusement, by the trouble of searching into books, for the accurate topographical descriptions of towns, cities, buildings, &c. &c. I think I may spare myself that labour for the future, and confine myself to those points that more immediately apply to the enlargement of the mind ---I mean, the government, laws, manners, and character of the people of each country; and only use the former as subservient to the latter purpose, at least until I come to those places where, the ground being but little trodden by British feet, more precise description may become necessary.

But, before I leave the Netherlands, I must make a few remarks upon the country and people, which it would be unpardonable in me to omit, after having been already so minutely particular in things of inferior merit to the scope of my plan.

Although personal appearance be, in the eye of Moral Philosophy, a very inferior consideration, and mind the proper study of man; yet in describing a people, I cannot think it altogether unnecessary to include their personal appearance, as it will be found that there exists a greater analogy between the person and the mind of men than is generally perceived. Thus the lively hilarity, the restless activity, the levity and fantastic character of the French, are strongly pourtrayed in the national person. In like manner, the lusty, fat, clumsy and misshapen person of the people of the Netherlands, is strongly illustrative of the temper and habit of their mind, intellects and spirits: industrious and heavy; dull of understanding, but not defective in judgment; slow in work---but, persevering in effort, and unerring in the process, they are generally successful in the end: in war, cold and backward at offensive operations, but inflexible and terrible in resistance; like the boar of the forest, they seek not the combat with any, but will not go out of their way to decline it with the most powerful: their appetites and defires cooler than other nations, but lefs fubject to change or caprice: never violently in love, but rationally attached to their wives; and both men and women faithful to their conjugal vow, as well from natural temperament, as from a principle of virtue.

Thus conftituted by nature, the effects of their induftry are wonderful in every thing, but chiefly in their canals and fluices, which ferve not only for the fupport of their commerce, and the facility of intercourfe, but for their defence againft enemies: this was in other times; but, alas! the former of thefe ufes, commerce, has fo entirely abforbed all their intellect, and poffeffed their very fouls, that they feem almoft entirely negligent of the latter; and from being, of all people, the moft wife and vigilant in determining and afcertaining their rights, the moft zealous afferters and defenders of their independence, the moft ardent friends to liberty, and the moft determined enemies to flavery, they are become a fort of ftrange, inconfiftent, hotchpotch politicians, whom ingenuity itfelf would find a difficulty in defcribing. They retain fo much of their ancient and noble vigilance as ferves to make them fufpicious—fo much of their independence as difpofes them to change—fo much of their jealoufy as ftimulates them to refiftance—but not one particle of their former wifdom, to inftruct them where they fhould attach themfelves, where refift, or where refolve to act—nor of their courage to carry any refolution they might form into effect.

In the year 1781, the Emperor Joseph the Second came to Bruffels, in order to indulge his paternal feelings as a monarch with the contemplation and view of his fubjects, and alfo to be inaugurated; and perhaps upon no occafion that has ever occurred in the moft volatile nation, was there greater joy more univerfally expreffed. For fome time before his arrival, the whole country was in motion,

G

and, even with them, domestic industry stopped its usual persevering pace, suspended in the eager, anxious expectation of his arrival. Every thing in the birth, education, natural disposition and person of the young Emperor, united to impress his subjects with the most exalted opinion of his goodness, and to inspire all ranks of people with the most fortunate presages of a wise and beneficent government. Nor did he disappoint them: his conduct, when among them, is handed over to remembrance, by a variety of acts of benevolence and condescension, which showed that the grandeur of the monarch had not made him forget the nature of the man, and that his heart was better fitted for the mild, domestic enjoyments of a subject, than the stern and unbending hardihood fit for a King: for I am perfectly of opinion with the celebrated JUNIUS, that there are virtues in a private man which are vices in a King; and that the monarch of a country, in order to preserve respect, should avoid familiarity, and keep his person sacred from too general observation. SHAKSPEARE has put into the mouth of his HENRY the Fourth, a beautiful expression on this subject, well worth the attention of Kings—

> "Had I so lavish of my presence been,
> So common hackney'd in the eyes of men,
> Opinion, that did help me to the Crown,
> Had still kept loyal to possession,
> And left me in reputeless banishment,
> A fellow of no mark, nor likelihood.
> By being seldom seen, I could not stir,
> But, like a comet, I was wonder'd at:
> That men would tell their children, This he he."

Of the number I have heard, I will mention one anecdote only, and one remarkably expression of JOSEPH's, which will serve to shew in its true light what his disposition was; and when you consider them as the act and sentiment of a young man nursed in the lap of despotism and pride, you cannot but consider them as marvellous.

In his journey to the low countries, he visited Wurtzaurg; and, in his perambulating alone and *incog*, stopped at a little public-house, where the people were busily employed in entertaining themselves: he went in, and inquired why they were so merry—" Sir," said one of the country people, " we are celebrating a marriage." " May I be permitted to join the company?" said the disguised Emperor. The host obtained that permission for him. When he entered the room, the married couple were presented to him, and he received them with great gaiety, sat down, drank their health, and, having informed himself of their situation, took leave of the company: but what was their astonishment, when, on lifting up a bottle of wine, they found a draft for six hundred florins, signed JOSEPH, and payable for the use of the married couple.

At Luxembourg, when the people called aloud on Heaven to shower down blessings on him for his affability, he made use of this remarkable expression, while his feelings moistened his eyes: " I wish I could make you as happy in my care, as I am in your affection!"

The affability of monarchs has often been magnified by the foolish, and often blamed by the wise: But, if all the instances of condescension practised by kings were like that I have recited of JOSEPH; if they arose from a sound, unquestionable spirit of philanthropy, not from gaping curiosity, broad folly, or a peurile inquisitive habit; and if, instead of conceiving those they visit paid for their intrusion with the honour of having conversed with majesty, and leaving them churlishly, they would generously pay them with hard cash, as the good Emperor JOSEPH did; then, indeed, their affability might defy the exaggeration of fools, and must certainly command the applause of the wise.

On the 13th of July, the ceremony of inauguration took place at Brussels. Nothing could equal the splendour of the place but the general joy of the people: the crowds were beyond all conception immense, and every thing was carried on with regularity till evening, when, in playing off some fire-works, that noble building the town-house took fire, and was burnt: six unfortunate persons lost their lives, and twenty were dangerously hurted: those who perished were absolutely roasted, and their cries were beyond description piercing. To such a temper as JOSEPH's, you will readily conclude that this must be a most afflicting circumstance—it was so; and he left Brussels under the pressure of very different feelings from those with which he entered it, and was followed by the prayers and blessings of all the people.

But now we are to view the reverse of the medal. The sound of their prayers for his welfare, and praises of his goodness, had hardly died away upon their lips, ere their minds turned to revolt and rebellion. I will not say that they were not right in one or other, or which of those two extremes: certainly they could not be right in both; much less can their subsequent conduct be justified, or accounted for, in any principle of human nature, but that of the most abject meanness, dastardly feebleness, and gross folly. They returned to their allegiance, and besought forgiveness: that forgiveness was granted. How they have behaved since, I have already informed you, (see Letter IV.); and I have now to add, that, pillaged by the French, and likely to be left unprotected, they have again held their necks out, soliciting the protection and the yoke of Austria, and have actually offered to raise 100,000 men for the Emperor, *if* he will again drive the French out of their territories—An excellent word that IF!

How a people, once formed for manly pith and love of freedom, could bend so low, is unaccountable. It is a question hard to be determined, whether an obstinate adherence even to a bad cause, is not more respectable, than a fickle, alternate dereliction, and adoption of right and wrong, as it suits the caprice or convenience of the moment? Of two things so very contemptible, I think the former the least odious and least unmanly.

At the same time, my observations on the country led me to conceive, that under the name of freedom, they groaned under the yoke of tyranny; for, though the country was, as I have described it, charming, its fecundity unsurpassed, its face decorated with the best gifts of Providence—I mean, smiling fields and bleating plains—though *Ceres* profusely repaid the labours of the husbandman, though every field had the appearance of a garden, and though, upon inquiry, I found that land which would bring in England five pounds an acre, rented at eight, nine, and ten shillings of our money at most—yet, in spite of all this, the farmers were rather poor in general—not even one of them to be found rich and substantial, like the middle rank of that class of men in England. They wanted the great stimulus to industry—security of their property: they were liable to be turned out by their landlords at pleasure, and be plundered when it should please some monarch to make war.

The first of these, however, you will observe, is not the oppression of the Emperor: it is a tyranny of that worst of all constituent parts of a state, an aristocracy—a vile aristocracy!—that universal, that every-day despotism, under which all places groan, more or less—which is exercised in all the various gradations of life that chequer society, from the great man who, under the name of minister, domineers over the peer, to the country fox-hunting savage, who puts a poor wretch in jail to pine for years, (his family, the while, supported by the parish charity), only for doing that which makes the enjoyment of his own life, killing a partridge or a hare!—that aristocratic tyranny which is seen scowling on the brows of a swaggering fellow in power, adopted by his secretary with increase, by him handed down to an upstart set of fellows in office, dependent on his smile, and by them displayed in all the nauseous, despicable forms which awkwardness and ignorance lifted above their stations, never fail to assume—the cold reserve, the affected stare, the listless nod, the feigned deafness, blindness, absence, and other fashionable perfections, which serve as vents for upstart arrogance, and indemnify the sycophant for the vile homage and submission which he has before paid some wretch, mean and arrogant as himself!—I tell you, my dear FREDERICK, it is this aristocratic usurpation of power, where power exists not, nor is necessary—this insulting assumption of superiority, this hidden petty oppression which rears its head in every manor, nay, almost every town and village in the kingdom, that put the nations out of tune, mars the harmony of social arrangement, and renders power in the aggregate obnoxious. Why, our very women have their saucy, aristocratic, supercilious front, their haughty stare, their contemptuous titter; and barter the winning softness of the sex, the dimples where the loves should dwell, for the haughty toss of the head, the ill-natured sneer, and the insulting Hector's frown—And thus the spirit of aristocracy, like a poisonous weed, grows and expands from one to the other with baleful luxuriance, gradually overspreading the whole face of humanity, stopping the wholesome current of the social atmosphere, and choaking up the less rank but more useful plants—Thus it goes round in shameful traffic; and, as the poet says,

> "The wh—re she kicks her cully,
> Court-waiters are kick'd at call;
> We are all kick'd, yet bully
> While int'rest kicks the ball."

I am persuaded, that if the grievances of the most despotic states were fairly estimated, and assigned to their real authors, the princes of such states would be found responsible for a very small share indeed, when compared with the aristocracy: and by aristocracy, I mean not merely lords, but all men who convert the wealth which Providence has bestowed upon them to the purposes of tyranny, exactions, imposition and oppression—under which four heads we will again find, not only imprisonment for begging alms, imprisonment for shooting a partridge, but often seduction, adultery, and persecution for resisting or resorting to law for punishment of that seduction or adultery. Of all those things, the proofs, I fear, in all nations, are abundant: I am sure they are so in the best governed state in Europe—I mean, England—

"Qui capit, ille facit."

I have thrown up a fool's cap: how many are there who will privately put it on!

LETTER XIV.

As the time of my departure from Brussels approached, I found the bitter sensations with which I left London, in some measure, returning.

My fortunate encounter with General LOCKHART had afforded me a temporary respite; but now I was once more to face an unknown country alone, without the chance of again meeting a friend to solace my mind, or mitigate my woe, on this side of India.

Having seen as much of Brussels as my time and occasions would at all allow, and, in truth, having rather trespassed on my plan, for the reasons just mentioned, I determined to push forward as fast as it was possible, and took post for Liege, where I arrived, after passing through a beautiful, fertile, well-cultivated country, to the charms of which the renewed agony of my feelings rendered me almost insensible.

As we have now almost the whole length of Germany before us to travel through, it will be proper, before I proceed further, to give you a general idea of the constitution of this vast empire—over all which, while one great monarch nominally presides, there are spread a number of petty potentates, who really rule after as distinct forms of government as almost any two governments, however remote in Europe.

Considering the nature of government abstractedly, one would suppose that it arose from the general will of the society governed, and was formed for their use and benefit alone: but if we view the different systems scattered over the civilized part of the earth, we shall find that they originated from force and fraud; and that, in their first formation, when bodily prowess, not intellectual power, bore sway—when he that could carry the strongest armour, and strike the heaviest blows, was sure to govern—when mere animal strength and ferocity disinherited reason of her rights, and robbed her of that ascendency to which the invention of gunpowder, aided by the art of printing, has since in some sort restored her—the basis upon which governments were raised was, one man, not the whole society; the point then was, how this or that strong ruffian could collect most slaves about him, not how this or that society should choose the best head: if he has strength to carry havoc through the ranks of their enemies, and then to overawe themselves, he was sure of dominion over the people, and left it to his son; but if it so happened that he did not also bequeath to him bodily prowess to preserve it, the next strong ruffian seized the reins, flung him from his seat and kept it till he, or some one of his heirs, was again served so in his turn by some other usurper. Hence arose the cabals and intrigues of courts, the spirit of party, and intestine commotion; till at length the people, for their own security, and to avoid the horrors of civil war, made choice (from dismal necessity) of some one family to rule them. As society advanced, and opulence held forth temptation, some greater ruffian, followed by a horde of needy, famished barbarians, made incursions on those rulers; and being irresistible, as well from numbers firmly connected, as from the powerful impulse of necessity, under whose banners they generally robbed and ravaged, was submitted to on terms, and became Lord Paramount of a number of petty sovereigns, who did homage to him, and fleeced the miserable subjects, to keep him in humour; and thus, in a series of time, the power of both took root, and remained immoveable, unless when torn up by some violent tempest that convulsed the state, and shook it to its foundations.

Reading this account, you will very naturally exclaim, "Good God! how absurd! how irrational!" Yet so it is; and from this source, muddy though it be, is modern honour, and modern greatness, and modern high blood, derived: from this foul and turbid fountain have most of the governments of the world issued; from those strong men of yore have most of our modern governors descended: and as it generally happens (so equally has Providence distributed the gifts of nature) that the strength of the intellectual part is in the inverse ratio of the animal, perhaps that is the reason why monarchs are formed, in general, of greater bodily vigour than mental endowments, and better fitted for the field than the cabinet—and for this reason are obliged to take from the puisne ranks of their subjects some assistant, so far removed from the great standard of antique dignity, as to possess understanding enough to govern.

Upon a retrospective view of the History of Europe, it will be found, that for a long time after the birth of CHRIST, Germany was divided among such petty rulers as I have described, who each held his little state in sovereignty, and was called *Princeps* in Latin, or, in plain English, *Prince*. After the downfal of the Western Empire, a nation called *Franks*, from that part called *Franconia*, over-ran a great part of Gaul and Germany, and in the fifth century took possession of that part of Gaul which lay north of the river Loire. In the year 800, CHARLEMAGNE, the son of PEPIN, their king, formed an immense empire in the west, comprehending a great part of Germany, France, Italy, and a part of Spain. About eighty years afterwards, the petty princes of Germany shook off the French Carlovinian race, and elected an emperor of their own from the House of Bavaria.

At last HENRY the Fourth, having displeased that grand arbiter the Pope, was put under the ban, and in consequence deposed by the states; on which occasion his Holiness had the address to make that great dignity elective, he having uncontroled power over the electors; since which it has continued so, with some modifications, and under certain regulations, formed by CHARLES the Fourth, at the diet of Nuremberg. The election, however, has been always so managed, that it has never departed from the regular line of succession but when there was an actual want of heirs.

In a country over which the Pope had such influence, it might reasonably be supposed that intolerance is carried to a great length; but it is not so, as a review of each particular state shews. The established religion, in general, is Popery. JOSEPH the Second, that good and wise monarh, displayed a greater spirit of toleration than any other Catholic prince since HENRY the Fourth of France. He was not murdered by a friar for it, it is true—those days of pious barbarity are past; but he was visited on the occasion by his Holiness, who, after a variety of remonstrances against the relaxation he gave to religious severity in his own dominions, finding him unmoved by papers, resolved to attack him in person; but, whether it was that the pontifical amulet lost its charm when out of the air of Rome, or that his Holiness was not properly anointed before (like *Hecate* in *Macbeth*) he took his flight, or that he forgot some of those reliques which were expected to operate on JOSEPH's mind, so it was, that the good emperor continued inflexibly attached to his former resolve; and, after kissing his Holiness' toe, and a thousand other pretty politenesses, sent him back to Rome again with his finger in his mouth; and a story to relate, that would, at one time, have set all Europe in a flame, and sent the good monarch, like HENRY the Second of England, to lash himself naked over the rotten remains of some vagabond fraudulent priest.

In the election of emperor, the laws of the empire have laid down no qualification but that which ought to be the *fine quá non* of all princes, namely, that he be *justus, bonus, et utilis*—Neither have they made any limitation in regard to religion, nation, state, or age; nevertheless, the majority of electors being Papists, a Roman Catholic prince is always chosen.

The rank of the emperor is very great: he is looked upon by all crowned heads as the first European potentate; and, as such, precedence is always given him and his ambassadors: he is the supreme head of the German empire; but his power in the administration thereof is very limited indeed. In ancient times, the emperor had considerable domains and incomes; but warfare and prodigality have dissipated the greatest part of them, and they have been successively alienated or mortgaged, so that his revenues were very inconsiderable lately, and now, since the French war, are almost as nothing.

The present emperor FRANCIS found the empire, when he was elected, incumbent with difficulties of the most enormous magnitude—a war on which the existence of every monarchy in Europe seemed to depend, an exhausted treasury, and a disposition to revolt in a part of his dominions, the Netherlands. At this present time, his situation is, beyond that of every other prince, lamentable:—almost all his resources gone, and an insolent, formidable, triumphant enemy, proceeding and carrying conquest by rapid strides through his country. He called upon his people to support him. The states of the Netherlands, instead of assisting him to stop the progress of the enemy, invited and opened their gates to them, put them in their bosom, and were stung. Of the other states, some refuse their aid, while some have recourse to feeble expedients; and, to evade the weight, temporise, procrastinate, and shuffle, till at length will come the French army, and force them to do for their enemy ten times more than (if done timely, and with a good grace) might save the empire and themselves. The KING of PRUSSIA, one of those states, on being called upon, says he is busily employed in securing the plunder of Poland, and cannot come—while the tyger is glutting in the blood of the harmless flocks, the huntsmen are coming upon him, to cut him off. As an Englishman, zealous for the welfare of my country, I wish the KING of PRUSSIA may not, by his attention to Poland, sacrifice all Germany to the French. As an honest man, I cannot help entertaining a wish, that the scandalous and outrageous wrongs done to Poland, and this treachery to the allies whom he himself brought into the present difficulties, may be expiated by any calamity, however great, that does not extend to the interest or wellbeing of Europe.

It is a maxim in courts of equity, that a man coming to demand redress, should come with clean hands, and, seeking equity, should do equity. This maxim has unfortunately never yet extended to decisions between states: power is their right, and force decides—Yet, in a contest like the present, the very foundation of which is hostility to kings, and which is carried on in the twofold way of arms, in the open field, and private negociation for insurrection; when, for the interest of the cause they espouse, as well as their own personal safety, kings should assume at once their best form to appreciate themselves, and discredit their enemies in the eyes of mankind—in such a state of things, I say, for the KING of PRUSSIA and the EMPRESS of RUSSIA to take the part they have done with regard to Poland, is so extravagant, that we can only account for it in the will of the ALMIGHTY predisposing them for some extraordinary crisis. No one would expect them to depart from their accustomed crooked path of policy, if safety did not loudly call upon them to proceed in the direct road. It is monstrous to see beings endowed with common sense, expending themselves in an unjust struggle for aggrandizement, while the sword of extinction is suspended by a hair over their heads.

H

But to return—in this state is the young emperor at this moment, deserted by his people in the Low Countries, unaided by his Continental ally, and supported only by Great Britain. What the issue may be, GOD alone can tell: but every one possessing a heart of feeling, or a single sentiment of honour or justice, must wish that young prince a fortunate delivery from the difficulties which the impolicy and wickedness of others have led him into, and which the treachery of some of them make more formidable, if not utterly insuperable.

LETTER XV.

THE various districts or territories into which Germany is divided, go under a variety of designations, not known among us as independent titles to power—principalities, seigniories, counties, electorates, margravates, and bishoprics lay and spiritual. Of the lay bishoprics, Osnaburg, the prince bishop of which is our DUKE OF YORK, makes one: and Liege, where we are now arrived is the territory of a bishop lay and spiritual, or spiritual and temporal, one of the fairest kind of that class —for he possesses temporalities, and enjoys them; whereas their lordships merely spiritual, enjoy and have the ingratitude and impudence to renounce them: but no matter for that; the bishop of Liege possesses a bishopric, fruitful in corn, wine, wood, and pasture, with air extremely pleasant and temperate; and while the latter gives his terrestrial clay health and appetite, the former afford him the means of preserving the one, and indulging the other, with true spiritual comfort, and high ecclesiastical voluptuousness. In cases of repletion, too, the mineral waters of the bishopric, particularly the well-known one of Spa, offer their aid; and some of the best beer in the world, which is brewed in these territories diversifies his spiritual Lordship's cup, and, with its pungent bitter, sends back his palate to his wine with renovated relish.

It is astonishing how inconsistent with themselves, and how discordant in their constituent principles, some very wise institutions are. Thus episcopacy, and all other branches, posts or ranks, high or low, commissioned or non-commissioned, of the church, publicly and systematically profess poverty, abstinence, and an utter indifference to temporal concerns, while their livings are enormous, and, themselves overfed. Nay, so cautiously has ecclesiastical law provided for that, even in our liberal establishments, that a bishop, at his instalment, positively declares, in the face of GOD, at the holy altar, that he is averse to being a bishop—*nolo episcopari*—Under such conditions, what must not the charity, the condescension, the mortifying submission of a divine be, to stoop to a bishopric, and suffer such a heavy load to be heaped upon his back—against his will! Assuredly, the imposing a bishopric upon him must be a great act of violence on his inclinations: for I cannot think it possible that a Christian divine would, in the first place, commit the crime of simony by seeking preferment, and gaining it by prostitution; much less can I believe that he would be guilty, at the holy altar, of a solemn act of perjury, by swearing *nolo episcopari*, if he was not actually, and *bonâ fide*, averse to a bishopric.

The bishop of Liege, however, may be fairly acquitted on the score of his temporal half, for the share of transgressions committed by his spiritual half. And unquestionably, as a Christian divine, he must groan in spiritual humiliation, when he reflects that his title is emblazoned with the gorgeous vanities of prince of Liege, duke of Bouillon, marquis of Franchemont, count of Looz, &c. Such a set of proud worldly titles are of themselves sufficient (putting the wine and beer, and repletion, out of the question) to annihilate the spiritual merits of the bishop, and expunge the grace of God from his name here, if not from himself hereafter.

Of all kinds of slavery, that nation groans beneath the worst, which has the name, without the essence, of a free constitution; and Germany abounds with such. By the constitution of this bishopric, the government consists of three states, the first is the chapter of Liege; the second, the nobility; and the third, the deputies of the towns and capital. These, however, are very seldom called together, except to *raise taxes*, or on some such *extraordinary* emergency: but there is a committee of the states who meet three times a-week, and in time of war daily; they are always about the prince bishop, to make remonstrances, and demand the redress of grievances—from whence we may reasonably infer, that the people are well protected, or at least well governed; the continual intercourse between the committee and bishops, no doubt, tending to promote a very happy influence in favour of the people!

In forming this constitution, special care has been taken to give the first state a great preponderance. The chapter is to consist of sixty persons, who must either prove their nobility for four generations, both by father and mother, or have been doctors or licentiates of divinity for seven years, or of law for five years, in some famous university, before they can be admitted.

How is it that the profession of the law should bear such potent sway in almost all countries—that even in Liege, a Catholic country and ecclesiastical government, five years study of the law should be deemed an equal qualification of seven of divinity?

In England, and its dependencies, the ascendancy of the law is still greater; and even in America, that profession is the first step to state honours. The truth is, that the science of the law, which, however despicable in practice, is the noblest of human sciences, quickens and invigorates the understanding more than all the other kinds of learning put together; while the study of divinity (I do not mean real divinity or morality, but that whimsical jumble of miracles and incongruities, of fulsome cant and senseless rhapsody, called to by churchmen) contracts the understanding, and bends it into a kind of crooked cunning. Formerly, the clergy were the dispensers of the laws, and they alone studied it—Happy times! happy people! When the united powers of both lawyers and priests were lodged in the same person, it is no wonder that they were able to enslave the persons, when they had got possession of the understanding, of the people—that we at this day see so many stupendous monuments remaining of their pride and power, and that the bloated load of episcopacy still has its votaries and supporters.

The bishopric of Liege is very populous and extensive, containing many large towns, many baronies and seigniories, seventeen abbeys for men, who must be all gentlemen, and eleven for ladies, exclusive of swarms of inferior note. In this distribution of the abbeys, male and female, I do not think that sufficient regard has been had to equality of numbers: I really think the fathers have been ill used. The ladies, though, I dare say, are well enough contented with the arrangement.

Although, as I have already apprized you, I do not mean to enter into a minute description of towns, so very easily found in many volumes of geography and history, there occasionally occur certain curiosities in some of those towns, which it would be unpardonable in me to pass over, as they may not perhaps be found in such books of those sciences as fall in your way.

Liege, the capital of the bishopric, is unquestionably a beautiful city, of immense size: its opulence, its pleasantness, its plenty, and salubrity, may be calculated from the name it has long been expressly called by way of eminence—*the Paradise of Priests.*—Indeed, it must needs be a holy and happy city; for it is chiefly occupied with convents, churches, and other religious foundations.

The Paradise of Priests!—Excellent! Why, if the genius of sensuality himself were to torture his invention for centuries, to strike out an appellation for the grand emporium of luxury, voluptuousness, and sensual enjoyment, he could not have hit on one so singularly appropriate as *the Paradise of Priests.*

In a grand cathedral here, are five great silver chests full of reliques, besides several silver statues of saints; and a Saint GEORGE on horseback, of massy gold; and in Saint WILLIAM's Convent, without the city, is the tomb of the famous English traveller, Sir JOHN MANDEVILLE, from whom all lying travellers have been since proverbially called *Mandevilles*—an appellation which, I promise you, I will hazard the imputation of dulness rather than incur. I suppose it was for his truly priestlike powers in the *marvellous* that he was honoured with a birth among their reverences. They have thought it necessary, however, to entreat, by an inscription in bad French, all persons who see it, to pray for his soul. In truth, poor Sir JOHN's marvellous stories were as harmless as ever were invented, and entertaining to boot. If so much could be said for their reverences, they might venture to rest their future safety on their own innocence and GOD's mercy: but I fear their miracles cut deeper, and will be found to go to a much more important and serious account.

In the bishopric of Liege, twenty miles from the capital, stands the famous town of Spa, so renowned for its excellent waters, that it has become a vulgar name for almost all mineral waters whatsoever. Those are said to open obstructions, concoct crudities, dry up excessive moisture, and strengthen the nerves and bowels; and such is their reputation, that prodigious quantities of them are carried into foreign countries.

Fortunate coincidence, to have such a choice and easy panacea for intemperance attached to *the Paradise of Priests!*

LETTER XVI.

Aix-la-Chapelle—The imperial city of Aix-la-Chapelle, by the Germans called Achen, lies at the distance of twenty-six miles, nearly east, of Liege. As it was a moderate stage, the weather fine, and the face of the country around beautiful, I found my journey extremely pleasant, and entered that famous city in as good a disposition to be pleased with it, as circumstances and reflections so melancholy as mine (which, in spite of every effort, would intrude themselves) may be supposed to allow. It is certainly a very fine city, and well deserves the reputation it has in all parts of the world.

Perhaps no city in Germany has a fairer claim to antiquity than Aix-la-Chapelle; for it was famous, even, in the time of the ancient Romans, for its waters, and was by them called *Aquisgranum,* or *Urbs Aquensis.* It was destroyed by the Huns, who, like the French now, destroyed and trampled under foot every vestige of refinement, wherever they carried their conquests; and it lay in ruins till it was rebuilt by CHARLEMAGNE, who made it the seat of his empire on this side of the Alps. By him it was ordained, the kings of the Romans should be crowned there: and it has been famous, since that time, for councils and treaties, particularly that famous one between France and Spain in 1663, and another lately between France and Great Britain.

Although there are many Protestants, both Lutherans and Calvinists, in this city, they are obliged to go to church two miles off, at a place called Vaels, in the dutchy of Limburg; so that Popery prevails with some portion of its intolerance. Here, as in all other places subject to its power, it has raised the Gothic gloomy pile, accumulated enormous masses of wealth, and hoarded up treasures, under the gulling pretexts of religious paraphernalia: a golden casket, set with precious stones of inestimable value, is hoarded up, not for the actual value of the moveable, but as the only fit receptacle for a relique it contains—a curious one, too, even of its kind—a bit of earth!—A bit of earth? yes! a bit of earth, common earth!—only with this fortunate circumstance in addition, that a drop of the blood of Saint STEPHEN fell, or is said to have fallen, upon it, as he was stoned to death! think of that, master FREDERICK! Why, when those things occur to me, I feel myself agitated by a whimsical tumult of sensations, serious and ludicrous, sorrowful and merry, that it is impossible to describe—something like that state in which the spirits flutter when a person whimpers between a laugh and cry. But, to carry the matter farther, when we recollect that some of the wisest and brightest of mankind, some of the bravest warriors, sternest philosophers, and ablest statesmen, that ever existed, have been the dupes of those shallow artificers, and actually have knelt in devout homage

ARRIVAL AT AIX-LA-CHAPELLE. 93

to these bits of earth, bone, sticks, and stone, &c. we must allow that it answers a great and noble end, by pointing out to us the infirmity of our nature, and shewing us, to use the words of one of our brightest luminaries, " what shadows we are, and what shadows we pursue !"

We have already had, and are likely yet to have such a clumsy load of cathedrals to attend to, that I should not mention that of Aix-la-Chapelle (a large, gloomy, dreary, old-fashioned, Gothic pile), were it not that it carries along with it some matters worthy of notice. What think you, then, of an emperor, a pope, and three hundred and sixty-five bishops, in one company ? Oh ! precious assemblage ! But where, I hear you ask—where, in the name of GOD, collect the bishops ? a pope and emperor are easily had ! My dear FREDERICK, three hundred and sixty-five bishops might easily be picked up in Christendom, and leave more behind, too, than would serve any useful purpose to the world.—Yes, the Emperor CHARLEMAGNE, and three hundred and sixty-five bishops, were present at the consecration of this cathedral by Pope LEO the Third. That emperor lies now in great state under the altar of the choir : Pope LEO, rots in Rome ; and for the bishops, they are gone, perhaps, as *Hamlet* says, " to stop a beer barrel."—

" Th' imperial CÆSAR, dead, and turn'd to clay,
Might stop a hole, to keep the wind away "

From such a splendid and opulent attendance at the consecration, one would naturally expect that this cathedral would have been, at the very outlet, enriched with costly and valuable trappings : but no---one image of that of Liege would purchase the whole. It should be recollected, however, that they were all, excepting the emperor, Churchmen ---a class, whose charity, generally speaking, has, like a ring, neither end nor beginning ; or at least ends and begins in itself, where nobody can see it; or, according to the old proverb, begins at home.

To compensate, however, for those worldly, worthless vanities, gold, silver, and jewels, his Holiness, and their three hundred and sixty-five Graces, presented the cathedral with some exquisite pieces of relique, of more inestimable value, by their account, than the mines of Potosi or Golconda: the first, an old covering—it would be folly for me to say, whether gown, petticoat, or shift—but they, that is to say, the priests, say, and the faithful believe them, that it was the shift worn by the Virgin MARY at the birth of CHRIST—how their Holinesses came by it, is hard to conjecture: —in the next place, a piece of coarse cloth, which, they also say, and are believed when they say, was girt about CHRIST on the cross: thirdly, a piece of cord, with which they say he was bound:—fourthly, some of the blood of Saint STEPHEN, now eighteen hundred years old;—and, fifthly, a picture of the Virgin and Child, embossed on a jasper, by Saint LUKE. With all due deference to their Reverences' knowledge, I should think a dozen statues in gold of the apostles would be rather a more valuable gift, and more ornamental, than these rags and cords, which I dare say did not cost altogether six pence. We talk here of our blue ribbons, our red ribbons, and our stars as great donations; but I think the presents of the Pope and three hundred and sixty-five bishops to the cathedral of Aix-la-Chapelle, beat them out of the field, whether we consider the magnificence of the gift, or the generosity of the givers.

But that which, above all things, renders Aix-la-Chapelle worthy of notice, is the salubrity of its waters, which bring from England, and all other European nations, a vast concourse of valetudinarians, who contribute at once to the gaiety and opulence of the city and adjacent country. Some of those waters are used for drinking, and others for bathing, resembling very much, in their quality, the virtues of those of Bath in Somersetshire, but that some of them are still hotter and stronger: they are unpleasant to the taste till use reconciles the palate to them, and most of them have a very offensive smell; but they are often powerful in effect, and give relief in a great variety of maladies; and they are rendered still more palatable by the commodious neatness of the baths, the excellence of the accommodations, and the great plenty of provisions, which are at once good and reasonable in this city.

I staid so short a time at Aix-la-Chapelle, that I could not, without the aid of some of the miracles wrought by the saints of the Romish church, or Sir JOHN MANDEVILLE, acquire a sufficient knowledge of the people, to attempt a description of them, or their manners—but it and Spa are so well known, that you cannot have much trouble in finding a description of them already written.

As far as my observations enabled me to judge, there was nothing in the German character that had the power either to create interest, or excite great attention.---They are rather to be approved than admired; and, wanting those prominent features that so whimsically chequer other nations with the extremes of bad and good, majestic and ridiculous, afford little subject to the traveller for the indulgence of sentimental reflection, or to the philosopher for the exercise of moral speculation.

LETTER XVII.

BIDDING adieu to the famous city of Aix-la-Chapelle, which, very untraveller-like, I passed without drinking of its waters, I pushed on, and soon arrived at the city of Juliers, the capital of a dutchy of that name, sixteen miles from Aix. The country itself is wonderfully fruitful, teeming with abundance of all sorts of corn, wood, pasture, woad, coal, and cattle; above all, a most excellent breed of horses, of which great numbers are exported.

As to the city, though a capital, there was nothing in it that I thought worth attention---that of neatness is its greatest praise. It is not, like Liege, overloaded with enormous church edifices; but, what is much better, the people are opulent, the poor well supplied, and all happy. In all likelihood, this is owing to the inhabitants being a mixture of Protestant and Roman Catholic; for, by a treaty between the Elector Palatine and the Emperor of Brandenburg, respecting the succession of the territories of the Duke of Cleves, both the Lutherans and Calvinists of this dutchy, and of Berg, are to enjoy the public exercise of their religion, and all other religious rites.

If experience would allow us to wonder at any thing in the management of the rulers of nations, it must surely be matter of astonishment, that in an article of such consequence as eternity, and which must be directed by private sentiments alone, such violence should systematically be offered to opinion, and that mankind should be dragooned, as they have been for so many weary centuries, into the profession of particular modes of faith. Combating opinion by force is so absurd, that I am sure those who attempted it, never could flatter themselves with the slightest hopes of success. It is therefore clear, that it was in motives very different from real wishes for the eternal welfare of man's soul, that religious persecution originated. Political finesse and state stratagem are the parents of persecution: and until every constitution is clean purged of religious prejudices, it must continue to be clogged with obstructions, and involved in confusion. If it be objected that certain religious sects are hostile to certain states, it may be answered, that they are so because the state is hostile to them. Cease to persecute, and they will cease to be hostile—*Sublata causa tollitur effectus.* It is folly, broad folly, to suppose that there are in any particular religion, seeds of hostility to government, any more than in any particular name, complexion, stature, or colour of the hair. Put, for experiment, all the men in the kingdom, of above five feet ten inches high, under tests and disqualifications, (and it would be full as rational as any other tests)—and, my life for it, they would become hostile, and very justly, too; for there is no principle, human or divine, that enforces our attachment to that government which refuses us protection, much less to that which brands us with disqualifications, and stigmatises us with unmerited marks of inferiority.

The states of this dutchy, and that of Berg, consist of the nobility and the deputies of the four chief towns of each; and they lay claim to great privileges in their diets—but they are subject to the Elector Palatine, to whom they annually grant a certain sum for the ordinary charges of the government, besides another which bears the name of a free gift.

I

Some authors say that this town was founded by JULIUS; others deny it; the dispute has run high, and is impossible to be determined: fortunately, however, for mankind, it does not signify a straw who built it; nor could the decision of the question answer any one end that I know, of instruction, profit, or entertainment. *Parva leves capiunt animos.* Those who rack their brains, or rather their heads, for brains they can have none, with such finical impertinent inquiries, should be punished with mortification and disappointment, for the misuse of their time. But what else can they do? You say, Why, yes; they might sit idle, and refrain from wasting paper with such execrable stuff; and that would be better. By the bye, if there were two good friends in every library in Europe, licensed to purge it, like the Barber and Curate in *Don Quixotte*, of all its uselels and mischievous stuff, many, many shelves that now groan under heavy weights would stand empty.

Travelling over a very even road, and a country extremely flat, (for from Aix-la-Chapelle I met with but one hill), I arrived at Cologne, the capital, not only of the archbishopric of that name, but of the Circle of the Lower Rhine. My spirits, which were not in the very best tone, were not at all raised on entering the city, by the ringing of church-bells, of all tones and sizes, in every quarter. Being a stranger, I thought it had been a rejoicing day; but, on inquiry, found that it was the constant practice. Never, in my life, had I heard such an infernal clatter: never before had I seen any thing so gloomy and melancholy—the streets black—dismal bells tolling—bald-pated friars, in myriads, trailing their long black forms through the streets, moulding their faces into every shape that art had enabled them to assume, in order to excite commiseration, and begging alms with a melancholy song calculated for the purpose, somewhat like that

of our blind beggars in London, and productive of
the same disagreeable effect upon the spirits. In
short, I was not an hour in Cologne, when those
circumstances, conspiring with the insuperable
melancholy of my mind, made me wish myself out
of it.

Nevertheless, Cologne is a fine city; and if it be
any satisfaction to you to spin those fine imaginary
ligaments that, in the brain of the book-worm, con-
nect the ancient and modern world, I will inform
you, that it was anciently called *Colonia Agrippina*,
because AGRIPPINA, the mother of NERO, was
born there, and honored it with a Roman colony,
because it was her birth-place. The mind, forced
back to that period, and contemplating the mischiefs of that monster NERO, cannot help wishing
that Cologne had been burnt the nigth of her birth,
and Miss AGRIPPINA buried in the ruins, ere she
had lived to give birth to that scourge of the world.

Although the established religion here be the
Roman Catholic, extraordinary as it may appear,
they are very jealous of power; and though the
elector, by his officers, administers justice in all
criminal causes, they will not permit him, in person, to reside above three days at a time in the city,
nor to bring a great train with him when he visits
it; for this reason he commonly resides at Bonne.

Cologne has a very considerable trade, particularly
in Rhenish wine; and its gin is reckoned the best
in the world, and bears a higher price than any
other in all the nations of Europe.

Like all great Roman Catholic cities, it had a
profusion of churches, crosses, miracles, saints, and
church trinkets; and I really think it has more
steeples and bells than any two cities in Germany.
As Liege was called the Paradise of Priests, this
ought to be called the Golgotha of Skulls and
Skull-caps. In the church of Saint URSULA, they
shew, or pretend at least to shew, the bones of

eleven thousand virgin martyrs. The skulls of some of those imaginary virgins are in silver cases, and others in skull-caps, of cloth, of gold, and velvet. And in the church of Saint GERION, are no less than nine hundred heads of Moorish cavaliers, of the army of the Emperor CONSTANTINE, (previous to that saint's conversion to Christianity), who, they say was beheaded for refusing to sacrifice to idols: by the bye, the Popish divines burn, instead of beheading, for not sacrificing to idols—Every one of those heads, however, has a cap of scarlet, adorned with pearls. The whole forms a spectacle no doubt equally agreeable and edifying. It struck me, however, as an extremely ludicrous sight, malgre the solemnity of so many death's heads: and when their story was recounted, I could not help internally chuckling, and saying (rather punningly, to be sure), " Ah! what *blockheads* ye must have been, to suffer yourselves to be separated from your snug warm bodies, rather than drop down and worship an idol, in which so many good Christian divines have shewn you an example!" This, you will conclude, I said to myself: an avowal of my sentiments in that place might have given my head a title to a scarlet cap and pearls; and as I had some further use for it, I did not think it expedient to leave it behind me in the church of Saint GERION —so, very prudently, kept my mind to myself.

Coming out of the church, a multitude of beggars, all in canonicals, or student's habits, surrounded, beseeching me for alms—one, pour l'amour de DIEU; another, pour l'amour de la Sainte Vierge; a third, pour le salut de notre Redempteur; a fourth, pour l'amour de Saint GERION; and so on!

When I had gone as far as I wished in donations, another attacked me: though I told him my charity-bank was exhausted, he persevered, and was uncommonly solicitous—till at length, having exhaunted the whole catalogue of faints that are to be found in the calendar, he raifed his voice from the miferable whine of petition, and exclaimed with great energy, " Par les neuf cent tetes des Cavaliers Maures qui font fanctifies au Ciel, je vous conjure de me faire l'aumone!" This was too formidable an appeal to be flighted; and fo, in homage to the fkulls and red caps, I put my hand in my pocket, and ftopped his clamours.

Thofe miferable modes of peculation are the moft pardonable of any produced by the church: we have no right to regret a trifle facrificed at the fhrine of compaffion, even when that compaffion is miftaken; but our reafon revolts at impofition, when it calls coercion to its aid, and affumes the name of right.

Without any national predilection, which you know I am above, I think our church affairs in Scotland are arranged upon a better fyftem than any other that I know of: hence their clergy are in general examples worthy of imitation, for learning, piety, and moral conduct.

LETTER XVIII.

LABOURED inveftigations to eftablifh connections between the hiftory of the ancient and bufinefs of the modern world, and virulent difputes about trifles of antiquity, fuch as in what year this place was built, or that great man was born, when and where JULIUS CÆSAR landed in England, whether he paffed this road or that, what route HANNIBAL took over the Alps, and fuch like, are fo effentially uninterefting, ufelefs, and unimportant, fo unprofitable, and, one would think, fo painful too, that it is wonderful how so many men of great learning have been unwise enough to employ their lives in the research.

It does not follow, however, that when information that tends to recall to our minds the great men of antiquity is presented to us, we should reject it. A man of classical taste and education feels a delight in those little memorials of what gave him pleasure in his youth. I know a gentleman, who, being at Seville, in Spain, travelled to Cordova, for no other purpose but to see the town where LUCAN and SENECA were born: and I dare say, that if you were at Cologne, you would be much pleased to see the town-house, a great Gothic building, which, contains a variety of ancient inscriptions; the first to commemorate the kindness of JULIUS CÆSAR to the Ubii, who inhabited this place, and of whom you have found mention made by him in his Commentaries, and also his building two wooden bridges over the Rhine: a second commemorates AUGUSTUS sending a colony here. There is also a crossbow of whalebone, twelve feet long, eight broad, and four inches thick, which they who speak of it conjecture to have belonged to the Emperor MAXIMIN. There are also some Roman inscriptions in the arsenal, the import of which I now forget.

It is very extraordinary, but certainly a fact, that there are, about Cologne, families yet existing, who indulge the senseless ambition of pretending to be descended from the ancient Romans, and who actually produce their genealogies, carried down from the first time this city was made a colony of the Roman empire. Of all kinds of vanity, this is perhaps the most extravagant; for, if antiquity merely be the object, all are equally high, since all must have originated from the same stock; and if it be the pride of belonging to a particular family who were distinguished for valour or virtue, a claim which often only serves to prove the degeneracy of the claimant, it could not apply in the case of a whole people: but this is among the frailties of humanity; and we are often so dazzled with the splendour of terrestrial glory, that we endeavour to be allied to it even by the most remote and ridiculous connections. I heard of a man, whose pride and boast, when drunk, was, that Dean SWIFT had once thrown his mother's oysters (she was an oyster-wench) about the street, and then gave her half a crown as an atonement for the injury. On the strength of this affinity did he call the Dean nothing but *Cousin Jonathan*, though the Dean was dead before he was born!

But of all the stories I have ever heard as illustrative of this strange ambition, that which the late Lord ANSON has left us is the most striking. When that great man was travelling in the East, he hired a vessel to visit the island of Tenedos: his pilot, a modern Greek, pointing to a bay as they sailed along, exclaimed in great triumph, "There, av, there it was that our fleet lay."—"What fleet?" interrogated ANSON—" Why, our Grecian fleet, at the siege of Troy," returned the pilot.

While those doughty descendants of the ancient Romans indulge the cheerless idea of their great and illustrious line of ancient ancestry, the prince who rules them felicitates himself with the more substantial dignities and emoluments of his modern offices. As elector and archbishop of Cologne, he has dominion over a large, fruitful, and opulent country: he is the most powerful of the ecclesiastical electors: he has many suffragan princes, lay and spiritual, under him; and he is archchancellor of the Holy Roman Empire. The revenues of his archbishopric amount annually to one hundred and thirty thousand pounds Sterling; and as elector, he is possessed of several other great benefices. I presume, because he is a prince, that he is a man of sense; and, I will venture to say, that, as such, he would not barter those good things for the power to demonstrate that LUCRETIA was his aunt, BRUTUS his grandfather, and the great JULIUS CÆSAR himself his cousin-german.

CHRIST chose his disciples out of fishermen. The Chapter of Cologne is, perhaps, on the contrary, the very most aristocratic body existing, being composed of forty canons, who are princes or counts of the empire—Of those, twenty-five choose the archbishop, and many advance one of their own body to that great and wealthy dignity, if they please.

From Cologne I proceeded to the town of Bonne, which is said to take its name from the pleasantness of its situation. Here the elector resides, and has a very fine palace. The country around is extremely fruitful and pleasant, and is blessed with most of the good things which render the rich magnificent and happy, and remind the poor of their inferiority and wretchedness—particularly wine, which is here remarkably excellent. It contains churches, priests, convents, cloisters, &c.; but I need not mention them—what place could exist without them?

I should not forget to tell you, that, at this place, JULIUS CÆSAR built one of his bridges across the Rhine—works which would have handed down to posterity the name of a common man, for the magnitude of the structure and ingenuity of the contrivance, but are lost in the crowd of astonishing talents which distinguished that brightest of mortals. The greatest biographer of antiquity says of him, that he was as great a general as HANNIBAL, as great an orator as CICERO, and as great a politician as AUGUSTUS; but it might be added, that he was among the first poets of his day—that he was of the first mechanical genius, and the finest gentleman, in Rome.

Nature seems to have formed, in CÆSAR, a compendious union of all human talents, as if to demonstrate how unavailing they were when opposed to strict rigid honesty and virtue in the character of BRUTUS.

To go from Bonne to Frankfort, there are two ways—one over the mountains of Wetterania, the other up the river Rhine. I made no hesitation to adopt the latter, and was rewarded for my choice with the view of as fine a country, inhabited by as fine a race of people, as I had ever seen. Valleys filled with herds, plains enamelled with corn-fields, and the hills covered with vineyards, regaled the eye, and conveyed to the mind all the felicitating ideas of plenty, natural opulence, and true prosperity. My anxiety, however, to get forward, and disengage myself from a species of solitude in a country where, though travelling is cheap, accommodations of most kinds in the public houses are bad, induced me to push on, without taking the time necessary for making accurate observations on the country as I passed; so that, gliding, as it were, imperceptibly, through a number of towns, of which I recollect nothing distinctly but the names of Coblentz and Mentz, I arrived at the great, free, and imperial city of Frankfort on the Maine.

Here I shall stop, for a short time, my relation, in order to give you time for just reflection and examination of what I have already written: and as, in the latter part of it, I have skimmed very lightly over the country, I desire that you will supply the deficiency of my information by close research in books; inform yourself of the great outlines of the Germanic Constitution; look back to its origin, its progress, and its establishment; thence proceed to the distinct parts, or inferior states, of which it is composed; ponder them all well; and from those draw your own inferences, and let me hear what they are with freedom: should they be wrong, I will endeavour to set them right; but should they be right, they will afford me the most lively satisfaction; for they will serve to correct one of the greatest errors under which youth labours—an overweening, sanguine imagination, that things in this life are, or at least can be modelled into perfection; whereas experience, and a just observation of the history of mankind, will shew, that on this ball things will never be as they ought, but must remain as they are—imperfect.

LETTER XIX.

THE country about Frankfort is delightful, rich and fruitful, and watered by the beautiful river Maine, which divides the city into two parts, that on the north being called Frankfort, and that on the south, Saxenhausen, from the Saxons, who are supposed to have been the founders of it. The city itself is large, populous, and rich, and distinguished for being the place where the emperor and king of the Romans is elected—though, by the appointment of CHARLEMAGNE, Cologne has a superior claim to that honor. The magistrates, and great part of the inhabitants, are Lutherans or Calvinists; notwithstanding which, most of the churches are in the hands of the Roman Catholics—a laudable instance of the true tolerant spirit of a wise and virtuous institution, and a heavy reflection upon, as well as a noble example to the Popish Powers of Europe.

The territory belonging to Frankfort is of very considerable extent; and the trade carried on through it, by means of the rivers Rhine and Maine, of very great importance, not only to the country itself, but to other commercial nations, and particularly to Great Britain, whose manufactures are sent to Frankfort, and thence circulated through the Continent, in amazing quantities.

The fairs of Frankfort are talked of all over Europe—of such importance are they in the world of commerce. They are held, one at Easter, and another in September, and continue for three weeks, during which time the resort of people there from all quarters is astonishing. Every thing is done by the government to render them as attractive to merchants as possible; and taxes or duties are extremely low—a bale of the value of ten or twenty thousand crowns paying duty only about ten or eleven pence of our money. All commodities from all parts of the world are sold there, and circulated through the empire; but, particularly, books are sold in prodigious quantities. After the fairs are over, the shops of the foreign merchants are shut up; and their names written over their doors.

To give an idea of the great importance these fairs are to commerce, I need only mention, that in the present war, the impediments thrown by the French in the way of the transit of goods up the Rhine, and the shutting up that fair, gave a most alarming paralysis to the manufacturing establishments of England, and a shock to public credit in consequence, that would, but for the timely interference of Parliament, have, in all probability, been fatal to the national credit.

Frankfort is in many respects a pleasant place: the merchants are extremely convivial and sociable, and form clubs, where they meet to drink tea and coffee, and play at cards. There is a playhouse also, a great number of coffee-houses, and other houses of entertainment in abundance. The country around is covered with woods and vineyards, and the circumjacent villages are very pleasant, and well supplied with houses of entertainment, to which the inhabitants of the city resort in the

Summer season: and the inns in Frankfort are excellent.

A singular custom prevails here, which I think worth mentioning: Taverns are denoted by pine-trees planted before the doors of them; and the different prices of the wines in their cellars are marked in ciphers on the door-posts.

In the town here is presented the original Golden Bull, or Pope's Authority, which contains the rules and orders to be observed at the election of the Emperors. The Golden Bull is never shown to strangers but in the presence of two of the council and the secretary—It is a little manuscript in quarto, consisting of forty-two leaves of parchment, with a gold seal of three inches diameter, of the value of twenty ducats, hung to it by a cord of yellow silk. It is said to be written in Latin and Gothic characters, without diphthongs; and kept in a black box together with two written translations of it into the German language.

It is said of Frankfort, that the Roman Catholics possess the churches, the Lutherans the dignities, and the Calvinists the riches. It is therefore one of the few places in Christendom where the churches and the riches do not go into the same hands.

From Frankfort to Augsburgh, I passed through a number of towns, all of them so very inconsiderable as not to merit any particular description. The way lies from the Palatinate though the Circle of Suabia. In the extreme end of the Palatinate, and immediately before entering the Dutchy of Wirtemberg, the country is covered with fir-trees, and money is so scarce in it, that a loaf of wheaten bread, weighing eight pounds, costs but two pence.

This city of Augsburgh is the capital of a bishopric of that name in the Circle of Suabia, and is worthy of the attention of the classical traveller for its antiquity. About twelve years before the birth of Christ, Augustus Cæsar subdued all this country, and, on the place where Augsburgh now stands, formed a colony, gave the town the name of Augusta Vindelicorum, and put it under the government of Drusus the brother of Tiberius, afterwards emperor of Rome. The inhabitants of this place were the Vindelici, a branch of the Illyrians. But, ancient though it be, it has little more of antiquity to entitle it to notice than the bare name; for it has been pillaged so often, particularly by that monster Attila, that there are scarcely any remains of its antiquity to be found.

Augsburgh, is now, however a handsome city—the public buildings in general magnificent, and adorned with fountains, water engines of a curious construction, and statues.

The most rich and splendid part of the town belongs to a family of the name of Fuggers (originaly descended from a weaver), who enriched themselves by commerce, and one of whom rendered not only himself, but the whole family, conspicuous, by entertaining the emperor Charles the Fifth in a superb manner, and supplying him with money, and then throwing his bond into the fire; in return for which, the emperor, made him a count of the empire.

This city is remarkable for goldsmiths' ware; and its mechanics are equal to any in the world, for works in gold, ivory, clocks, and time-pieces; and they engrave better than any people in Germany, which brings them considerable profits. But what they are, above all other people, eminent for, is the manufacturing steel-chains so prodigiously fine, that when one of them, of a span in length, has been put about the neck of a flea, it lifts up the whole of it as it leaps; and yet those are sold for less than a shilling of our money a piece.

Controversy, and difference in religious opinions, which has almost, ever since the commencement of

Christianity, disgraced the human understanding, and defaced society, imposes upon the liberal, well-thinking traveller, the office of satirist but too often. Augsburgh, however, is a splendid exception, and holds up a most glorious spectacle of manly sense, generous sentiment, justice, and I will say policy too, vanquishing that shark-jawed enemy of mankind, bigotry. The magistracy of Augsburgh is composed of about an equal number of Protestants and Roman Catholics—their senate consisting of twenty-three Roman Catholics and twenty-two Lutherans, and their common Council of a hundred and fifty of each : The executive power is lodged in the senate—the legislative authority in both bodies. But, what is hardly to be found any where, they all, as well as the people, agree together in the most perfect harmony, notwithstanding the difference of religion ; and at all tables but the communion table, they associate together, dip in the same dish, and drink of the same cup, as if they had never heard of the odious distinction of Papist and Protestant, but as being bound to each other by the great and irrefragable bond of humanity : fellow-creatures, affected by the same feelings, impelled by the same passions, labouring under the same necessities, and heirs to the same sufferings, their means of assuaging the one, gratifying or resisting another, and supplying the third, are the same, though chequered and varied a little in the mode—the road alone different, the ends alike. Is it not cruel, then—is it not intolerable, that the calamities inseparable from humanity should be aggravated with artificial stings, and the nakedness of human nature exposed, and rendered more offensive, by factitious calamities of human contrivance ? Cursed were those who first fomented those disputes, and cast those apples of discord through the world : blind were they who first were seduced from the paths of peace by them ; and more cursed, and more blind, must they be, who, in this time of intellect and illumination, continue on the one hand, to keep up a system so wicked and so detestable, or, on the other, to submit to error at once so foolish and so fatal.

LETTER XX.

FOR the reasons mentioned in my last, Augsburgh is a most agreeable place to live in. Touched with the sensations natural to a man who loved to see his fellow-creatures happy, my heart expanded to a system of peace and harmony, comprehending the whole globe: my mind expatiated involuntarily on the blessings and advantages derived from such a system; and, taking flight from the bounds of practicability, to which our feeble nature is pinned on this earth, into the regions of fancy, had reared a fabric of Utopian mold, which, I verily believe, exceeded in extravagance the works of all the Utopian architects that ever constructed castles in the air.

Hurried on by this delightful vision, my person paid an involuntary obedience to my mind; and the quickness of my pace increasing with the impetuosity of my thoughts, I found myself, before I was aware of it, within the chapel-door of the convent of the Carmelites. Observing my error, I suddenly turned about, in order to depart, when a friar, a goodly person of a man, elderly, and of a benign aspect, called me, and, advancing towards me, asked, in terms of politeness, and in the French language, why I was retreating so abruptly—I was confused: but truth is the enemy before whom confusion ever flies; and I told him the whole of my mistake, and the thoughts from which they arose.

The good father, waving further discourse on the subject, but with a smile which I thought carried a mixture of benevolence for myself, and contempt for my ideas, brought me through the church, and shewed me all the curiosities of the place, and particularly pointed out to me, as a great curiosity, a sun-dial made in the form of a Madonna, the head enriched with rays and stars, and in the hand a sceptre which marked the hours.

Quitting the chapel, and going towards the refectory, the friar stood, and, looking at me with a smile of gaiety, said, " I have yet something to shew you, which, while lady Madonna marks the time, will help us to pass it ; and, as it will make its way with more force and subtlety to your senses than those I have yet shewn you, will be likely to be longer retained in remembrance."

He spoke a few words in German, which of course I did not understand, to a vision bearing the shape of a human creature, who, I understood, was a lay-brother ; and, turning down a long alley, brought me to his cell, where we were soon followed by the aforesaid lay-brother, with a large earthen jug of liquor, two glasses, and a plate with some delicately white biscuit.

" You must know," said the friar, " that the convent of Carmelites at Augsburgh has for ages been famed for beer unequalled in any part of the world ; and I have brought you here to have your opinion—for, being an Englishman, you must be a judge, the Britons being famed for luxury, and a perfect knowledge of the *scavoir vivre*." He poured out, and drank to me : it looked liker the clearest Champaigne than beer—I never tasted any thing to equal it ; and he seemed highly gratified by my expressions of praise, which I lavished upon it, as well from politeness, as regard to truth.

After we had drank a glass each, " I have been reflecting," said the friar, " on the singular flight of fancy that directed your steps into this convent—Your mind was diseased, my son! and a propitious superintending Power has guided your steps to a physician, if you will but have the goodness to take the medicine he offers."

I stared with visible marks of astonishment.

" You are surprised," continued he; " but you shall hear! When first you disclosed to me those sickly flights of your mind, I could on the instant have answered them: but you are young—you are an Englishman—two characters impatient of reproof: the dogmas of a priest, I thought therefore, would be sufficiently difficult to be digested of themselves, without any additional distaste caught from the chilling austerity of a chapel!"

I looked unintentionally at the earthen jug, and smiled.

" It is very true," said he, catching my very inmost thoughts from the expression of my countenance—" it is very true! good doctrine may, at certain times, and with certain persons, be more effectually enforced under the cheering influence of the social board, than by the authoritative declamation and formal sanctity of the pulpit; nor am I, though a Carmelite, one of those who pretend to think, that a thing in itself good, can be made bad by decent hilarity, and the animation produced by a moderate and wise use of the goods of this earth."

I was astonished—

" You fell into a reverie," continued he, " produced by a contemplation of the happiness of a society existing without any difference, and where no human breath should be wasted on a sigh, no ear tortured with a groan, no tears to trickle, no griefs or calamities to wring the heart."

" Yes, father!" said I, catching the idea with my former enthusiasm; "that would be my wish— that my greatest, first desire."

"Then seeſt thou," interrupted he, "the extent of thy wiſh, ſuppoſe you could realize it, which, thank GOD! you cannot."

"What! thank GOD that I cannot? are theſe your thoughts?"

"Yes, my ſon; and ere Madonna marks the progreſs of ten minutes with her ſceptre, they will be your's too."

"Impoſſible!"

"Hear me, my ſon!—Is not death a horrible precipice to the view of human creatures?"

"Aſſuredly," ſaid I—"the moſt horrible: human laws declare that, by reſorting to it for puniſhment, as the ultimatum of all terrible infliċtions."

"When, then," ſaid he, "covered as we are with miſery, to leave this world is ſo inſupportable to the human reflection, what muſt it be if we had nothing but joy and felicity to taſte of in this life? Mark me, child!" ſaid he, with an animated zeal that gave an expreſſion to his countenance beyond any thing I had ever ſeen: "the miſeries, the calamities, the heart-rendings, and the tears, which are ſo intimately interwoven by the great artiſt in our natures as not to be ſeparated in a ſingle inſtance, are in the firſt place our ſecurity of a future ſtate, and in the next place ſerve to ſlope the way before us, and, by gradual operation, fit our minds for viewing, with ſome ſort of fortitude, that hideous chaſm that lies between us and that ſtate—death. View thoſe miſeries, then, as ſpecial acts of mercy and commiſeration of a beneficent Creator, who, with every calamity, melts away a link of that earthly chain that fetters our wiſhes to this diſmal world. Accept his bleſſings and his goods, when he ſends them, with gratitude and enjoyment: receive his afflictions, too, with as joyous acceptance, and as hearty gratitude. Thus, and not otherwiſe, you will realize all your Utopian flights of deſire, by turning every thing to matter of comfort, and living contented with dispensations which you cannot alter, and, if you could, would most certainly alter for the worse."

I sat absorbed in reflection—The friar, after some pause proceeded—

"Errors arising from virtuous dispositions and the love of our fellow-creatures, take their complexion from their parent motives, and are virtuous. Your wishes, therefore, my son! though erroneous, merit reward, and, I trust will receive it from that Being who sees the recesses of the heart; and if the truths I have told you have not failed to make their way to your understanding, let your adventure of to-day impress this undeniable maxim on your mind—so limited is man, so imperfect in his nature, that the extent of his virtue borders on vice, and the extent of his wisdom on error."

I thought he was inspired; and, just as he got to the last period, every organ of mine was opened to take in his words.

"'Tis well, my son!" said he—"I perceive you like my doctrine: then" changing his manner of speaking, his expressive countenance the whole time almost anticipating his whole words, "take some more of it," said he gaily, pouring out a fresh glass. I pleaded the fear of inebriety—"Fear not," said he; "the beer of this convent never hurts the intellect."

Our conversation continued till near dinner-time; for I was so delighted, I scarcely knew how to snatch myself away: such a happy melange of piety and pleasantry, grave wisdom and humour, I had never met. At length, the convent-bell tolling, I rose: he took me by the hand, and, in a tone of the most complacent admonition, said, "Remember, my child! as long as you live, remember the convent of the Carmelites; and in the innumerable evils that certainly await you if you are to live long, the words you have heard from old Friar AUGUSTINE will afford you comfort."

"Father!" returned I, "be assured I carry away from you a token that will never suffer me to forget the hospitality, the advice, or the politeness of the good father AUGUSTINE. Poor as I am in natural means, I can make no other return than my good wishes, nor leave any impression behind me: but as my esteem for you, and perhaps my vanity, make me wish not to be forgotten, accept this, (a seal ring, with a device in hair, which I happened to have on my finger); and whenever you look at it, let it remind you of one of those, I dare say innumerable, instances, in which you have contributed to the happiness and improvement of your fellow-creatures."

The good old man was affected, took the ring, and attended me to the convent gate, pronouncing many blessings, and charging me to make Augsburgh my way back again to England if possible, and take one glass more of the convent ale.

LETTER XXI.

LEAVING Augsburgh, I travelled thro' Bavaria a long way before I reached the Tyrol Country, of the natural beauty of which I had heard much, and which I therefore entered with great expectations of that sublime gratification the beauties of nature never fail to afford me. I was not disappointed; indeed, my warmest expectations were exceeded.

The first thing that strikes a traveller from Bavaria, on entering it, is the fort of Cherink, built between two inaccessible rocks which separate Tyrol from the bishopric of Freisingen. So amply has nature provided for the security of this country against the incursion of an enemy, that there is not a pass which leads to it that is not through some narrow defile between mountains almost inaccessible; and on the rocks and brows of those passes, the emperor has constructed forts and citadels, so advantageously placed, that they command all the valleys and avenues beneath.

After a variety of windings and turnings through mountains of stupendous height and awful aspect, I began to descend, and entered the most delightful valley I had ever beheld—deep, long, and above a mile in breadth—surrounded with enormous piles of mountains, and diversified with the alternate beauties of nature and cultivation, so as to form an union rarely to be met with, and delight at once the eye of the farmer, and the fancy of him that has a true taste for rural wildness. From the heights in descending, the whole appeared in all its glory; the beautiful river Inn gliding along through it longitudinally, its banks studded with the most romantic little villages, while a number of inferior streams were seen winding in different courses, and hastening to pour their tribute into its bosom.

Here I felt my heart overwhelmed with sensations of transport, which all the works of art could never inspire: here nature rushed irresistibly upon my senses, and, making them captive, exacted their acknowledgement of her supremacy: here vanity, ambition, lust of fame and power, and all the tinselled, gaudy frippery to which habit and worldly custom enslave the mind, retired, to make way for sentiments of harmony, purity, simplicity, and truth: here Providence seemed to speak in language most persuasive, "Come silly man, leave the wild tumult, the endless struggle, the glittering follies, the false and spurious pleasures which artifice creates, to seduce you from the true—dwell here, and in the lap of nature study me:" Here, oh! here, exclaimed I, in a transport which bereft me, for the time, of every other consideration, here will I dwell for ever. The charm was too finely spun, to withstand the hard tugs of fact; and all its precious delusions vanished before a host of gloomy truths—deranged affairs—family far off, with the distance daily increasing—the hazards and the hardships of a long untried journey—and the East Indies, with all its horrors, in the rear. I hung my head in sorrow; and, offering up a prayer to protect my family, strengthen myself, and bring us once more together in some spot heavenly as that I passed through, was proceeding on in a state of dejection proportionate to my previous transports, when I was roused by my postillion, who, pointing to a very high, steep rock, desired me to take notice of it. I did so; but seeing nothing very remarkable in its appearance, asked him what he meant by directing my attention to it—He answered me in the following manner, which, from the singularity of the narrative, and his strange mode of telling it, I think it would injure to take out of his own words: I will, therefore, endeavour, as well as I can, to give you a literal translation of it; and, indeed, the impression it made on my memory was such, that, I apprehend, I shall not materially differ from his words:

"You must know, Sir, (for every one in the world knows it), that all these mountains around us, are the abodes of good and evil spirits, or genii—the latter of whom are continually doing every malicious thing they can devise, to injure the people of the country,—such as leading them astray—smothering them in the snow—killing the cattle by throwing them down precipices—nay, when they can do no worse, drying up the milk in the udders of the goats—and, sometimes, putting between young men and their sweet-hearts, and stopping their marriage. Ten thousand curses light upon them! I should have been married two years ago, and had two children to-day, but for their schemes. In short, Sir, if it were not for the others—the good ones—who are always employed (and the blessed Virgin knows they have enough on their hands) in preventing the mischiefs of those devils, the whole place would be destroyed, and the country left without a living thing, man or goat!"

Here I could not, for the life of me, retain my gravity any longer, but burst, in spite of me, into an immoderate fit of laughter, which so disconcerted and offended him, that he sullenly refused to proceed with the story any farther, but continued marking his forehead (his hat off) with a thousand crosses, uttering pious ejaculations, looking at me with a mixture of terror, distrust, and admiration and every now and then glancing his eye askance toward the hills, as if fearful of a descent from the evil spirits.

My curiosity was awakened by the very extraordinary commencement of his narrative; and I determined, if possible, to hear it out: so, assuring him that I meant nothing either of slight or wickness by my laughter—that I had too serious ideas of such things to treat them with levity---and, what was more convincing logic with him, promising to reward him for it---he proceeded with his story as follows:

"Well, Sir, you say you were not sporting with those spirits---and fortunate it is for you: at all events, Saint JOHN of GOD be our guide, and bring us safe to Innspruck. Just so the great MAXIMILIAN was wont to laugh at them; and you shall hear how he was punished for it---and that was the story I was about to tell you. The Emperor MAXIMILIAN, that glory of the world, (he is now in the lap of the blessed Virgin in Paradise), once on a time, before he was emperor, that is to say, when he was archduke, was always laughing at the country people's fears of those spirits—and an old father of the church forewarned him to beware, lest he should suffer for his rashness: so one day he went out hunting, and at the foot of that mountain a most beautiful chamois started before him; he shot at it, and missed it---(the first shot he had missed for many years, which you know was warning enough to him)---however, he followed, shooting at and missing it, the animal standing every now and then till he came up within shot of it: thus he continued till near night, when the goat disappeared of a sudden, and he found himself buried, as it were in the bowels of the mountain: he endeavoured to find his way out, but in vain; every step he took led him more astray, and he was for two days wandering about, CHRIST save us! in the frightful hollows of those mountains, living all the time on wild berries: on the second night he bethought himself of his want of faith, and of the saying of old Father JEROME: and he fell on his knees, and wept and prayed all night; and the Virgin heard his prayers, he being a good man, and, above all, an emperor---GOD bless you and me! we should have perished---In the morning a beautiful young man, dressed in a peasant's habit, came up to him, gave him victuals and wine, and desired him to follow him, which he did, you may be sure, joyfully---but, Oh blessed Virgin! think what his surprise must have been, when, getting again into the plain out of the mountain, the young man disappeared and vanished all of a sudden. Just at the foot of that steep rock which I shewed you, and which ever since goes by the name of the emperor's rock---You see what a dangerous place it is, and what dangerous spirits they must be that would not spare even the holy Roman emperor. In my mind, the best way is to say nothing against those things, as some faithless people do, and to worship the Virgin and keep a good conscience, and then one will have the less to fear."

By the time he had ended his narrative, we were in sight of Innspruck, when I annoyed and terrified him afresh, by laughing immoderately at the end of his story—but atoned in some measure for it, by giving him half a florin.

'On inquiring at Innspruck, I found that MAXIMILIAN had actually lost his way in the mountain, and had been conducted out of it by a peasant, who left him suddenly; the rest was an exaggerated traditionary tale, arising from the superstitious fears of the country people.

LETTER XXII.

IN all nations under Heaven, and at all times since the creation there have been men formed to make a noise in the world—to increase or impede, to direct or disturb, the calm, sober progress of social life—and, in the eagerness and violence of their efforts to reach the goal of superiority, overturn or thrust out of their ordinary path the rest of mankind, till either they provoke against them a general conspiracy of their fellow-creatures, or, till reaching the point of their pursuit, they become elevated objects of homage and admiration. Such men are generally composed of great materials for mischief:—having strong natural talents and violent ungovernable spirits; according to the direction these get, they are harmless or mischievous —but, like morbid matter in the animal system, if not let loose by some channel or other, they never fail to disturb the whole economy of the body they belong to, and produce fatal consequences to it and to themselves: Colonial possessions have therefore, in some views, been of use (as America formerly to

L

England) to draw off those dangerous spirits, who, though they are in times of peace better at a distance, in times of war are found to be the toughest sinews of a nation.

The country of Tyrol, such as I have described it, formed by nature for the residence of the Sylvan deities, rich in the products of the earth, the people contented and happy, and the whole the region of peace; manufactures, the first root of low vices, and commerce, the great instigator of war, have scarcely been able to set their feet there: hence it happens, that there is no channel through which those exuberant spirits I have alluded to can take their course, or expand their force. Home, therefore, is no place for those of the Tyrolese, who are cursed or blessed (call it which you please) with those very combustible qualities; and they are obliged to roam abroad in search of opportunities of distinguishing themselves, giving vent to their spirits, and manifesting their talents. They are found, therefore, scattered all over the Continent: and as it rarely happens that opportunities occur in life of signalising such talents in a dignified line, rather than be idle they do what they can, and apply to chicanery as a wide and appropriate field for their genius and vigour to work on--the emigrant Tyrolese are, therefore, by most nations of the continent, reckoned among the most expert and accomplished sharpers in the world--the people, however, who remain at home, are of a different character--they are, generally speaking, tall, robust, and vigorous; the women strong, and very fair; and both sexes exhibit a very pleasing mixture of German phlegm and Italian sprightliness; or, to speak more properly, they are a mean between those two extremes.

Innspruck, though a small city, is handsome and agreeable, standing in a very beautiful valley, surrounded with mountains, which, while their lower parts are well cultivated, are capped on the tops with perennial snow. The castle formerly the residence of the Austrian princes is stately and magnificent, adorned within with fine paintings, and decorated without by natural and artificial fountains, statues, pleasant gardens, groves, walks, and covered galleries, leading to five different churches.

A-propos—Let me not forget the churches! In a chapel of the Franciscan church, there is an image of the Virgin MARY as big as the life, of solid silver, with many other images of saints of the same metal. If some of those silver deities were transferred to Paris, I fear their divinity would not save them from the hands of the sacrilegious Convention. One thing, however, is well worth the attention of travellers, particularly those who wish to wipe away the sins of a deceased friend, and get them a direct passport to happiness—This Franciscan church is held to be one of the most sacred and venerable in the world, on account of the indulgences granted to it by several popes; so that one single mass said in it, is declared to be sufficient to deliver a soul from the pains of purgatory. When we consider the great and important extent of their power in that respect, we cannot wonder if they had all the saints in the calendar, and the Virgin MARY to boot, in solid silver, even of the size of the Colossus at Rhodes.

Hall, the second city in Tyrol, lies one league from Innspruck: it is famous for its salt-works, and for a mint and silver mines, in which seven thousand men, women, and children are constantly employed.

At a royal palace and castle called Ombras, lying at equal distance from Innspruck and Hall, there is an arsenal, famous for a prodigious collection of curiosities, such as medals, precious stones, suits of armour, and statues of several princes on horseback, in their old rich fighting accoutrements; besides great variety of military spoils and trophies taken by the House of Austria; in particular, a statue of Francis the First and his horse, just as they were taken at the battle of Pavia, and two others of Turkish bashaws, with the costly habits and appointments with which they were taken, embellished with gold, silver, and precious stones. But, above all their curiosities, the most extraordinary is an oak inclosing the body of a deer: this last, however unaccountable, is fact; and equals, I think, any of the wonders in the metamorphoses of Ovid.

Leaving Innspruck, I proceeded on my journey, and soon entered into the mountains, which are there of a terrible height---I was the best part of a day ascending them: as I got near the top, I was shewn, by my driver, the spot where Ferdinand, king of Hungary, and the Emperor Charles the Fifth, met, when he returned from Africa, in the year 1500. It is marked with an inscription to that effect, and has grown into a little village, which, from that circumstance, bears the name of the Salutation.

Although this mountain, called Bremenberg (or Burning-hill), is covered with snow for nine months in the year, it is inhabited to the very top, and produces corn and hay in abundance; at the highest part there is a post-house, a tavern, and a chapel, where the traveller is accommodated with fresh horses, provisions, and, if he chooses, a mouthful of prayers---I availed myself of the two first; but the latter being not altogether in my way, I declined it, for which I could perceive that I was, by every mouth and eye in the place, consigned to perdition as a heretic.

Just at this spot there is a spring of water which falls upon a rock, and divides into two currents, which, at a very small distance, assume the appearance, and, in fact, the magnitude too, of very large rivers. The mountain is sometimes difficult to pass, sometimes absolutely impracticable---I was fortunate, however, in this respect; for I got over it without any very extraordinary delay, and on my way was regaled with the most delicious venison that I have ever tasted in my life; it was said to be the flesh of a kind of goat.

Although it is but thirty-five miles from Innspruck to Brisen, it was late when I reached the latter; and as it contained nothing worth either the trouble or delay attending the search of it, I set out the next morning, and, travelling with high mountains on one side, and a river all along upon the other, arrived at a town called Bolsano, in the bishopric of Trent. The country all along was thickly inhabited, and the mountains perfectly cultivated and manured even to their highest tops. On entering the valley of Bolsano, I found the air becoming obviously sweet, delightful, and temperate; the vineyards, and all the trees and shrubs, olives, mulberries, willows, and roses, &c. of all the most lively green, and every thing marking the most luxuriant vegetation.

Bolsano is a small, but extremely neat and pleasant town—but nothing I saw about it pleased me so much as their vineyards, which are planted in long terraces along the sides of the hills, and are formed into the most beautiful arbours, one row above another.

From Bolsano to Trent, is fifty-one miles, a good day's journey: almost the whole of it lies through the valley of Bolsano, a most fruitful and pleasant —indeed, delightful road, which made the day's journey appear to me much shorter than it really was.

Perhaps no part of the habitable globe is, within the same comparatively small compass of earth, so wonderfully diversified by the hand of nature in all her extremes, as that through which I have just carried you. There, under almost the same glance of the eye, were to be seen the stupendous, the rugged, the savage, and the inaccessible—the mild, the fruitful, and the cultivated. Here, the mountain capped with perpetual snow, gradually falling in blended gradations of shade, far beyond the reach of the artist's pencil, into the green luxuriant valley; and there, the vineyard, the olivary, and the rich corn-field, bursting at once from rugged rocks and inaccessible fastnesses: the churlish aspect of the tyrant winter for ever prowling on the mountain's head above—perpetual spring smiling with all her fascinating charms in the plains below. Such scenes as these would baffle all efforts of the poet's pen or painter's pencil: to be conceived, they must be seen. I shall therefore close my account of them with a strong recommendation to you, that whenever you travel for improvement, you go through the Country of Tyrol, and there learn the great and marvellous working of nature.

LETTER XXIII.

PERHAPS the learned unwise men of the world, who spend their lives poring after impossibilities, have never met with a more copious subject of puzzle-pated enjoyment than the derivation of the names of places. In all disputed cases on this subject, the utmost within human reach is conjecture; but the joke of it is, that, fortunately for mankind, the certainty of it would not be of a single button advantage to them, even if it could be acquired by their search. Doctor GOLDSMITH, in his *Citizen of the World*, has thrown this matter into high ridicule; and I recommend it to your perusal, lest this shadow of literature should one day wheedle you from more respectable pursuits. Trent has afforded vast exercise to book-worm conjectures in this way; for, while some pronounce it to be derived from Tridentum, and for this purpose will have it that NEPTUNE was worshipped there, though so far from the sea—others claim the discovery of its derivation from Tribus Torrentibus, or three streams which run there. Now, as to the first, exclusive of forcing NEPTUNE all the way from the Gulph of Venice to their temples, I cannot find any such similarity in the sound of Trent and Trident to warrant the inference; and as to the Tribus Torrentibus, they might as well say that a primmer or hornbook was found there, and that thence it was derived from the alphabet, since the same analogy subsisted between them, namely, that the letters T, R, E, N, T are to be found in both. But, in the name of God, what signifies what it was called after? Its name is Trent; and if it had been Putney, or John o' Groat's house, the town would be neither the better nor the worse, nor the treasures of literature suffer any defalcation from the difference.

The bishopric of Trent is about sixty miles long, and forty broad—fertile, and abundant in wine, oil, fruit, and pasture—and pleasant, the beautiful river Adige meandering through the whole of it from north to south. The inhabitants are bigoted Roman Catholics—you will the less wonder, then, that the bishop should have so extensive a principality, and an annual revenue of forty thousand crowns.

As I receded from Germany, and advanced towards Italy, I found the air, the persons, and the manners of the people, to display a very great difference, and to resemble those of the Italians more than those of the Germans. Though Popish bigotry be pretty strong in many parts of Germany, it no where there assumes the gloomy, detestable aspect that it does in Italy.

And now, since I have happened to mention the characters of these two people, I may as well, once for all, more particularly as we are got to the verge of both, give you them in full; in both which I am warranted in saying, that all who know the two will agree with me.

Perhaps contrast was never more perfectly exemplified than in a comparison between the Germans and Italians; and that contrast strikes more forcibly and suddenly in passing from one country to the other, than it would in so short a space between any two people existing. The Italians, jealous, revengeful, treacherous, dissembling, servile, vicious, sanguinary, idle, and sensual. The Germans, on the contrary, open, good-natured, free from malice and subtlety, laborious, sincere, honest, and hospitable—and, with those valuable qualities, properly complaisant. So happy is the character of this people, that to be German-hearted has long been a phrase signifying an honest man who hated dissimulation: and their hospitality was, even in the days of Julius Cæsar, remarkable; for we learn from him, that their houses were open to all men—that they thought it injustice to affront a traveller, and made it an article of their religion to protect those who came under their roof. Did not intemperance in eating and drinking detract from their virtues, no people on earth would bear comparison with them for intrinsic worth, and particularly for integrity in dealing.

The city of Trent, though not very large in circumference, is populous. The high mountains which surround it, subject it to all the inconveniences of heat and cold—rendering the air excessively hot in summer, and extremely cold in winter; besides which, they expose the town to dreadful inundations—the torrents that descend from the mountains being sometimes so impetuous as to roll large pieces of rock with them into it, and having several times laid the whole place waste.

There are in Trent many stately palaces, churches, and religious houses. The only one, however, that I will particularize, is that of Saint MARY MAJOR, noted for a prodigious large organ, which can be made to counterfeit all sorts of musical instruments, together with the singing of birds, the cries of several beasts, and the sounds of drums and trumpets, so exactly, that it is difficult to distinguish between the imitation and the reality. To what an end such an instrument should be set up in a place of worship, I am at a loss to divine, unless it be to add to the rich, useless lumber that fills all those of Popish countries.

But that which distinguishes this church still further, is, that it is the place where the famous Council of Trent was held, concerning the Reformation, at which four thousand persons of a public character, laymen and ecclesiastics, assisted. This Council sat eighteen years before it did any thing; but at last the Pope contrived to get the ascendant; and, after debating and deliberating so long, not only the Protestants, but even the German and French nations, refused to receive its decrees. Certain of the clergy, finding the ascendancy that the negotiation of the Pope was getting in this council, said that the Holy Ghost had been sent there from Rome in a *cloakbag!*

Trent once boasted a curiosity---which indeed still remains, though out of use---that, I think, would be found serviceable in most towns in Christendom, and elsewhere too, and particularly at Bath, and such places. It was a tower on the river Adige, into which the stream was conducted, for the purpose of drowning such of the clergy as were convicted of having been too familiar with their neighbours' wives and daughters!

The people of Trent speak promiscously, an dindifferently, both the German and Italian languages; but whether well or not, I was not adept enough to discover.

My next stage was Baſſano, a town in the territory of Vincenza in Italy, situated at the end of a very long norrow valley. It is watered by the river Brenta, which waſhes that very rich, fertile, ſerene, healthy, and plentiful diſtrict of Italy, ſo celebrated for its admirable wines, as well as for its fine paſture-grounds, rich corn-fields, and prodigious abundance of game, cattle, and mulberry-trees; from all which it is called the Garden and Shambles of Venice.

The next day I arrived at an early hour at Venice, the deſcription of which I ſhall not injure by commencing it with the mutilated fragment of a letter, and ſhall therefore poſtpone it to my next.

Thus, my dear FREDERICK, have I, in order to preſerve the unity and order of my progreſs, brought you through Germany with a preciſe regularity, that, if I was not wiſhing for your improvement, might be diſpenſed with—yet have left much, very much indeed, untouched, in the confidence that you will yourſelf have the induſtry to find it out.

I confeſs, my dear boy, that I have often, as I wrote, detected myſelf in excurſions from the road into moral reflection—but I could not ſtop: your improvement was my object in undertaking the buſineſs; and I could not refrain from endeavouring to inculcate ſuch leſſons as the progreſs of the work ſuggeſted, and as impreſſed my mind with a conviction of their truth and utility.

You muſt have obſerved, that there are two topics on which I dwell very much—one, LIBERTY—the other, an abhorence of bigotry and ſuperſtition. But, before I proceed further, I muſt call to your remembrance what I have often ſaid, that by liberty I do not mean that which ſome people now give that name to---nor do I mean religion when I ſpeak of bigotry; for true liberty is ſtill more incompatible with anarchy than with deſpotism, and superstition is the greatest enemy of religion. Let the first object of your heart and soul be true morality---the next, rational liberty: but remember, that the one is not to be found independent of religion, nor the other over to be enjoyed but under the restraining hands of wholesome laws and good government---such as England now boasts.

In these times, when human opinion is actually polled on the two extremes of political judgment, I know, that to speak rationally, is to incur the censure of both, or to be, as POPE somewhere says, " by tories called a whig, by whigs a tory:" but I care not---I speak my opinion with the fair face of independence; nor would scruple to tell the KING of PRUSSIA my hatred of despotism, or the Convention of France my abhorrence of anarchy---between both of which the true and genuine point of liberty lies; and England, thank God! draws the line.

LETTER XXIV.

As I approached Venice, I was much delighted with its appearance. Its stately steeples and noble buildings seemed as if just emerging from the sea, and floating on the surface of it; and it required no great stretch of fancy to imagine, that it undulated with the agitated waves of its parent the Adriatic. On all the surrounding coasts, nature and art seemed to have vied with each other in pouring the greatest profusion of their gifts, while thousands of masts, scattered like forests over the surrounding bays, denoted that Venice, not content with her own, shared in the wealth and luxuries of other climes.

It is indeed difficult to conceive a more extraordinary and pleasing appearance than this city makes at a distance, whether you approach it from the sea or from the continent. Built not like towns in Holland, where immense moles and walls push the sea forward, and encroach on his dominion, it stands on piles erected in the sea; and the foundations of the houses almost touching the water, gives it the appearance of floating on its surface. The steeples are seen at sea at the distance of thirty miles; and the prospect becomes more beautiful the nearer it is approached—presenting in many views the appearance of floating islands.

To erect a city thus upon the water, while so many thousands of acres stand unoccupied, at first sight seems extraordinary—but all those great and strange deviations from the ordinary path presented by nature, have their source in necessity; and it is not till long after the necessity has been first lamented, and afterwards obviated, that experience comes into aid, and demostrates, that, from her, security and utility have often arisen. Thus it is with Venice, who, fortified by her local situation (the effort of necessity), sits secure, and bids defiance to the world.

The place where Venice now stands, is supposed to have been formerly a marshy ground, on which the Adriatic Sea had gradually encroached, leaving the more elevated parts of it above water, and thereby forming a vast number of little islands, hence called Lagunes: on those the fishermen of the neighbouring shores built their huts; and when Italy was invaded by the Goths under ALARIC, and afterwards by that barbarous race the Huns, under ATTILA, both of whom spread ruin and desolation wherever they came, vast numbers of people from the circumjacent shores of the Adriatic, particularly from Padua and Aquileia, fled hither, and brought along with them immense wealth. Here

DESCRIPTION OF VENICE.   133

they laid the first foundations on seventy-two distinct little islands, and certainly with huts, of a city which afterwards stood almost foremost in the naval and commercial world: as those islands were built upon, and became over-people, they gradually pushed forward their piles, and built upon them aga n, till the whole became one vast city, extending to many more of those islands beyond the original seventy-two.

As it was indebted in a great measure, for its rise and importance to the commerce of the East, which then was carried on by way of the Red Sea and Alexandria, when the passage by the Cape of Good Hope was discovered, that trade declined and Venice declined gradually along with it.

It is amazing, what an extent of territory and accumulation of power the Venetians once poss s-sed. Besides their present possessions, which comprehend the territories of Padua and Verona, the Vincentine, the Brescians, the Bergamases, the Cremasco, the Polesin of Rovigo, Marca Trevigiana, the Patria del Friuli, and Istria, they had under their dominion the islands of Rhodes, Scio, Samos, Mytilene, Andros, Candia, the Morea, and the cities of Gallipoli and Thessalonica: besides which, they, in conjunction with France, took Constantinople, and remained for some time masters of that part of the Empire; and disputed the dominion of Sclavonia, Croatia, Morlachia and Dalmatia, with the Kings of Hungary, and contended with the Genoese for the empire of the sea: but of a great part of these, and their other conquests, they have since been stripped, almost entirely, by the Turks.

As to the government of Venice, I shall not enter into any particulars of its history—It is called a republic, and was once a democracy. The name remains, while that which gave it is gone. It is, certainly, now a downright aristocracy—the

M

privilege of sitting in the great Council being confined to the nobility; and the doge, under the name of head, being no more than a gaudy slave, loaded with fetters: yet, such is the idle fondness of man for superficial pomp, that this office is sought after with avidity; for though his power be small, his state is very splendid. Hence it is said, that the doge of Venice is a king in his robes, a senator in council, a prisoner in the city, and a private man out of it; and what is more extraordinary, is, that though he may be deposed, he cannot resign—nor even decline the office, if he be once chosen, without exposing himself to banishment, and his effects to confiscation.

The established religion of this state is the Roman Catholic; but the Venetians are not bigots, and reject the supremacy of the Pope. Jews, Armenians, Greeks, and Protestants, are allowed the exercise of their religion there; and, provided they do not intermeddle with state affairs, of which they are extremely jealous, even their priests, monks, and nuns, may take almost any liberties they please—a privilege that you may be assured is not neglected by any of them.

As few places have excited greater admiration and attention than Venice, so none have been more copiously described by travellers, every one of whom may, when he returns to his native country, give a very accurate account of the public buildings, curiosities, paintings, &c. by only translating the book given to him by his valet de place, or cicerone, on his arrival there—It is certain, Venice abounds with all those, particularly paintings; but I had not the time minutely to investigate; nor should I have the inclination, if I did, to describe such things: they are open to you in many well written volumes, which I recommend to your perusal. Such things, however, as strike me for their novelty, or difference from those in other places, I will, as well as I can recollect them, give you an idea of.

To their local situation they own their security—separated from *terra firma* by a body of water of five miles in breadth, too deep to be forded, and too shallow for vessels of force to pass; and on the other sides, by scattered shallows, the channels between which are marked out by stakes, which, on the appearance of an enemy, they can take away; they bid defiance to hostile army or navy, and have not been reduced to the necessity to erecting walls or fortifications for their defence.

The first peculiarity that strikes me, as arising immediately from their living, I may say, in the sea, is the total exclusion of all sort of carriages; for those streets that are on firm ground are extremely narrow and crooked; and on most of the canals, so far from having a quay on either side to walk on, the water comes up to the doors of the houses; so that walking is but little known, for they get into a boat off their threshold, and their first step out of it again is, ten to one, on the threshold of another. This circumstance, though in some respects it has its uses, is, in others, extremely disagreeable, as well as injurious; for, though those who have occasion to labour have a sufficiency of exercise, those whose condition exempts them from labour, and who, therefore, in all other countries, resort to artificial labour (exercise) for the promotion of health, are here entirely cut off from all such means of it as we practise, having neither hunting, shooting, riding, bowling, &c. &c. nor can they have them, unless they go to the Continent for them: The chief amusements of the Venetians are reserved for the carnival time, which commences about a week after Christmas, and which, therefore, I could not see; but, from the concurrent testimony of all travellers and the people themselves, as well as from the evidence of my own observation on the manners of the people, I am well warranted in saying, are festivals of debauchery, riot, and licentiousness. This is a subject on which I am, nevertheless, disposed to believe, that more has been said than truth will bear out—yet, a bare statement of the truth, would, I fear, bear hard enough upon the moral character, or at least the piety, of the Venetians.

That masquerades are the very worst schools of vice, the private anecdotes of the *beau monde* even in England might suffice to demonstrate—That courtezans are found lost to all sense of modesty and common decency, the streets of London afford nightly proofs——Therefore, that masquerading (which is the amusement of the Venetians) should cloak many crimes, and that their courtezans should be shameless and their women lewd, is no such wonder, seeing, as we do, those things in this Northern clime; but we may, without any illiberality, suppose, that, from physical causes of the most obvious kind, they are carried to a greater extent there than here: though one of the most enlightened and amiable of all travellers says it would be hard to be proved, yet, with deference to him, I think it may be rationally supposed.

There is an active principle in the mind of man which will not suffer it to rest; it must have some materials to work upon. Men, enlightened by science, have within themselves a fund, and can never want food for contemplation; but the many, in those hours when a suspension of labour or worldly business drives them to expedients for the employment of their time, are but too prone to leave the mind to the guidance of the senses, and to cogitate on vice till they wish to practise it. Hence that homely but true saying, " Idleness is the root of all evil." In England we have a variety of expedients which the Venetians want, whose minds being besides naturally more vivid, are more prompt to give a loose to the warm illusions of sensual fancy. Thus prepared, they meet the carnival, when every thing conspires to give circulation to indulgence; and when those operations of the mind which with us have so many channels to discharge themselves, with them, like a vast stream suddenly confined to one narrow channel, burst forth with an irresistable torrent, and carry away before them every bond that religion or morality has laid down as restraints on the exhuberance of human passion. The customs and habits of the place and time contribute to it; for, while the severe restrictions of the female sex for the rest of the year sharpen both inclination and invention on the one hand—on the other, the unbounded licenfe, the universal change of habits, customs and laws—the total suspension of all distinction, care, or business which take place at that time, aided by perpetual masquerade—and those most convenient of all receptacles, the gondolas, with those most expert and forward of all pandars, the gondoliers—afford ample scope to their wishes, and form altogether a mass of circumstances in favour of vicious indulgence, not to be found in any other part of Christendom; to resist which, they must be more virtuous than any other people—a point never yet laid to their charge by the best-natured and most extenuating of all those who have written upon that subject.

LETTER XXV.

PROFLIGATE though the people of London are, I will not allow that it is so vicious a city as Venice. That there are in it, and indeed in all capitals, individuals who have reached the highest acme of shameless debauchery and depravity, it would be foolish to deny: but that concubinage is practised in the same open way, so generally, or so systematically as at Venice, no one will venture to assert. I trust the day of depravity and indelicacy is far removed from us, that will exhibit a British mother arranging a plan of accommodation for her son, and bargaining for a young virgin to commit to his embraces—as they do in Venice— not as wife, but as concubine. On that one custom of the Venetian ladies I rest my position; and have no hesitation to avow, that all the private concubinage of London amounts not to such a flagrant consummation of moral turpitude and shameless indelicacy as that practice to which I allude.

The Venetian men are well-featured and well-shaped—the women, well-shaped, beautiful, and, it is said, witty: but I had *that within* which robbed every object of its charms; and I might say with HAMLET, that " man delighted not me, nor woman either."—In short, not all the beauties and novelty of the place, not all the pleasures that stare the traveller in the face, and solicit his enjoyment, not all the exquisite looks of the ladies, could rouse my mind from its melancholy, or fix my attention— I grew weary of Venice before I had been many hours in it, and determined to grasp at the very first opportunity that offered for my departure.

I had arranged, in my own mind, a plan to proceed to Latichea, a considerable sea-port town in Syria, and thence to Aleppo, whence, as it was a great Eastern mart, I entertained hopes that I should find a speedy, or at least a certain conveyance, by a caravan, across the deserts, to Bassorah, and little doubted but that I should find a vessel at some of the Venetian ports, either bound, or belonging to a sea-port of such commercial consequence, upon which I could procure a passage— But in this I was disappointed; for, on the fullest inquiry that I could make, I found that there was only one ship ready to sail; and no probability of any other for a considerable time after—I did every thing I could to avail myself of this conveyance, but was disappointed, owing to a young lady being passenger, who was daughter to the owner of the vessel—and the old gentleman did not approve of an English officer being of the party with his daughter. I used every argument without success, urging the resident, Mr STRANGE, who had behaved very politely to me during my short residence at Venice, to interest himself about it: I likewise entreated Mrs. STRANGE, an affable, pleasant woman, to exert her endeavours, and made her laugh, by proposing to her to give me a certificate of my behaviour, and to pledge herself to the old gentleman that the happiness or honour of his family would not be disturbed by me during the passage.

Hearing, however, that a ship lay at Trieste, which was to sail thence for Alexandria in Egypt, I determined to embrace that opportunity, and, instead of my former intended route, go to Grand Cairo, thence to Suez, and so down the Red Sea, by way of Mecca, to Moca, and thence to Aden, which company's vessels, or India country traders are always to be found going to one or other of the British settlements.

I accordingly set out for Trieste, with all the impatience of a sanguine mind, anxious to change place, eager to push forward, and full of the new route I had laid down—the charms of which, particularly of seeing Grand Cairo, the Land of Egypt, and the Pyramids, were painted by my imagination in all the glowing exaggerated colours of romance. The captain of the vessel was then at Venice, and I accompanied him to Trieste, which is about sixty miles from Venice.

Soon after our arrival at Trieste, I had the mortification to find, that the vessel was by no means likely to keep pace with the ardour of my mind, and that, owing to some unforeseen event, her departure was to be delayed; so, after a few of those effusions which may be supposed on such an occasion to escape a man of no very cool temper hanging on the tenter-hooks of expectation, I found it necessary to sit down, and patiently wait the revolution of time and event, which nothing could either impede or accelerate.

It has often been remarked, and is held as a point of faith by Predestinarians, that some men are doomed by fate to disappointment—and that, when they are so, no wisdom can obviate, no vigilance provide against, nor no resolution resist, her decrees; but, that, in spite of all the efforts of reason and industry, a series of sinister events shall pursue them through life, and meet them at every turn they attempt to take. Such has been my lot for the greatest part of my life---but I have neither faith enough in predestination, nor self-love enough so far to blind me to my own faults, as to suppose that lady Fate had any thing at all to do with it. No, no; it was often owing to a temper, warm, impatient, and uncontroled, which, in almost all cases of momentary embarrassment, chaled reason from her office, usurped her place, and decided as chance directed. Let every man examine the grounds of all his serious disappointments in life with candour, and he will find physical causes to which to assign them, without resorting to supernatural. For my part, when I hear a man say that he has been all his life pursued by ill-fortune, I directly conclude, that either he has been a blunderer, or those he dealt with, brutes. In the ordinary operation of earthly contingencies, mischances will happen; but an uniform life of mischance can only arise from mismanagement, or a very extraordinary chain of human injustice.—

These reflections arose from the following incident:

I had procured a servant to attend me on my journey, who, from my short observation of him, promised to contribute very considerably to my comfort, my convenience, and, indeed, to my security, as he was apparently honest, sincere, active, and clever in his duty, and master of several languages, and particularly of the *lingua Franca*, a mixture of languages, peculiarly useful in travelling through the East. Finding that I was likely to be delayed at Trieste, and conceiving that in this interim letters from England, for which I most ardently longed, might have arrived at Venice for me, I imprudently and impetuously sent him to Venice, for the purpose of taking them up, and carrying them to me. But guess what must have been my feelings when I found, almost immediately after his departure, that the vessel was preparing to sail, and that I must either lose my passage or my servant: anxious though I was to get forward, and grievous though my former delay had been to me, I hesitated which to do; but prudence, for once, prevailed over inclination; and I determined, at all events, to depart, under all the embarassment attending the want of a servant and linguist, and all the poignant feelings of having been accessary to the disappointment, and perhaps the injury of a poor fellow, whom I really conceived to be a person of merit. In our passage to Alexandria we touched at Zante, an island on the coast of Greece, belonging to Venice; it was anciently called Zacynthus—is about fifty miles in circumference, and contains fifty thousand inhabitants. Never before had I tasted any thing equal to the delicious flavour of the fruits of this island---the grapes exquisite, and the melons and peaches of prodigious bigness and unequalled flavour. The island is abundantly fruitful in wine, currants, oil, figs, and corn, but is very subject to earthquakes. Near the sea-port which we entered is as great a curiosity in nature as is any where, I believe, to be found. Two spring wells of clear fresh water throw up large pieces of real pitch in such quantities, that, it is said, the people collect, one year with another, one hundred barrels of it, which they use in paying their shipping and boats.

In the first stages of melancholy, consolation is rejected by the mind as premature. The heart, intent, as it were, upon supping full of woe, disclaims all advances of comfort, and feeds on grief alone. Hence the truly skilful in the human heart consider premature consolation as an aggravation of woe, and comfort only with condolence, well knowing that the tide of grief must take its course, and that, until it be first full, no hopes can be had of its retiring. The full force of this I began now to feel. The disquietude of domestic embarrassment---the bitterness of separation from all I loved---the solitary sadness of my situation; wandering through unknown countries---myself unknown and unfriended---aggravated at length by the loss of my servant, who was a sort of prop to my spirits---and my being cast into a ship among a people whose language I little understood, without any soul or one circumstance to mitigate my sorrow, or console me under it; all these, I say, had wound up my feelings to the highest pitch of fortune—More miserable I could not be when the island of Zante received me, and, for the first time for a sad series of days, railed me with the transporting sound of an English voice.

I have promised my FREDERICK, to give you a candid relation, in hopes that you will improve by it: but if I thought, that, on the contrary, any thing I said should tend to raise in your mind a sentiment injurious to your principles, or reflective on your father's conduct, but to be an example and admonitory guide to your own, I should condemn my candour and curse the hour that I wrote—but, I trust to your good sense and disposition, with my care to direct them; and shall, but not without hesitation, proceed. But, as I have already spun out this letter to such an extent, I will defer my further relation to another.

LETTER XXVI.

AT the time I set out upon my journey over land to India, I was (though married, and the father of children) very young, naturally of a sanguine constitution: my attachment to the fair sex was no ways diminished by a military education; and a warmth of temper, an ardent sensibility of mind, and a frank unsuspicious disposition, left me but too often to regret the facility with which I yielded to the charms of women. But the regret for each error was wilfully smothered in vain determinations of amendment—and the promised amendment again broken in upon by some new error. Thus it was, till riper years and circumstances of weight strengthened my reason, and gave it in some greater degree that dominion it should have over my actions.

Circumstanced as I have in my last letter described myself to be, and constituted by nature and education as I have mentioned above, I landed in the charming island of Zante, where nature herself seems to have conspired against chastity--making the very air breathe nothing but transport and delight. There I met a young lady, a native of England—extremely pretty, highly accomplished, and captivating in the extreme: she had been at Venice for her education—was a complete mistress of music, and expressed an intention of following it professionally on her arrival at England, whither was going passenger in a vessel bound there from Zante. To have accidentally met with a native of England, even of my own sex, in such a distant corner of the world, under such circumstances as mine, just escaped from the horrid life I had for some time led, must have filled me with joy: allowance, therefore, may be made for my feelings on meeting this young lady, and for my thinking of some expedient to prevent our separation. She laboured, perhaps, under the pressure of feelings as disagreeable as my own, and expressed her satisfaction at meeting with a countryman so very unexpectedly. Reserve was soon thrown off on both sides: we entered into a conversation interesting and confidental, which increased my anxiety to keep her with me, and in order to persuade her to accompany me, I pointed out in the strongest colours possible, the great advantages she might derive from her accomplishments in India, where her musical talents alone, exclusive of her various captivating qualities, would be an inexhaustible mine of wealth. In short, I so very eagerly enforced my proposal to accompany me, and time was so very short, that she consented, and in two hours we had arranged every thing for our departure together---and here with shame and horror I confess (nor shall ever cease to regret it), that this ecclaircissement communicated the first ray of substantial pleasure to my heart that it felt since I left London.

Thus far, our project sailed before the wind: wayward imagination had decked it out in the most alluring drapery that fancy could fabricate, and prevented us from seeing the impracticability of it, as it stood in the nakedness of truth; and when it came to be carried into execution, a thousand difficulties occurred, that the wildness of passion, and the warmth of our feelings, had before concealed from our view. In the first place, it was necessary for her to obtain the consent of a lady to whose care and protection she was committed: in the next place, accommodations were to be procured for her in the same ship with me—a circumstance of most arduous difficulty; besides which, a variety of other impediments—insuperable indeed—concurred to frustrate our views, and put an end to our project. If my pleasure at meeting her was great, my anguish at parting with her was inexpressible. I had once more to face the world alone; and, on the second day of my sojourning at Zante, embarked with a heavy heart, and set sail for Alexandria. The last disappointments we undergo, seem always the heaviest; and this at Zante I thought at that time to be the greatest of my life. But—oh! short-sighted man! bubble of every delusive shadow! I never reflected, as I have since done, what serious mischiefs, what endless misery, what loss of time, means, and reputation, I may by that providential disappointment have escaped—for these are the almost never-failing consequences of such affairs. It too often happens, that the syren who deludes a man into her snares, is the very person who inflicts the deadly wound into his heart. Avoid, my dear FREDERICK! avoid all such, as you would avoid plague, pestilence, or ruin—steel your heart by timely reflection against their advances. In all your transactions with women, like a good general in warfare, secure for your heart a retreat; for it will be too late to find that they are unworthy when your heart is ensnared—and when you find them worthy of your affection, it will be time enough to give a loose to the sensibility of your heart. A virtuous woman is beyond all calculation to be valued, when she is found; but, alas! in finding her, you may pass through so many fires ordeal, and run such danger, that it is almost a doubt, whether a wise man (if he can fetter his passions) had not better dispense with the blessing, than run the hazard of searching for it.

On my arrival at Alexandria, I found, to my fresh mortification, that the plague was raging all over Egypt—and as, if this was not of itself sufficient to block up my intended route, an irruption of the Arabs, who in formidable bodies infested all the roads, put a period to all my hopes of seeing Grand Cairo, and viewing the curiosities of that country, which all who, like us, have the Bible put early into their hands, are taught to venerate as soon as they are taught to read. Here I thought to have viewed the pyramids, whose antiquity, origin, or intended use, have baffled the learned and ingenious inquiries of so many ages—of beholding Mount Sinai, the stone of Moses, the tract of the Israelites, all of which are said to be clearly pointed out, and geography by that means brought into the support of Sacred History. These, and many things, I did wish to see—they are worth it: but I have had since reason to believe, that my ill luck was not so great as I then thought it; for the search is dangerous, and made prodigiously expensive by the exactions of the Mahomedan magistrates. It is as well, therefore, to travel over this country in books, which afford us good information, and more of it, at an easier rate than you could purchase it in the country.

Alexandria was built by ALEXANDER the Great, soon after the overthrow of Tyre, about 333 years before CHRIST, and is situated on the Mediterranean, twelve miles west of that mouth of the Nile, anciently called Canopicum. A very extraordinary circumstance is related as a proof of the suddenness of ALEXANDER's resolution to build it: After he had directed the number of public structures, and fixed the places where they were to stand, there were no instruments at hand proper for marking out the walls, according to the custom of those times: upon this, a workman advised the King to collect what meal was among the soldiers, and lift it in lines upon the ground, in order to mark out the circuit of the walls: the advice was followed, and the king's soothsayer interpreted it to be a presage of the future prosperity and abundance of the city. This prophecy was certainly afterwards verified; for it soon became the emporium of commerce, of arts, and of sciences.

By the description of STRABO and other ancients, it appears that this city was built upon a plan well worthy the vast mind of its founder; and the fragments of its ornaments afterwards made part of the grandest embellishments of Rome and Constantinople. In the museum of the royal palace, which occupied a fourth part of the city, the body of ALEXANDER was deposited in a golden coffin—but the detestable SELEUCUS CIBYOFACTES violated the monument, took away the golden coffin, and substituted a glass one in its place.

This city like most others of antiquity, has been the scene of terrible massacres. About two hundred years after its foundation, it was totally depopulated by PTOLEMY PHYSCON—the very few who escaped slaughter, flying into other countries. Desirous, however, not to reign over empty houses, he seduced inhabitants from the neighbouring countries; and again, for some slight offence, determined on a general massacre of the young men; and accordingly, when they were one day assembled in the Gymnasium, or place of public exercise, he ordered it to be set on fire, so that all perished, either in the flames, or by the swords of his mercenaries, whom he had placed at all the avenues. Afterwards, in the year of CHRIST 215, the Emperor CARACALLA, having been lampooned by some of the inhabitants, ordered a general massacre by his numerous troops, who were dispersed over the city. The inhuman orders being given, all were murdered, without diftinction of age or fex; fo that, in one night's time, the whole city floated in blood, and every houfe was filled with carcafes: the monfter himfelf, retiring to the temple of Serapis, was all the time imploring the protection of the Deity—a proof that practical devotion and the moft atrocious inhumanity may meet in the fame bofom. As if this had not been fufficient vengeance, he ftripped the city of all its ancient privileges—ordered all ftrangers who lived there to depart—and, that the few who remained might not have the fatisfaction of feeing one another, he cut off all communication of one ftreet with another, by walls built for the purpofe, and guarded with troops.

Notwithftanding thefe maffacres, Alexandria again recovered its former fplendour—and was again facked by AMROU, the infamous Saracen—and all the intrepid youth of the city perifhed with arms in their hands. The magnificence of the city may be eftimated from the account written by AMROU to the Caliph: "I have taken," faid he, "the City of the Weft; it is of an immenfe extent; I cannot defcribe to you how many wonders it contains, there are 4000 palaces, 4000 baths," &c. &c.

The great advantages of the Eaft India trade, which was then carried on by the Red Sea, preferved Alexandria through feveral revolutions; but having fallen under the dominion of the Turks, and the paffage round the Cape of Good Hope being difcovered, a fatal blow was given to its commerce, and it has fince fallen to decay. It is, however, even now, worth the attention of the claffical traveller. Entering the harbour, we paffed by the Ifland of Pharos, were PTOLEMY built the enormous tower which was once the wonder of the world: and, when riding within the port, nothing could be more gratifying than to fee from thence that mixture of ancient and modern monuments that presented themselves to the view, on which ever side the eye could be turned.

Of myriads of antiquities which this place affords for the inspection of the curious, I shall mention only two—One, the column of POMPEY, on viewing of which, the remembrance of that great and good man's most unmerited and cruel fate extracted a sigh from the bottom of my heart: this pillar engages the attention of all travellers; it is composed of red granite; the capital is Corinthian, with palm leaves, and not indented; the shaft and the upper member of the base are of one piece, ninety feet long; and nine in diameter; the base, a square of fifteen feet on each side; the whole column is one hundred and fourteen feet high, perfectly well polished, and only a little shivered on the eastern side. Nothing can equal the majesty of this monument: seen from a distance it overtops the town, and serves as a signal for vessels; approaching it nearer, it produces an astonishment mixed with awe: one would never be tired of admiring the beauty of the capital, the length of the shaft, nor the extraordinary simplicity of the pedestal. Some years ago, a party of English seamen contrived, by flying a kite, to draw a line over the pillar, and by that means made a kind of a shroud, by which they got up, and on the very top of it drank a bowl of punch, to the utter astonishment of a multitude who came to see them; they broke off one of the volutes of the column, but amply compensated for this mischief by a discovery they made, as, without their evidence, the world would not have known, at this hour, that there was originally a statue on this column, one foot and ancle of which, of enormous size, are still remaining.—The other is the obelisk of CLEOPATRA, of immense size, and of one single piece of granite marble. Here I observed, too, a thick wall, with towers mouldering under extreme age, which conained, in its face, fragments of architecture of the most exquisite workmanship, such as broken columns, friezes, &c.; those were the antique ruins of some fallen pieces of antiquity, at the time that this antique wall was built: what then must be the length of time since they had first undergone the hands of the workman? These circumstances tend to demonstrate, that, far back beyond the reach of our calculation, the arts flourished: and when one thinks of the miraculous masses of work done in former ages—the magnitude of the pieces of which those works were composed, such as whole columns and obelisks of a single block of marble—the Colossus of Rhodes, made of brass, one foot of which was placed on one side of the harbour, and another on the other side, so that ships passed between its legs—we cannot help yielding up the palm to the ancients for stupendous magnificence, however we may surpass them for the useful, the elegant, and the good.

At Alexandria I remained about twelve days, till, wearied of the confined state I lived in on account of the plague, I resolved to devise some means, if possible, to get away, and at length hired a boat to carry me to the island of Cyprus, from whence I concluded, that I should find no sort of difficulty in procuring a conveyance to Latichea, and to proceed by my first intended route. I accordingly arrived at Cyprus in perfect safety, where, to my great sorrow and astonishment, I found that an epidemical fever, equal in its effects to a plague, prevailed: however, there was no alternative; I must run the risque, and I dismissed the boat that carried me from Alexandria.

Although the etymologies of the names of places are of very little importance, and most frequently uncertain, I think it probable that the learned are right, who assert the name of this is derived from Cyprus, or Cypress—with which shrubs the island abounds. It had, in ancient times, a number of other names—one of which was Paphia, whence Venus, who was worshipped in it, was called the Paphian Goddess. It lies thirty miles west of Syria, whither I was bound, stretching from the south-west to the north-east, one hundred and fifty miles in length, and seventy in breadth in the widest part of it.

This island holds a very high rank in classic lore—It gave birth to some great philosophers and considerable poets—The Apostle BARNABAS was a native of it, and, assisted by ST. PAUL, first introduced Christianity among them. Famagusta, a town on the eastern part of the island, opposite to the shore of Syria, is the ancient Salamis, built by TEUCER the son of TELAMON, and brother of AJAX.

Symisso, on the south-east, the best port in Cyprus, is the *Amathus* mentioned by VIRGIL, in his Æneid, and by OVID in his Metamorphoses. And Baffo, on the Western coast, is the Paphos of antiquity, famous for the Temple of Venus.

As the branches of an empire most remote from the great seat of government are always more despotically governed than those near the source of redress, Cyprus has been continually ruled with a rod of iron since it came into the hands of the Turks. While it was under the dominion of Christians, it was well peopled, having no less than eight hundred or a thousand villages in it, besides several handsome cities; but the Turks have spread ruin and desolation over the country, and it is now so thinly inhabited that more than half the lands lie uncultivated.

The air of this island is now for the most part unwholesome, owing to the damps arising from the many fens and marshes with which the country abounds—while, there being but few springs or rivers in the island, the want of a plentiful fall of rain, at proper periods, diſtreſſes the inhabitants very much in another way; and by means of the uncultivated ſtate of the country, they are greatly infeſted with poiſonous reptiles of various kinds.

The moſt remarkable mountain in Cyprus is called Olympus—a name common to ſeveral other mountains in Greece, particularly to that in Theſſaly, ſo famous in the poetry of the ancients. That in Cyprus is about fifty miles in circumference: great part of it is covered with woods; and at the foot of it are fine vineyards, which produce admirable wine, not only in a ſufficiency for their own conſumption, but ſome alſo for exportation. And although the greater part of the iſland lies uncultivated, as I have before obſerved, it produces a ſufficient quantity of corn, unleſs in ſeaſons when their harveſt fails, in which caſe the people are eaſily ſupplied from the continent. They have, beſides, cattle enough for their own conſumption. Many parts of the country abound in wild fowl, and ſeveral ſorts of game, and they have plenty of fiſh upon the ſea coaſts.

The trade of Cyprus is not inconſiderable, and carried on chiefly by Jews and Armenians: the commodities in which they deal are wine, oil, cotton, wool, ſalt, ſilk, and turpentine—beſides, it produces ſeveral ſorts of earth, fit for the uſe of painters, particularly red, black, and yellow.

Its moſt wonderful production, however, is the famous ſtone (Aſbeſtos) inextinguiſhable, or (Amiantos) impollutus, ſo called from its extraordinary property of reſiſting fire. It is related that the ancients made out of this ſtone a kind of thread that would remain unconſumed in the moſt intenſe fire. It is even ſaid, that ſome experiments have been made in modern days, which have ſufficiently proved that the thing is not a fiction. In ſuch extraordinary queſtions as this, though I do not poſitively contradict, I always ſuſpend my belief, till ſomething stronger than mere affertion is offered to convince me.

There is one dreadful mifchief to which this ifland is fubject. In the hot feafon, locufts come from the Continent, in fwarms fo vaft and fo thick as to darken the fky like clouds. Thofe would certainly devour all the fruits of the earth, if they were not driven to fea by a north wind that ufually blows at the time of their coming. When that wind happens to fail, which fortunately is feldom, the confequence is a total demolition of the fruits of the country.

The whole ifland, as well as particular towns, was entirely confecrated to the goddefs VENUS, who thence was called VENUS CYPRIA, or DEA CYPRIA, and is reprefented by the poets as taking a peculiar pleafure in vifiting it; and this unqueftionably arofe from the loofe habits and lafcivious temperament of the women there, who certainly are, at this time, not remarkable for chaftity.

I muft confefs, however, that I felt great pleafure in entering Cyprus; it was, as I have already ftated, claffic ground, and dedicated to the Queen of Love. But a traveller who vifits it with hopes of amufement, will be much difappointed; for in no one particular did it feem to me to refemble that Cyprus famed in the Heathen Story and Mythology. Of the Cyprian queen's favours the ladies feemed to boaft no one mark, fave the moft naufeous, difgufting lewdnefs; and the natural fertility of the foil is half loft beneath the oppreffive yoke of the fervants of the Turkifh government. Thus, in the extraordinary revolutions that human affairs are inceffantly undergoing, that ifland which for its fuperior beauties was fuppofed to be the refidence of love, which gave birth to the philofophers ZENO, APPOLLONIUS, and XENOPHON, is now a miferable, half-cultivated fpot, peopled with a mixture of wretched Turks, Jews, Greeks, and Chriftians

—groaning under the tyranny of a barbarous despotic abuse of delegated power---infested with locusts which devour the fruits of the earth---and disgraced by a race of ignominious women, who esteem it to be an act of religion to prostitute themselves to all strangers.

Our RICHARD the First made a conquest of this island on his way to the Holy Land, and conferred the royalty of it on GUY LUSIGNAN, king of Jerusalem. The Venetians possessed themselves of it in the year 1480---but, in the sixteenth century, the Turks dispossessed them, and have ever since kept it under the yoke---I should have remarked that their wine is excellent.

Continuing my route, I hired another boat, after only forty-eight hours stay at Cyprus, and proceeded for Latichea, which, as I have somewhere before mentioned, is a considerable sea-port town of Syria, built on a promontory of land, which, running into the sea, occasions its being continually refreshed with breezes. Fortune, who had hitherto been not very liberal in her dispensations, now favoured me; for, just as I arrived at Latichea, a caravan was preparing. The consul of the Turkish Company at Cyprus received me with great politeness and hospitality—gave me a letter to the resident at Latichea; and by his instruction and assistance, after a very short stay, I set out on my way to Aleppo with the caravan.

As I shall hereafter have occasion more particularly to describe the nature of those caravans, I shall, for the present, tell you, that this was composed of no other beasts of burden than mules and asses, of which there were not less than three or four hundred in number.

Mounted on a mule, I travelled along, well pleased with the fertile appearance of the country, and delighted with the serenity of the air—We were, as well as I can now recollect, near ten days on the road; during which time we travelled only in the morning early, and in the heat of the day reposed under the shade of trees.

I was informed, that if, instead of going to Latichea, I had gone to Scandaroon (otherwise Alexandretta), I should, in the road from thence to Aleppo, have travelled through a country, in which the most singular and extravagant customs prevail that exist in any country emerged from barbarism—Several of those I heard; but one in particular was, that the men prostituted their wives and daughters to all comers—and that this originated from a principle of religion, though there was every reason to believe, that, like many of their religious institutions, it was made at last subservient to the gratification of avarice.

On my way to Aleppo, I was met by a Mr. ―, an English gentleman, who had heard of my coming, and who, in the most kind and hospitable manner, insisted upon my living at his house instead of the British consul's, where I should otherwise have resided during my stay there; and his manner of asking me was so engaging, interesting, and impressive, that I found it impossible to refuse him.

As the great public caravan had departed from Aleppo before my arrival, and the expence of forming a private one on my account was too great, as I was travelling on my own account, and had no dispatches to authorise or enforce my departure, or bear me out in the expence; I was constrained to remain at Aleppo till some eligible mode of travelling occurred, or another public caravan was formed. This delay gave me an opportunity of seeing and informing myself of the city and surrounding country; the result of which, I shall, in as short a manner as possible, relate to you in a future letter. It also gave occasion to one of those unhappy incidents which I have often had occasion to lament, not from any consciousness of direct criminality, but for the scope it gave to misrepresentation, and the injury which that misrepresentation did me in the opinion of some of my friends. *(End of Part First.)*

A JOURNEY TO INDIA, &c.

PART II.

LETTER XXVII.

My dear Frederick,

So long as the route of my journey lay through European regions, little presented itself respecting human nature of such very great novelty as to excite admiration or awaken curiosity. In all the various nations through which we have passed, a certain parity of sentiment, arising from the ore great substratum, Christianity, gave the same general colouring to all the scenes, however they might differ from each other in their various shadings. Whatever dissimilitude the influence of accident, climate, or local circumstance, may, in the revolutions of ages, have introduced into their manners, customs, municipal laws, and exterior forms of worship—the great code of religion and moral sentiment remains nearly the same with all: and right and wrong, good and evil, being defined by the same principles of reason, and ascertained by the same boundaries, bring the rule of conduct of each to so close an approximation with that of the others, that, when compared with those we are now to attend to, they may really be considered as one and the same people.

In the empire now before us, were we to leave our judgment to the guidance of general opinion of Christian nations, we should have, on the contrary, to contemplate man under a variety of forms and modifications, so entirely different from those to which habit has familiarised our minds, as at first to imprefs us with an idea of a total disruption from our nature, and induce us, as it has already the generality of our people, to divorce them from a participation of all those sympathetic feelings which serve to enforce the discharge of mutual good offices among men. Deducing all their principles, not only of moral conduct, but municipal government, from a religion radically different from, and effentially adverse to, ours; deluded by that system into a variety of opinions which liberality itself must think absurd; unaided by that enlightened philosophy which learning, and learned men, acting under the influence of comparative freedom, and assisted by the art of printing, have diffused through the mass of Europeans; and living under a climate the most unfavourable to intellectual or bodily exertion, they exhibit a spectacle which the philosophic and liberal mind must view with disapprobation, regret, and pity—the illiberal fierce Christian with unqualified detestation and disgust: while, on their part, bigoted to their own principles and opinions, they look on us with abhorrence, and indulge as conscientious a contempt of, and antipathy to Christians, which I apprehend no lapse of time, without a great change of circumstance, will be able to eradicate. Should Mahomedanism and Christianity ever happen to merge in Deism (but not otherwise), the inhabitants of Syria and Europe will agree to consider each other even as fellow-creatures. In Spain and Portugal, Jew, Turk, and indeed Protestant, are without distinction called hogs. In Turkey, Jews and Christians are discriminately called dogs; each thinking the other completely excluded from the pale of humanity, and well worthy the dagger of any TRUE BELIEVER who would have the *piety* to apply it.

You will allow, my dear FREDERICK, that it muſt have been rather an important contemplation to your father, to have perhaps two thouſands miles to travel through the immenſe and almoſt trackleſs wilds of a country inhabited by ſuch people, without the conſolation of any others to accompany him in his journey; for, unleſs a public diſpatch was to overtake me, there was little probability of my having a ſingle European partner of my fatigue and perils.

However, as the period was not yet arrived at which I was to go forward, or even determine my mode of travelling, I endeavoured to ſoothe my mind as much as I could into content, and to take advantage of my ſtay at Aleppo, to acquire all the knowledge poſſible of the place, that is to ſay, of that city in particular, and of the Turkiſh government and manners in general.

A diſtant view of Aleppo fills the mind with expectations of great ſplendour and magnificence. The moſques, the towers, the large ranges of houſes with flat roofs, riſing above each other, according to the ſloping hills on which they ſtand, the whole variegated with beautiful rows of trees, form altogether a ſcene magnificent, gay, and delightful: but, on entering the town, all thoſe expected beauties vaniſh, and leave nothing in the ſtreets to meet the eye, but a diſmal ſucceſſion of high ſtone walls, gloomy as the receſſes of a convent or ſtate priſon, and unenlivened by windows, embelliſhed, as with us, by the human face divine. The ſtreets themſelves, not wider than ſome of the meaneſt alleys in London, overcaſt by the height of the priſon-houſes on either ſide, are rendered ſtill more formidably gloomy by the ſolitude and ſilence that pervade them; while here and there a lattice towards the top, barely viſible, ſtrikes the soul with the gloomy idea of thraldom, coercion, and imprisonment.

This detestable mode of building, which owes its origin to jealousy, and the scandalous restraints every man is empowered by the laws and religion of the place to impose upon the women consigned either by sale or birth to his tyranny, extends not to the inside of the houses, many of which are magnificent and handsome, and all admirably suited to the exigencies of the climate, and the domestic customs and manner of living of the inhabitants.

The city is adorned, it is true, here and there, with mosques and appendant towers, called Minarets, from which cryers call the faithful to prayers; and in some of the streets there are arches built at certain distances from each other, so as to carry the eye directly through them, and form a vista of considerable grandeur: but all these are far from sufficient to counterbalance the general aspect of gloominess and solitude which reigns over the whole, and renders it so peculiarly disgusting, particularly at first sight, to an Englishman who has enjoyed the gaiety and contemplated the freedom of a city in Great Britain.

The mosques (Mahomedan temples) are extremely numerous in this city; indeed almost as much so as churches and convents in the Popish countries of Christendom. There is nothing in their external appearance to attract the notice of the traveller, or indulge the eye of the architect; they are almost all of one form—an oblong quadrangle: and as to the inside, I never had an opportunity of seeing one; none but Mussulmen being permitted to enter them, at least at Aleppo.

The next buildings of a public kind to the mosques that deserve to be particularly mentioned, are the caravanseras—buildings which, whether we consider the spirit of beneficence and charity that first suggested them, their national importance, or their extensive utility, may rank, though not in splendour of appearance, at least in true value, with any to be found in the world.

Caravanseras were originally intended for, and are now pretty generally applied to, the accommodation of strangers and travellers, though, like every other good institution, sometimes perverted to the purposes of private emolument or public job: they are built at proper distances through the roads of the Turkish dominions, and afford the indigent or weary traveller an asylum from the inclemency of the weather; are in general very large, and built of the most solid and durable materials; have commonly one story above the ground floor, the lower of which is arched, and serves for warehouses to stow goods, for lodgings and for stables, while the upper is used merely for lodgings; besides which, they are always accommodated with a fountain, and have cooks shops and other conveniencies to supply the wants of the lodgers. In Aleppo the Caravanseras are almost exclusively occupied by merchants, to whom they are, like other houses, rented.

The suburbs of Aleppo, and the surrounding country, are very handsome, pleasant, and, to a person coming out of the gloomy city, in some respects interesting. Some tossed about into hill and valley lie under the hands of the husbandman; others are covered with handsome villas; and others again laid out in gardens, whither the people of Aleppo occasionally resort for amusement.

The roofs of all the houses are flat, and formed of a composition which resists the weather effectually. On those most of the people sleep in the very hot weather: they are separated from each other by walls; but the Franks, who live contiguous to one another, and who, from their disagreeable circumstances with regard to the Turks, are under the necessity of keeping up a friendly and harmonious intercourse together, have doors of communication, which are attended with these fortunate and pleasing advantages, that they can make a large circuit without descending into the streets, and can visit each other during the plague, without running the risk of catching the infection by going among the natives below.

There is a castle in the city which I had nearly forgotten to mention—The natives conceive it to be a place of great strength. It could not, however, withstand the shock of a few pieces of ordnance for a day. It is esteemed a favour to be permitted to see it; and there is nothing to recompense one for the trouble of obtaining permission, unless it be the prospect of the surrounding country, which from the battlements is extensive and beautiful.

Near this castle stands the seraglio, a large old building, where the bashaw of Aleppo resides: the whole of it seemed to me to be kept in very bad repair, considering the importance of the place. It is surrounded by a strong wall of great height: besides which, its contiguity to the castle is very convenient; as, in case of popular tumults, or intestine commotions, the bashaw finds an asylum in the latter, which commands and overawes the city, and is never without a numerous garrison under the command of an Aga.

Such is the summary account I have been able to collect of Aleppo, the capital of Syria; which, mean though it is when compared with the capitals of European countries, is certainly the third city for splendour, magnificence, and importance, in the vast extent of the Ottoman Empire—Constantinople and Grand Cairo only excelling it in those points, and no other bearing any sort of competition with it.

LETTER XXVIII.

However faction may agitate or abuse, irritate the minds of men against the executive branch of their government, the people of every nation under Heaven are disposed to think their own constitutional system the best; and the artful intertexture of religion with governments confirms them in that opinion, and often consigns the understanding to unalterable, error and illiberal prejudice. It would be wonderful, then, if the Turkish constitution, founded on the Koran, was not looked upon with abhorrence by the bulk of the Christian world; and more wonderful still, if the outrageous zealots of the Christian church, who for so many centuries engrossed all the learning of Europe to themselves, should not have handed down with exaggerated misrepresentation every circumstance belonging to the great enemies of their faith. But that, at this day of intellectual illumination, mankind should be enveloped in such error and darkness, with regard to the government of so large a portion of the globe as Turkey, is extraordinary; and only to be accounted for by a reference, in the first place, to those religious prejudices which we suck in from our nurse, and which habit, incessant document, and every part of our education, tend to confirm in our mind; and in the next, to that indisposition the human mind feels to part with its old prejudices, and the general indolence and incapacity of men to acquire knowledge by the arduous and fatiguing paths of study.

The Turkish government is grossly misrepresented. Were our opinions to be directed by the general belief of Europeans, we should suppose that the life and property of every being in that vast empire were irremediably at the mercy of the Grand Seignior—and that, without laws to protect, or any intermediate power whatever to shield them, they were entirely subject to the capricious will of an inexorable tyrant, who, stimulated by cruelty, sharpened by avarice, and unrestrained by any law human or divine, did every thing to oppress his subjects, and carry destruction among mankind. I firmly believe, that, from the combination of ideas arising from those prejudices, there are few Christians who think or hear of the grand Turk, that do not, by an involuntary act of the mind, instantly think of blood and murder, strangling with bowstrings, and slicing off heads with cimeters.

As there is no part of your education more near my heart than the eradicating illiberal prejudices from your mind, and fortifying you against their assaults; I find it impossible to refrain from giving you my opinion of the Turkish government, which I have been at some pains to collect, as well from oral information as from the best authors; and which, though very far from what a generous and universally philanthropic disposition would wish them to have, is very different from that which is generally attributed to them, and unquestionably far more limited in its powers than the governments of several Christian countries I could mention.

The constitution of that country is laid down expressly in the Koran. The emperor of Turkey (commonly called the Grand Seignior) is a descendant of Mahomet, who pretended he had the Koran from Heaven: and he is as much bound by the institutes of that book as any subject in his realm—as liable to deposition as they to punishment for breach of them, and indeed has been more than once deposed, and the next in succession raised to the throne. Thus far, it is obvious, his power is limited and under control. But that is not all—It is equally certain that the Turkish government is partly republican; for, though the people at large have no share in the legislation, and are excluded by the Koran from it (which Koran has established and precisely ascertained their rights, privileges, and personal security), yet there is an intermediate power which, when roused to exertion, is stronger than the Emperor's, and stands as a bulwark between the extremes of despotism and them. This body is the ULAMA, composed of all the members of the Church and the law, superior to any nobility, jealous of their rights and privileges, and partly taken from the people, not by election, but by profession and talents.—In this body are comprised the Moulahs, the hereditary and perpetual guardians of the religion and laws of the empire: they derive their authority as much as the Emperor from the Koran, and, when necessary, act with all the firmness resulting from a conviction of that authority; which they often demonstrate by opposing his measures, not only with impunity, but success. Their persons are sacred; and they can, by means of the unbounded respect in which they are held, rouse the people to arms, and proceed to depose. But, what is much more, the Emperor cannot be deposed without their concurrence.

If, by this provision of the constitution, the power of the monarch is limited, and the personal security of the subject ascertained, on the one hand; the energy of the empire in its external operations is, on the other, very frequently and fatally palsied by it. Declarations of war have been procrastinated, till an injurious and irrecoverable act of hostility has been sustained; and peace often protracted, when peace would have been advantageous. The Ulama being a numerous body, it has been found always difficult, often impossible, to unite so many different opinions; and nothing being to be done without their concurrence, the executive power finds it often impossible to take a decisive step in a crisis of advantageous opportunity. But as this code of laws and government is received as a divine revelation, binding both prince and people, and supposed to be sealed in Heaven, the breach of it would be sufficient to consign even the monarch to deposition and death.

As to the military force, which in the hands of all Despots has been made the instrument of the people's slavery, that of the Turk could avail him nothing; and, whenever it does interfere, acts only to his overthrow. The very reverence they have for his person arising from obedience to their religion, they are, *à fortiori*, governed by it, not him. He holds no communication with them; and the standing force of the Janissaries is, compared with the mass of the people, only a handful. Some wild accounts, indeed, have stated it at 300,000; but the best informed fix it below 60,000, of which a great part consists of false musters and abuses—great multitudes being enrolled to obtain certain privileges annexed to the office of Janissary. The fact is, that the chief force of the empire is a militia composed of the people; who, with respect to obedience and subordination, are so loose that they leave their duty whenever they please, without receiving any punishment. How far the people of Turkey are protected from the encroachments of power, will appear from the recital of a fact related by one of the best and most liberal of our historians on that subject, and which is of too great notoriety to be doubted.

In the year 1755, the Porte, as it is called, or Palace of the Grand Vizir at Constantinople, was burnt down: in laying the plan for rebuilding it on the former site, the leading consideration was, how to contrive matters so as to render it secure from accidents of a like nature in future; and it was determined that the only certain means to do so was, to leave a space of clear ground all round it, for which purpose the contiguous houses should be purchased from the proprietors, and demolished. All the owners of the houses agreed to the sale, except one old woman, who pertinaciously refused: she said she was born, and had lived all her life, in that spot, and would not quit it for any one. Now, in England, for the convenience of a private canal, the Parliament would force her to sell. But what did they say in Turkey? When all the people cried out, "Why does not the Sultan use his authority, and take the house, and pay her the value?" No! answered the magistrates and the Ulama, it is impossible! it cannot be done! it is her property. While the power of the monarch is thus limited, and the rights of the people thus ascertained by the Koran, and in things manifest and open to view rigidly adhered to, justice between man and man is rarely administered; for, though the laws themselves are good, the corrupt administration of them disarms their effect, and distorts them from their purpose. The venality of the judges is beyond conception flagitious and barefaced; and their connivances at false witnesses so scandalously habitual, that testimony is become an article of commerce, and can be procured with a facility and at a price that at once stamps an approbrium on the country, and furnishes matter of wonder to the considerate mind, how, if judges are flagitious and shameless enough to be guilty of it, the people can bear such a pernicious system so long. Hence flow all the censures on the laws and government of that country—hence most of the impediments under which its commerce and agriculture languish; while the actual written laws of the realm are, if duly administered, sufficiently adequate to the security of property, the regulation of commerce, the repression of vice, and the punishment and prevension of crimes.

In endeavouring to guard your mind against an illiberal, vulgar prejudice, I have stated to you what the Turkish constitution is, and what the laws; but you must not carry what I have said to an overstrained or forced interpretation. I would not have you infer that the people are well governed; I only say, that their constitution contains within it the means of better government than is supposed. I would not have you infer that property is always secure; I barely say there are laws written to secure it. This too I wish to impress on you, that the common people are more free, and that property and life are better secured, in Turkey, than in some European countries. I will mention Spain for one. Like the country we are now contemplating, fear keeps them, as disunited individuals, under passive obedience in ordinary cases; but, unlike the Spaniards, when notoriously aggrieved: when their property or religious code is forcibly violated: when the prince would riot in blood, and persist in an unsuccessful war: the Turks appeal to the law; they find a chief; the soldiery join their standard, and depose or destroy him, not on the furious pretext of popular hatred, but upon the legitimate ground of the Koran, as an infidel, and a violator of the laws of God and Mahomet—They always, however, place his regular successor on the throne. Yet, notwithstanding the general venality which pollutes the fountains of justice, and notwithstanding the great abuse of power to which I have alluded, their internal policy is, in many respects, excellent, and may be compared with advantage to that of any nation in Europe. Highway-robbery, house-breaking, or pilfering, are little known and rarely practised among them; and at all times the roads are as secure as the houses. Ample provisions too are made against those petty secret frauds which many who carry a fair face in England, and would bring an action for damages against on that should call them rogues, practise every day. Bakers are the most frequent victims of justice, and are not unfrequently seen hanging at their own doors. They are mulcted and bastinadoed for the first and second offence, and on the third, a staple is driven up into their door-case, and they are hanged from it. Notwithstanding which, men are constantly found hardy enough to pursue the same course of practice; and this is more extraordinary, as the police is so strictly attended to, that the bashaw or vizir himself goes about in disguise, in order to discover frauds and detect the connivances of the inferior officers of justice. But what will our great ladies, who consume their nights, destroy their constitution, and squander their husband's property in gambling; who afterwards, to repair their shattered finances, have recourse to the infamous expedient of keeping gaming-houses, and endeavour to recover by degrading means what they have lost by folly, to the disgrace of themselves and family, and the shame of their sex and rank—What will they say when I tell them, that gaming is held among the Turks to be as infamous as theft, and a gamester looked upon with more detestation than a highway robber? The Turkish ambassador and his train will, on their return to their country, have to tell a curious tale of this much-famed island, in that and other respects.

LETTER XXIX.

PREJUDICE, that canker of the human heart, has injured mankind by impeding personal intercourse, and thereby clogging the channel of intellectual improvement: it forbids that interchange of sentiment—that reciprocal communication of opinion—that generous circulation of intellectual wealth, which, while it enriches another, advances itself—it dissevers the bond of social union, and makes man sit down the gloomy, selfish possessor of his own miserable mite, with too much hatred to give, and too much pride to receive, those benefits, which Providence, by leaving our nature so unaccommodated, has pointed out as necessary to pass between man and man: under its influence we spurn from us the good, if we dislike the hand that offers it, and will rather plunge into the mire than be guided by the light of any one whose opinion is at variance with our own.

Thus it is between the Turks and us—the little of their affairs which the prejudice of the Mahomedans have allowed themselves to communicate, or suffered others to glean among them, has been in general so misused, distorted, and misrepresented by the prejudices of the Christians, that it is not going beyond the truth to say, there exist not a people in the civilized world whose real history and genuine state are so little known as those of the Turks: and the worst of it is, that not one misrepresentation, not one single mistake has fallen on the generous, charitable side; but all, all without exception tend to represent the Turk in the most degraded and detestable point of view. As the purity of the Christian does not allow him to be guilty of a wilful, uncharitable misrepresentation, we should attribute it to unavoidable error, were it not that, till some late authors whose liberality does them honour, they all walked in the very same track, and could hardly have been so uniformly erroneous from design. We must therefore attribute it to religious zeal and mistaken piety; in which, in this instance alone, they seem to be reputable competitors with the Turks. The moroseness, the animosity, and the supercilious self-

P

possession of the bigot, each holds in common with the other.

One striking feature in the constitution of Turkey is, that neither blood nor splendid birth are of themselves sufficient to recommend a man to great offices. Merit and abilities alone are the pinions which can lift ambition to its height. The cottager may be exalted to the highest office in the empire; at least there is no absolute impediment in his way; and I believe it has often happened. Compare this with France under its late monarchy, where no merit could raise a man from the Canaille: this, I say, is one of the criterions of a free constitution, and Turkey is so far democratic.

The very first principle ingrafted in the minds of the Mahomedan children, is a high contempt of all religions but their own; and from the minute babes are capable of distinguishing, they are taught to call Christians by the name of Ghiaour, or Infidel: this grows up in their manhood so strong in them, that they will follow a Christian through the streets, and even justle against him with contempt, crying, Ghiaour! Ghiaour! or, Infidel! Infidel!—Men of dignity and rank, indeed, will treat Christians with courtesy; but as soon as they are gone out of hearing, will call them dog! This is monstrous! But let us recollect how a Turk would be treated in Spain or Portugal, and we shall see that inhuman bigotry may be found in a greater degree among Christians than even Mahomedans. In Spain or Portugal they would treat them thus:—the common people would call them hogs; they would justle them also in contempt; and what is more, they would stab them (it has often happened) *por amor de Dios;* and as to the people of rank, they would very conscientiously consign them to the Inquisition, where the pious fathers of the church would very piously consign them to the flames, and coolly go to the altar, and pray to GOD to damn them hereafter to all eternity. So far the balance, I think, is in favour of the Turks. Need I go further?—I will.—

The Mahomedans are divided into two sects, as the Christians are into many. Those are the sect of Ali, and the sect of Omar. Now, I have never heard among them of one sect burning the other deliberately: but the Roman Catholics, even now, burn Protestants by juridical sentence—burn their fellow Christians to death for differing from them in a mere speculative point of doctrine. Which then are the better men? I am sure it is unnecessary to say: though bad are the best.

The Turks are allowed, by those who know them best, to have some excellent qualities; and I think, that in the prodigality of our censure, which, tho' slow acquainted with them, we are forward to belittle, it would be but fair to give them credit for many of those good qualities, which even among ourselves it requires the greatest intimacy and the warmest mutual confidence and esteem to disclose or discover in each other. That they have many vices is certain. What people are they that have not? Gaming they detest; wine they use not, or at least use only a little, and that by stealth; and as to the plurality of women, it can in them be scarcely deemed a vice, since their religion allows it. One vice, and one only, of a dark dye is laid to their charge; and that has been trumpeted forth with the grievous and horrid addition, that though contradictory to nature, it was allowed by their religion. This I have reason to believe is one of the many fabrications and artifices of Christian zealots, to render Mahomedanism more odious: for I have been informed from the most competent and respectable authority, and am therefore persuaded, that the detestable crime to which I allude, is forbidden both by the Koran and their municipal laws; that it is openly condemned by all, as with us; and that, though candour must allow there are many who practice it (by the bye there are too many in England who are supposed to do the same), there are none hardy or shameless enough not to endeavour to conceal it; and, in short, that it is apparently as much reprobated there as any where; which, at all events, rescues the laws and religion of the country from that stigma.

Perhaps there is no part of the world where the flame of parental affection burns with more ardent and unextinguishable strength, or is more faithfully returned by reciprocal tenderness and filial obedience, than Turkey. Educated in the most unaffected deference and pious submission to their parents' will; trained both by precept and example to the greatest veneration for the aged, and separated almost from their infancy from the women, they acquire a modesty to their superiors, and a bashfulness and respectful deportment to the weaker sex, which never cease to influence them through life. A Turk meeting a woman in the street, turns his head from her, as if looking at her were criminal; and there is nothing they detest so much, or will more sedulously shun, than an impudent, audacious woman. To get the better of a Turk therefore, there is nothing further necessary, than to let slip a virago at him, and he instantly retreats.

Since the arrival of the Turkish ambassador in London, I have had frequent occasion to observe, that the people of his train have been already, by the good example of our British belles and beaux, pretty much cased of their national modesty, and can look at the women with as broad and intrepid a stare, as the greatest puppy in the metropolis.

Their habitual tenderness and deference for the fair sex, while it speaks much for their manly gallantry, must be allowed by candour to be carried to an excess extravagant and irrational. It is the greatest disgrace to the character of a Turk to lift his hand to a woman: this is, doubtless, right, with some limitations; but they carry it so far as to allow no provocation, be it what it may, sufficient to justify using force or strokes to a woman; the utmost they can do is, to scold and walk off. The consequence of this is, that the women often run into the most violent excesses. There have been instances where they have been guilty of the most furious outrages; where they have violated the laws in a collected body, and broke open public stores of corn laid up by the government: the magistrates attended, the Janissaries were called, and came running to quell the riot—but, behold they were women who committed it: they knew no way of resisting them, unless by force; and force they could not use: so the ladies were permitted quietly to do their work in defiance of magistrates, law, right, and reason.

Among the variety of errors and moral absurdities falsely ascribed to the Mahomedan religion, the exclusion of women from Paradise holds a very conspicuous place, as a charge equally false and absurd; on the contrary, the women have their fasts, their ablutions, and the other religious rites deemed by Mahomedans necessary to salvation. Notwithstanding, it has been the practice of travellers to have recourse to invention, where the customs of the country precluded positive information; and to give their accounts rather from the suggestions of their own prejudiced imagination, than from any fair inferences or conclusions drawn from the facts that came under their observation.

LETTER XXX.

THE subject I touched upon in my last three letters, and on which this, and probably some succeeding ones, will turn, is attended with circumstances of great delicacy, and may possibly bear the aspect of at least a dubious import, as touching the great point of religion. I will therefore, before I proceed further, explain to you (lest it should require explanation) the whole scope of my meaning.

My object throughout the whole of what I have said respecting the Turks, is to war with prejudice, not to draw comparisons:—to shew that where the Mahomedans are vicious or enslaved, it is not the fault of their religion or their laws:—to convince you, the Turks are not the only people in the world, who, under all the external forms of sanctity and religion, are capable of the most detestable crimes, and sometimes, utterly bereft of all pretensions to charity—and that, while they have been held up as a perpetual subject of reproach and accusation, they were committing only just the same crimes that conscience might have retorted on their accusers. If allowance can be at all made for historical misrepresentation, we may perhaps be disposed to consider that of the ignorant Catholic missionaries of the early ages, as entitled to some excuse, or at least mitigation. The intemperate zeal of those times forbade the full exercise of the rational faculties; but in this age of illumination and liberality, he that falsifies from polemical malice should meet little quarter and less belief. And it must be grievous to all men of virtue and religion to reflect, that churchmen, disciples of the Chriſtan church, which ſhould be the fountain of purity and truth, have been foremoſt in the liſt of falſifiers.

The difficulty of obtaining information of any kind in Turkey, is very great; of their religion chiefly they are extremely tenacious; and as to their women, it is allowed by the beſt informed men, who have lived there for many years, in departments of life that gave them the beſt means of obtaining information Europeans can have, that, at beſt, but a very imperfect knowledge can be had of them. Yet travellers who probably never migrated farther than "from the green bed to the brown," have given us diffuſe accounts of their religion; and adventurers who never were beyond the purlieus of Drury, have ſcaled Seraglio walls, and carried off the favorites of Sultans.

The truth is, my dear FREDERICK, the Turks, like all other people, have their ſhare of vices, but are by no means countenanced in them by their religion; and from what I have been able to collect, as well from my own inquiries and obſervations, as from reading the beſt hiſtorians, I am perſuaded that they have not, in the whole ſcope of Mahomedaniſm, one doctrine ſo ſubverſive of virtue, or ſo encouraging to the indulgence of vice, as many that are to be found in that curious code, Popery.

The malice of our intemperate zealots againſt Mahomedaniſm has been of courſe extended to its founder with more than common exaggeration and additions. They have repreſented Mahomet to be a man of mean origin, poſſeſſing a mind unenlightened by ſcience or literature, and an underſtanding and faculties naturally groſs. All thoſe ſuggeſtions are undoubtedly falſe;—he ſprung from the moſt noble of all the Arabian tribes—the Coraiſhités: at his time, poverty, ſo far from being a reproach among them, was a mark of every thing that was great and dignified, if ſupported with magnanimity and fortitude; and the two firſt caliphs lived as poor as Mahomet himſelf, although they had immenſe revenues, commanded vaſt armies, and were lords of great provinces. As to his underſtanding I can only ſay, that perhaps he was the very laſt man in the world whoſe intellectual powers ſhould be called in queſtion. His genius was unbounded, his ſpirit enterpriſing, his powers of addreſs were unequalled, he was allowed to be the greateſt orator of his time; and yet, with all theſe qualifications, his underſtanding was ſlighted. It is a logical truth, that when people prove too much, they prove nothing at all: our Chriſtian zealots, in this inſtance, have overſhot the mark, and thereby rendered all their other information at leaſt doubtful. Perhaps the conſummation of all policy was Mahomet's pretending to be an idiot, in order to make his great and wonderful effuſions appear to be the immediate inſpiration of Heaven—He called himſelf THE IDIOT PROPHET.*

The whole of Mahomedaniſm may be reduced ſimply to this one article of faith—" There is but one GOD, and MAHOMET is the prophet;" but upon this they have ſuperinduced, from time to time, ſuch a variety of abſurdities as would require volumes to deſcribe: however, in ſtrict candour let us reflect, and aſk our own hearts the queſtion, whether ſprinkling with holy water, or worſhipping a bit of white wafer as GOD, can be exceeded, or are leſs abſurd than the periodical ablutions of the Turks, or their going on a pilgrimage to Mecca?

With regard to the women, I have ſaid before that the beſt information we can obtain is very imperfect; all I have been able to collect, you ſhall have. They are formed in a ſtyle of the moſt exquiſite ſymmetry, particularly about the cheſt and boſom: they have delicate ſkins, regular features, black hair and eyes, and are, above all other beings,

* Mohammed.

cleanly and neat in their persons, bathing twice a day regularly, besides on other occasions, and not suffering even the smallest hair to remain upon their bodies. They are kept in the most rigorous confinement, and only persons of ill fame paint. Women of character are there chaste—nor is their chastity to be attributed to restraint merely, for, from their infancy they are trained to discretion and self-subjection, and the modesty natural to the sex is cherished from its first dawnings. When they grow up, they are not, like our women here, subjected to the contagion of infamous gallantry; neither are the men trained to, nor do they pride themselves, like some among us, on the arts of seduction. In fact, that practice makes no part of the accomplishments of their fine gentlemen; nay, it is held by them to be infamous. There are no such characters to be found in Turkey as your box-lobby loungers—none of your upstart cubs like those who doudle the best part of the day through Pall-Mall, St. James's-street and Bond-street; who, without birth, wealth, education, or parts, fancy themselves fine fellows, and powder their noses in ladies' head-dresses, whispering them in order to get the reputation of gallantry; who strut like Bantam cocks, and assume a fierce air to conceal their conscious want of spirit; and dressed in a suit of regimentals bought by papa, at mama's request, to exhibit sweet Master Jacky to advantage in the Park—though never to be soiled with gunpowder, or personated with a ball in the nasty field of battle!!!—my dear FREDERICK, I have often told you that you shall make choice of your own profession. If you should choose any of the learned professions, you may fail in it without dishonour; for many of the ablest men have failed before: but, mark me! avoid the military as you would ruin, unless you have the requisites; let not the glitter of a scarlet coat, or the empty name of a soldier, tempt you to be like one of those miserable animals I have described. There may be characters more wicked—I know none so utterly contemptible.

All extremes are bad; but the exceedings of virtue even where they run into error, are still preferable to vice. However ludicrous it may appear, we cannot absolutely despise or condemn the prudery of the Turkish women, though it runs into such extravagance, that, when feeding their poultry, they keep carefully vieled if there happens to be a cock among them, so fastidiously averse are they to the odious male creature seeing their pretty faces.

When the circumstances under which the Turkish women stand are considered, it must appear amazing, that chastity, from principle, is universal among them, as it is confessed to be: the nature of man urges him to desire, with greatest ardour, that which is most forbidden; and women who are much confined, may well be supposed to have their passions inflamed by the exaggerated workings of the imagination. Infidelity, however, to the marriage-bed, is much less frequent among the men there, than among the women here; and the tide or fashion, which in this country gives such a rapid and irresistible circulation to vice and adultery, runs there in an opposite direction; and contrary to our customs, no man is so unfashionable in Turkey as he that has interrupted the domestic peace of a family by seduction.

Among the many virtues which may with strict justice be ascribed to the Turks, hospitality holds a conspicuous place. It is not confined to common civility, it extends to personal protection. Many deem it absolutely their duty to risk their lives in defence of their guests; nor will any motive, however cogent, be allowed to justify the violation of it. Nay, to such a system is it carried up, that an engagement with a stranger is accepted as an excuse for not obeying the fummons of a great man, when no other apology, not even that of indifpofition, would be admitted.

While the Turks abhor and defpife all other religions but their own, their government is by no means intolerant in fpiritual concerns. The exercife of all religions is free, and at Conftantinople (we are told) Monks drefs in their habits, and are allowed at funeral proceffions to elevate the crofs, which is more than the Englifh tyranny allowed the Roman Catholics of Ireland to do, till very lately: a Turk, however, convicted of apoftacy, could not by any means efcape death. Meantime it muft be obferved, that if they keep up a decent femblance of the forms of their religion, no intrufive inquiry is made unto their real faith: and though it is one of the injunctions of Mahomet to endeavour to convert unbelievers, and they fometimes in obedience to that command folicit the converfion of Chriftians and others; they never fail to confider any renegado, or perfon who becomes a convert, with contempt, if not diflike.

I will conclude this letter with an extract from that moft valuable and accurate work, Ruffel's Hiftory of Aleppo, which will give you a better, becaufe a true, notion of Turkifh morals, than you are likely to receive from general opinion. "Upon the whole," fays he, "whether it be afcribed to the influence of their political conftitution, or to the abfence of various temptations, which in Europe often lead to the violation of better laws; there are perhaps few great cities where many of the private and domeftic virtues are in general more prevalent than at Aleppo."

LETTER XXXI.

THE use of periodical stated times of devotion is universally admitted, and the necessity of adopting them makes a part of the Christian code. The Mahomedan religion, however, exceeds it far in the rigid attention to, and frequency of, devotion. There are no less than five stated times of prayer in every twenty-four hours, fixed as indispensable, at none of which a true believer fails; and the fervency of their praying exceeds even the frequency. I have heard it asserted, that if the house was to take fire while they are at their devotion, they would not break off; and so rigidly intent do they conceive it their duty to be during the time of prayer, that if in the midst of it they were interrupted by a fit of sneering or coughing, they consider all already done as gone for nothing, and always begin them again. And to tell a truth of them, if the Christians curse them, they are pretty even with them in return, never failing to pray for discord, enmity, and dissension among their enemies, as well as health and prosperity to themselves; and to the efficacy of those prayers they fondly attribute all the wars and dissensions which incessantly harass Christendom. A bell tolls as a public notice of prayer; and when a true Mahomedan hears it, let him be where he will, whether at home or abroad, in the highway or in the market, be the place dirty or clean, wet or dry, he immediately falls down and worships.

As subsidiary to prayer they have their ablutions, in which they are full as scrupulously punctual as in their prayers. One is preparatory to prayer, another after cohabitation with women, a third before eating, and another again incidental. Those they never neglect to perform, unless some insuperable obstacle lies in the way. Charity, that most glorious doctrine of any religion, is enjoined by the Koran under the most heavy denunciation of heavenly vengeance, in case of neglect; and by it they are charged to regard no bounds in liberality to the poor. Many Mussulmen in their zeal to discharge this duty have given a fourth, many a third, and some one half of their property. Nay, the instances are not unfrequent of men giving away their all, and living afterwards themselves upon alms. To do strict justice it must be said, that poverty is no where so respectfully attended to, honoured, or reverenced, as among the Mahomedans; who have a saying among them, " that the fear of want is a mark of the judgment of GOD."

Abstinence is considered as a virtue among them, and very strictly enjoined as a religious duty. The great fast appointed by the Koran continues for the month of Ramedan, during which time they neither eat, drink, nor converse with their wives, from sun-rise till the stars appear, or the lamps are hung out at the mosques. Any man who breaks it is punished with death; but the worst of it is, that they will not allow even travellers, the sick or the wounded, to plead a right to exemption: some of the Turks, however, and all the Christians, have hit upon expedients to pass the month without much mortification; that is, sleeping in bed all day, and sitting up and carousing all night, to evade the restraint.

The last and greatest ordinance of their religion is the pilgrimage to Mecca, which when once accomplished is supposed to be a direct passport to Heaven; and there are few of them who do not at one time or other of their lives take that painful and hazardous journey. As this is a very interesting journey, however, to travel in the closet, as it includes the description of a caravan, and serves to shew to what extremeties enthusiasm can influence men, I will give you a description of it as handed to me by a very accurate and ingenious person, on whose precise veracity I can rely; first making some remarks upon the preceding part of this letter.

You will observe from what I have already said, that, excepting the mere points of religious faith, the moral ordinances of Mahomedanism comprehend most of those parts of the Christian religion, on the practice of which the reputation of piety is founded; and that for strict obedience to those ordinances the Mahomedans are more remarkable than we are. Adultery is not frequent among them; wine is seldom or never used; theft is little known; so is murder. Then in the practical parts of devotion, there are in the first place prayers; secondly, abstinence or fasting; thirdly, charity. Those are all Christian doctrines, more zealously observed by them than by us. Their ablutions are at least no injury to the cause of morality or piety; but rather, being done as a religious exercise, serve to keep up the series of intercourse which should subsist between the creature and his Creator: besides, I cannot help thinking with our inimitable poet Thomson, that

————from the body's purity, the mind
Receives a secret sympathetic aid. SEASONS—Summer.

And as to the pilgrimage to Mecca, however irrational it may appear to us, it is at least recommended by sincerity and zeal, and is doubtless in the eye of an all-seeing Providence meritorious. HE, we are to suppose, will judge, not by the value of the act, but the purity of the motive; and will accept it as the offering of a frail, blind mortal, bending in obedience to that which he conceives to be the will of Heaven. Besides, for the life of me I cannot see why a pilgrimage to Mecca is at all more culpable than a pilgrimage to Jerusalem; not to mention the thousand other holy places to which well-meaning Christians go, for their soul's sake, at imminent hazard of their lives, and certain mortification and hardship to their bodies.

Banish then, my FREDERICK! banish from your heart all illiberal and uncharitable prejudices, if any have yet found their way to it. Revere and cling to your religion as the best and most conducive to eternal and temporal happiness; and the more good because it enjoins us to be charitable even to the Jews as well as to the Gentiles: but never think that you advance the cause of that religion, or do service to your GOD, by waging war against your fellow-creatures for opinions they can no more help entertaining than you can help having yours, or by denouncing against them that eternal sentence which rests with the Almighty alone to judge of or to pronounce.

To a benevolent mind the animosities of mankind present a most afflicting picture; and the frivolous pretexts upon which those animosities are grounded render it only the more horrible. One would think that the substantial traffic of life, and the struggle of mankind for the superfluities of it, of themselves afforded ample materials for scuffle, without resorting to the shadows of speculation for contention. Yet experience has shewn us that opinion is a much more copious source of animosity and warfare; and that for one man who has been cursed, murdered, or destroyed by his fellow-creatures in a contest for property, there are a thousand who have fallen sacrifices to the vengeance of hostile opinion.

Were it possible that I could obtain from the bounty of Heaven a grant of the first wish of my heart, that wish should be to see all mankind in harmony and mutual good will, ranging without distinction under the one great name of man and brother. As those who foment the disunion between them are the most pernicious monsters of society, so he who endeavours to bring them one step nearer to a general accommodation of sentiment, who strives to inculcate the principles of mutual toleration, and encourage the growth of reciprocal affection between men as fellow beings, may be justly ranked among the best friends of mankind, and the most faithful servants of Him who gave being to all.

Among the gross misrepresentations of which I complain, and which for the sake of mankind I lament, is that general falsehood, the infidelity of the Turkish women. The respectable author whom I have before taken the freedom of quoting, I mean Dr. Russel, declares that in twenty years residence at Aleppo, he did not remember a public instance of adultery; and that in the private walks of scandal those he heard of were among the lowest class, and did not in number exceed a dozen. "In respect to the Franks (continues he) the undertaking is attended not only with such risk to the individual, but may in its consequences so seriously involve the whole settlement, that it is either never attempted, or is concealed with a secrecy unexampled in other matters. I have reason to believe that European travellers have sometimes had a Greek courtesan imposed on them for a sultana; and after having been heartily frightened, have been induced to pay smartly, in order to preserve a secret which the day after was known to half the sisterhood in town." He remarks, however, that at Constantinople the state of gallantry is different.

On the subject of the Turkish moral character, I have endeavoured to be as concise as justice would allow me to be; and yet I find that I have gone to some length. I cannot however dismiss it without giving you a trait to which the most obstinate polemical prejudice, and the most inveterate hatred, must in spite of them pay the tribute of applause. Their treatment to their slaves is beyond all example among us humane, tender, and generous, and such as may well bring a blush into the faces of Christian dealers in human flesh. When young slaves, male or female, are bought by a Turk, they seem to be introduced into the family rather in the condition of an adopted child; they receive the same education, perform nearly the same offices, and are bound to no greater marks of respect than their master's own children—and in fact feel none of the galling circumstances of a state of servility; the very worst treatment they ever receive is to be put on a footing with the menial domestics, or ordered to the same duty as a valet or a page. It often happens, on the other hand, that they are married into the family, and very frequently are promoted to high offices in the state. If they adopt the religion of their masters, it is always spontaneously; and even to slaves taken in war, no compulsion is used to make them change their faith.

The following is the best description I am able to give you of an Eastern caravan. It exactly coincides with my own observations, and with the various accounts I have had from others. I owe it, as well as the account of the proceedings of the pilgrims at Mecca, to the kind offices of a friend, who took the pains to procure them for me.

DESCRIPTION OF A CARAVAN.
Inclosed in the preceding Letter.

A CARAVAN, which is so often mentioned in the history and description of the East, and in all the tales and stories of those countries, is an assemblage of travellers, partly pilgrims, partly merchants, who collect together in order to consolidate a sufficient force to protect them, in travelling through the hideous wilds and burning deserts over which they are constrained to pass for commercial and other purposes; those wilds being infested with Arabs, who make a profession of pillage, and rob in most formidable bodies, some almost as large as small armies. As the collection of such a number requires time, and the embodying of them is a serious concern, it is concerted with great care and preparation, and is never attempted without the permission of the prince in whose dominions it is to be formed, and of those also through whose dominions it is to pass, expressed in writing. The exact number of men and carriages, mules, horses, and other beasts of burthen, are specified in the license; and the merchants to whom the caravan belongs, regulate and direct every thing appertaining to its government and police during the journey, and appoint the various officers necessary for conducting it.

Each caravan has four principal officers: the first, the caravanbachi, or head of the caravan; the second, the captain of the march; the third, the captain of the stop or rest; and the fourth, the captain of the distribution. The first has the uncontrolable authority and command over all the others, and gives them his orders: the second is absolute during the march; but his authority immediately ceases on the stopping or encamping of the caravan, when the third assumes his share of the authority, and exerts it during the time of its remaining at rest: and the fourth orders the disposition of every part of the caravan, in case of an attack or battle. This last officer has also during the march the inspection and direction of the distribution of provisions, which is conducted under his management by several inferior officers, who are obliged to give security to the master of the caravan; each of them having the care of a certain number of men, elephants, dromedaries, camels, &c. &c. which they undertake to conduct and furnish with provisions at their own risque, according to an agreement stipulated between them.

A fifth officer of the caravan is the pay-master or treasurer, who has under him a great many clerks and interpreters, appointed to keep accurate journals of all the material incidents that occur upon the journey. And it is by these journals, signed by the superior officers, that the owners of the caravan judge whether they have been well or ill served or conducted.

Another kind of officers are the mathematicians, without whom no caravan will presume to set out. There are commonly three of them attached to a caravan of large size; and they perform the offices both of quarter-masters and aides-de-camp, leading the troops when the caravan is attacked, and assigning the quarters where the caravan is appointed to encamp.

There are no less than five distinct sorts of caravans; first, the heavy caravans, which are composed of elephants, dromedaries, camels and horses; secondly, the light caravans, which have but few elephants; thirdly, the common caravans, where there are none of those animals; fourthly the horse caravans, where there are neither dromedaries nor camels; and lastly, sea caravans, consisting of vessels; from whence you will observe that the word caravan is not confined to the land, but extends to the water also.

The proportion observed in the heavy caravan is as follows: When there are five hundred elephants, they add a thousand dromedaries and two thousand horses at the least: and then the escort is composed of four thousand men on horseback. Two men are required for leading one elephant, five for three dromedaries, and seven for eleven camels. This multitude of servants, together with the officers and passengers, whose number is uncertain, serve to support the escort in case of a fight, and render the caravan more formidable and secure. The passengers are not absolutely obliged to fight; but according to the laws and usages of the caravans, if they refuse to do so, they are not entitled to any provisions whatever from the caravan, even though they should agree to pay an extravagant price for them.

Every elephant is mounted by what they call a nick: that is to say, a young lad of nine or ten years old, brought up to the business, who drives the elephant, and pricks it with a pointed iron to animate it in the fight: the same lad also loads the fire-arms of the two soldiers who mount the elephant with him.

The day of the caravan setting out being once fixed, is never altered or postponed; so that no disappointment can possibly ensue to any one.

One would suppose that so enormous and powerful a body, so well armed, might be certain of moving forward without fear of being robbed; but as most of the Arabian princes have no other means to subsist but by their robberies, they keep spies in all parts, who give them notice when the caravans set out, which they way-lay; and sometimes attack with superior force, overpower them, plunder them of all their treasure, and make slaves of the whole convoy—foreigners excepted, to whom they generally shew more mercy. If they are repulsed, they generally come to some agreement; the conditions of which are pretty well observed, especially if the assailants are native Arabians. The carrying on of robberies with such armies may appear astonishing; but when the temptation is considered, and when it is known that one caravan only is sometimes enough to enrich those princes, much of our surprise vanishes.

They are obliged to use great precautions to prevent the caravan from introducing that dreadful distemper, the plague, into the places through which they pass, or from being themselves infected with it. When therefore they arrive near a town, the inhabitants of the town and the people of the caravan hold a solemn conference concerning the state of their health, and very sincerely communicate to each other the state of the case, candidly informing each other whether there be danger on either side.—When there is reason to suspect any contagious distemper, they amicably agree that no communication whatever shall take place between them; and if the caravan stands in need of provisions, they are conveyed to them with the utmost caution over the walls of the town.

The fatigues, hardships, and hazards, attending those caravans, are so great, that they certainly would never be undertaken, if the amazing profits did not in some measure counterbalance them.—The merchant who travels in them must be content with such provisions as he can get, must part with all his delicacies, and give up all hope of ease; he must submit to the frightful confusion of languages and nations; the fatigues of long marches over sands, and under a climate almost sufficiently hot to reduce him to a cinder: he must submit cheerfully to exorbitant duties fraudulently levied, and audacious robberies and subtle tricks practised by the herd of vagabonds who follow the caravans —for preventing which, the merchants have a variety of well contrived locks, that can only be opened by those who know the knack of them.

But in some tracks of caravans there are dangers, and horrible ones against which no human foresight or power can provide, and beneath which whole caravans sink, and are never after heard of.

The Egyptian caravans are particularly subject to hazards in the horrid tracks they are necessarily obliged to take through sandy deserts, where, for boundless extents, nature has denied one single circumstance of favour; where a blade of grass never grew, nor a drop of water ever ran; where the scorching fire of the sun has banished the kindly influence of the other elements; where, for several days journey, no object meets the eye to guide the parched traveller in his way; and where the casual track of one caravan is closed by the moving sands, before another can come to take advantage of it. In those vast plains of burning sands, if the guide should happen to lose his way, the provision of water, so necessary to carry them to the place where they are to find more, must infallibly fail them; in such a case the mules and horses die with fatigue and thirst; and even the camels, notwithstanding their extraordinary power to subsist without water, soon perish in the same manner, together with the people of the caravan, wandering in those frightful deserts.

But more dreadful still, and still more inevitable, is the danger when a south wind happens to rise in those sandy deserts. The least mischief it occasions is, to dry up the leathern bags which contain the provision of water for the journey. This wind, to which the Arabs give the epithet of poisoned, often stifles in a moment those who have the misfortune to meet it; to prevent which, they are obliged to throw themselves immediately on the ground, putting their faces close to the burning sands which surround them on all sides, and covering their mouths with some linen cloth, lest by breathing they should swallow instantaneous death, which this wind carries with it wherever it extends.—Besides which, whole caravans are often buried under moving hills of burning sand, raised by the agitation of the winds.

All those horrors and dangers are so exquisitely described by our charming bard THOMSON, that I

DESCRIPTION OF A CARAVAN.   191

cannot refrain tranfcribing the paffage, as bringing them more immediately home to the underftanding and the heart, than volumes of common defcription could do.

>   ———Breathed hot
> From all the boundlefs furnace of the fky,
> And the wide glittering wafte of burning fand,
> A fuffocating wind the pilgrim fmites
> With inftant death.   Patient of thirft and toil,
> Son of the Defert! even the camel feels,
> Shot through his withered heart, the fiery blaft.
> Or from the black-red either burfting broad
> Sallies the fudden wirlwind.   Straight the fands,
> Commov'd around, in gathering eddies play;
> Nearer and nearer ftill they darkening come;
> Till; with the general all-involving ftorm
> Swept up, the whole continuous wilds arife;
> And by their noon-day fount dejected thrown,
> Or funk at night in fad difaftrous fleep
> Beneath defcending hills, the caravan
> Is buried deep.   In Caro's crowded ftreets
> Th' impatient Merchant wondering waits in vain,
> And Mecca faddens at the long delay.—

Yet, notwithftanding all thofe horrible circumftances of terror and danger—trade, and the defire of gain, on the one hand, induce multitudes of people to run the hazard.

> Impiger extremos currit Mercator ad Indos,
> Per mare pauperiem fugiens, per faxa, per ignes.
>   HORACE.

And on the other hand, enthufiafm and religious zeal fond thoufands to tempt their fate, and take a paffage to Heaven through thofe horrid regions. Thus we fee in what various ways delufion operates.—The merchant might find a livelihood, and the bigot his way to divine favour, juft as well by ftaying within the confines of their own native home.

ACCOUNT OF THE CEREMONIES OBSERVED BY PILGRIMS ON THEIR ARRIVAL AT MECCA.

The caravans are generally so ordered, as to arrive at Mecca about forty days after the Fast of Ramedan, and immediately previous to the Corban, or Great Sacrifice. Five or six days before that festival, the three great caravans, viz. that from Europe, that from Asia Minor, and that from Arabia, unite; and all, consisting of about two hundred thousand men, and three hundred thousand beasts of burthen, encamp at some miles from Mecca. The pilgrims form themselves into small detachments, and enter the town to arrange the ceremonies preparatory to the Great Sacrifice. They are led through a street of continual ascent, till they arrive at a gate on an eminence, called the Gate of Health. From thence they see the great mosque which incloses the House of Abraham. They salute it with the most profound respect and devotion, repeating twice, "Salam Alek Irusoul Allah!" that is to say, "Peace be with the Ambassador of God!" Thence, at some distance, they mount five steps to a large platform faced with stone, where they offer up their prayers; they then descend on the other side of it, and advance towards two arches, of the same kind of dimensions, but at some distance from each other, through which they pass with great silence and devotion. This ceremony must be performed seven times.

From hence proceeding to the great mosque which incloses the House of Abraham, they enter the mosque, and walk seven times round the little building contained within it, saying, "This is the House of God, and of his servant Abraham." Then kissing with great veneration a black stone, said to have descended white from Heaven, they go to the famous well called Zun Zun, which the angel shewed to Hagar when she was distressed in the desert, and could find no water for her son Ishmael, and which the Arabs call Zem Zem. Into this well they plunge with all their clothes, repeating "Toba Alla, Toba Alla!" that is to say, "Forgiveness, God! Forgiveness, God!" They drink a draught of that fœtid, turbid water, and depart.

The duty of bathing and drinking they are obliged to pass through once; but those who would gain Paradise before the others, must repeat it once a day during the stay of the caravan at Mecca.

At fifteen miles from the town of Mecca there is a hill called "Ghiabal Arafata," or "the Mount of Forgiveness." It is about two miles in circumference—a most delicious spot. On it Adam and Eve met, after the Lord had, for their transgressions, separated them forty years. Here they cohabited and lived in excess of happiness, having built a house on it, called "Beith Adam," that is to say, "the House of Adam." On the eve of the day of Sacrifice, the three caravans, ranged in a triangular form, surround this mountain—during the whole night the people rejoice, clamour, and riot—firing off cannon, muskets, pistols, and fireworks, with an incessant sound of drums and trumpets. As soon as day breaks, a profound silence succeeds—they slay their sheep and offer up their sacrifice on the mountain with every demonstration of the most profound devotion.

On a sudden a scheik (or head of the temple), a kind of prelate, rushes from amidst them, mounted on a camel—he ascends five steps, rendered practicable for the purpose, and in a studied sermon preaches thus to the people:

"Return praise and thanks for the infinite and immense benefits granted by God to Mahomedans, through the mediation of his most beloved friend and prophet, Mahomet: for that he has delivered them from the slavery and bondage of sin and ico-

R

latry, in which they were plunged; has given them the House of Abraham, from whence they can be heard, and their petitions granted; also the mountain of forgiveness, by which they can implore Him, and obtain a pardon and remission of all their sins.

" For that the blessed, pious, and merciful God, giver of all good gifts, commanded his secretary, Abraham, to build himself a house at Mecca, whence his descendants might pray to the Almighty, and their desires be fulfilled.

" On this command all the mountains in the world ran, as it were, each ambitious to assist the secretary of the Lord, and to furnish a stone towards erecting the holy house; all, except this poor little mountain, which, through mere indigence, could not contribute a stone. It continued therefore thirty years grievously afflicted: at length the Eternal God observed its anguish, and, moved with pity at its long suffering, broke forth, saying, I can forbear no longer, my child! your bitter lamentations have reached my ears; and I now declare, that all those who go to visit the house of my friend Abraham shall not be absolved of their sins, if they do not first reverence you, and celebrate on you the holy Sacrifice, which I have enjoined my people through the mouth of my prophet Mahomet! Love God! Pray! Give Alms!"

After this sermon the people salute the Mountain, and depart.

LETTER XXXII.

IN my last letters I endeavoured to give you an account of the Turkish government, laws, and constitution in general, so far as I was able to collect information on the subject. I will now proceed to a description of those particular parts of that vast empire through which I had occasion to travel.

During my stay at Aleppo, I experienced much politeness and hospitality from the European gentry resident there, and particularly from Mr. ——, at whose house I entirely resided; and as the Franks live on a very good footing with each other, the time passed so agreeably, that were it not for "that within," I should have been happy enough —We rode out occasionally, sometimes hunting, sometimes merely for the ride sake. Sometimes with an intelligent native whom I got to walk with me, or with some of the Franks, I walked about the town, in order to amuse away the time and see what was going forward, notwithstanding the cry of "Frangi Cucu!" or "Cuckold Frank!" which frequently followed us for the length of a street. Sometimes we went of evenings to some of the outlets, where preperation was made for our reception by servants, previously dispatched for the purpose, and there regaled with coffee, wine, fruits, &c.

The first day we went on a party of the last mentioned kind, Mrs. —— did us the honour to accompany us: the place appointed was in a range of beautiful rural gardens that lie along the side of a river; where the well cultivated earth teeming with a vast abundance of the best esculent plants, flowers, flowering shrubs and fruit-trees, afforded a most delicious regale to the senses; and the plane, the willow, the ash, the pomegranate, and a variety of other trees, clustered together in almost impervious thickets, yielded a delightful shady retreat from the piercing rays of the sun. It was on this occasion that I got the first specimen of Turkish illiberality, which, as I was entirely unprepared for it confounded me, and nearly deprived me of temper and of prudence. As we walked along, I observed several Turks addressing themselves to Mrs. ———— and me, who walked arm in arm, and speaking with a loudness of voice, contortion of countenance, and violence of gesticulation, attended with a clapping of hands, which, though I did not understand their language, I could plainly perceive carried the appearance of a menace or insult. I was at a loss what to think of it; Mrs. ———— blushed, and seemed much hurt: Mr. ———— and the other gentlemen were silent, and betrayed not the least mark of emotion or resentment. At length, when we got from them, I asked what it meant? and was told, that it was all aimed at Mrs. ————, or at least occasioned by her: that, bigoted to the customs of their own country, and utterly ignorant of those of any other, they were affected with great indignation at her dress, occasional derangement of her veil, and, above all, at the shameless and unpardonably wicked circumstance of a woman walking so openly and familiarly in the company of men.— Talking of this affair afterwards with Mr. ————, the lady's husband, he assured me, that there was not an opprobrious and infamous epithet which the vulgar ingenuity of the brightest quean in Billingsgate could think of, that they had not huddled upon us. I was beyond measure astonished at the coolness with which he bore it, and said, that if I had understood what they had said, I should most certainly have been unable to restrain myself, and would have knocked one of them down as an example to the rest. Had you done so, returned he, you would certainly have repented it: for, if you escaped being stoned, or put to death upon the spot, the legal punishment for an infidel striking a true believer, you could not escape; and probably we, and all the Franks in the city, would suffer for it: it would at all events cause a dreadful convulsion in the place, and you would yourself fall a sacrifice to it.

Not long since I was conversing on this subject with a gentleman of my acquaintance, and mentioned it with some asperity, as arising from a spirit of bigotry peculiar to Mahomedans. " My good Sir," said he, " let me undeceive you! the very same would be done in most parts of Spain. I was one day," continued he, " walking in a town in Spain, in company with the wife of a gentleman who resided there, who were both well known, and bore the most unexceptionable character. Seeing me however walking with her, the populace, as we passed, held up two fingers significantly, and cried to her, What a cuckold is your husband! and concluded with ' Todas las Inglesas son putas,' or, " All English women are ———s." He added, " that he was even in Cadiz, where commercial intercourse renders them rather more liberal than in other part of the country, frequently accosted by little children themselves, with ' Crees in Dios ?' Do you believe in God? and sometimes forming a cross with the thumb of the right hand and the forefinger, ' Crees en este? Crees en este? No! No! Ah Judio! Moro! Barbaro! Bruto! Protestante! Puerco! Voia al los Infernos!!' In English—Do you believe in this? Do you believe in this? No! No! Ah Jew! Moor! Barbarian! Protestant! Hog! Go to Hell!!"

So much for human beneficience and charity, under the fostering auspices of religion!

The house of Mr. ———, where I was so hospitably lodged, was a magnificent edifice, built in all the fulness of Eastern grandeur and luxury, and furnished with all the splendour and state of Turkey, united with the taste and opulence of Great Britain. It was indeed a house in which voluptuousness itself might sit down with satisfaction—The most unaffected hospitality and generous benevolence spread the board, and politeness and affability presided over all. Never shall I forget it—never shall I think of it without gratitude and esteem.

A gentleman of the opulence and consequence of Mr. ———, with a house such as I have described, and a disposition to social enjoyment, was not, you will conclude, without a resort of company and friends; in truth, he had friends even among the better sort of Turks. Parties of pleasure had no intermission while I was there; and as the ladies of Europe or of European extraction in that country are highly accomplished, speak many languages, are indefatigable in their efforts to please, and receive strangers from Europe with a joy and satisfaction not to be described, Aleppo would have been to me an Elysium, if the pleasures of the place did not from the beginning suffer diminution from my own painful sensations, which were aggravated at last by an incident that arose from my intercourse there—of which more hereafter.

While I remained at Aleppo, I walked as I before told you, frequently about the streets; and I think I never was witness to so many broils in all my life put together, as I was in my wanderings there—Not a time I went out that I did not observe one, two, three, and sometimes half a dozen or more. They have nothing terrible in them however, and, were it not extremely disgusting to see men scold, would be very entertaining; for I will venture to say that a street battle " à la Turque" is one of the most ludicrous exhibitions in the world. The parties approach to each other, and retreat mutually, as the action of the one gives hopes to the other of victory, lifting their hands, and flourishing them in the air, as if ready to strike every moment, grinning, and gnashing their teeth, while their beard and whiskers besprent with the spume of their mouths, and wagging with the quick motion of their lips and ghastly contortions of their jaws, present the most ridiculous spectacle imaginable. They reminded me at the time of a verse in an old English ballad:—

> 'Tis merry in the hall,
> When beards wag all.

Nothing, in fact, can exceed the extravagance of their gesture: the vehement loudness of their voice, or the whimsical distortions of their countenances, in which are displayed sometimes the quickest vicissitudes of fear and fury, and sometimes the most laughable combination of both. All this time, however, not a single blow is actually struck; but they compensate for the want of bodily prowess by the exercise of the tongue, denouncing vengeance against each other, threatening instant demolition, lavishing every bitter reproach, every filthy epithet, and every horrible imprecation that they can think of, and both boasting occasionally of their patience and forbearance, which fortunately enabled them to refrain from annihilating their adversary. At last the fray gradually decays: exhausted with fatigue, and half choaked with dust and vociferation, they retreat gradually backwards to their own doors; where summing up all their malignity into a most horrid execration, they part for the time, and retire to vaunt in empty threat, and growl away their rage, in the recesses of their haram.

Yet those people are found terrible in battle by the Christian troops that have from time to time been opposed to them: here, if proof be wanting of the effects of religion on the human mind, is an incontrovertable one of its powerful operations. Under the influence of their faith, which tells them that they go to Paradise instantly if killed in battle with Infidels, they perform prodigies of valour fighting against Christians; while, forbidden by that faith to imbrue their hands in the blood of a true believer, their passions have been gradually brought under the dominion of their religion, till that which at firſt was faith at laſt becomes habit, and the appropriate energy and courage of the man has ſunk into the degrading and emaſculant efforts of the woman.

The practice of fighting, or perſonal conflicts between individuals of the ſame ſociety, ſeems to have been condemned by the univerſal conſent of all religions. The Gentoos, as well as all the other ſects of the various parts of the Eaſt through which I have travelled, give vent to their paſſion in nearly the ſame manner as the Turks. The Chriſtians too are moſt ſtrictly forbidden to ſtrike one another by the great Author of their faith: but it is their good fortune, that they not only have the beſt religion in the world for their guidance, but that they are the only people in the world who claim exemption from the penalties of that religion, and think themſelves wronged and their perſonal rights infringed, if they are refuſed the privilege of breaking through its rules whenever thoſe rules are at variance with their convenience.

Be it your care, my dear child, to fortify your mind with the ſpirit of true religion and ſound morality, and let your practice in life be ever guided by their precepts.

LETTER XXXIII.

THE avidity with which human creatures ſearch for ſomething to recreate the mind and keep it in exerciſe, is of itſelf a convincing proof of the natural activity of our intellectual faculties, and ſhews that, like the different parts of the body, they were given by Providence to be called into effort and improved by practice. As they who by the favours of opulence are exempted from the necessity of actual bodily labour, are obliged to have recourse to artificial labour called exercise; so they who have the misfortune to be precluded from the employment of the mind by business, are obliged to seek mental exercise in a variety of expedients, some of which are criminal, some foolish, and some good for nothing or indifferent. Cards, dice, and games of chance are (according to the extent to which they are carried) of the two former—tale and novel-reading of the two latter. Those however serve to occupy the vacant hours of all the idle and unemployed. And when letters deny their friendly aid, we find among ourselves the deficiency supplied from the less ample resources of the memory; and story-telling, love tales, fairy tales, and goblin and ghost adventures, are recited round the villager's fire or the kitchen hearth in as great numbers, with as much ingenuity, and to as great effect, as they are to be found written in the innumerable volumes on the shelves of our circulating libraries.

In Turkey, where the art of printing has not yet been known, were the circulation of literary productions is chained down within the narrow compass of manuscript, and where therefore the efforts of genius are repressed by discouragement, the business of story-telling makes in itself a profession, which, as it is acquired by study and prosecuted with art, is followed with considerably profit.

One day a friend (a French gentleman) who escorted me through the town called to draw me out with him for a walk; he said he wished to shew me some of the caravanseras, observing that he thought I should be entertained with a view of them. I agreed to go; and he brought me to two, which after he had shewn to me and explained their principle, police, and etiquette, I could not help admiring and approving. To both these were attached eating-houses and coffee-houses, and every appendage that could render them convenient and comfortable. As we were about leaving the last I observed my friend stop and listen attentively. "Come hither," said he, after a minute's pause— "come into this coffee-house, here is something going forward that may amuse you."

We accordingly entered the coffee-house, where we saw a number of people, some seated in the Turkish fashion, some on low stools, and some standing; and in the middle a man walking to and fro, speaking in an audible voice, sometimes slowly, sometimes with rapidity, varying his tones occasionally with all the inflections of a corresponding sense. I could not understand him, but he seemed to me to speak with " good emphasis and good discretion :" his action was easy to him, though expressive and emphatical; and his countenance exhibited strong marks of eloquent expression. I could not help staring with astonishment at a scene so new to me, and felt great approbation of the tones and manner of this extraordinary orator, though I could not understand a single word he said. He was listened to by all with great attention, and the Turks (albeit not used to the laughing mood) frequently betrayed strong symptoms of risibility: but in the height and torrent of his speech he broke suddenly off, scampered out of the door and disappeard. I set it down that he was a maniac or lunatic of an ingenious kind, and was for going away. "Stay," says my friend, "rest where you are for a few minutes, let us hear further."

The orator had scarcely been gone three minutes when the room was filled with the buzz of conversation, a word of which I could not understand, but which my guide listened to very attentively. At length the buzz began to grow loud, and soon increased into clamour; when a scene ensued of so very ludicious a kind as forced me to cram my handkerchief into my mouth to suppress a laugh, or at least so to stifle it as to avoid observation. In short, they were disputing violently, and the beards were, as I once before mentioned to you, ALL WAGGING. I became more convulsed with mirth; and my friend seeing that I was likely to give offence, took me under the arm and hurried me out of the coffee-house: we retired into a porch in the caravansera, where I gave vent to my suppressed laughter till my sides were sore and my eyes ran tears.

"In the name of God, my friend!" said I, "tell me what is the meaning of all that extravagant scene to which we have just now been witness: who is that madman that spoke so much? and why did they all quarrel after he went away?"

"Come, come," said he, "let us retire to my house, and I will there explain the whole of it to you, from begining to ending."

I accordingly accompanied him home, where we found a very gay circle assembled, to whom he described my astonishment; recounting my immoderate laughter, till they all laughed very nearly as immoderately as myself. "You must know," said he, addressing himself to me, "that he whom you took to be a madman, is one of the most celebrated composers and tellers of stories in Asia, and only wants the aid of printing to be perhaps as eminent in reputation for making CONTES, as Marmontel or Madame D'Anois. As we passed along I heard his voice, and, knowing it, resolved to let you see him, and brought you in for the purpose. He was entertaining the company with a very curious, interesting, and comical story; the subject of which was avarice; the hero a miser of the name of Cassem. His misery and avarice are represented in it as bringing him into a variety of scrapes, which waste his wealth; and his character is drawn with such strength of colouring, and marked with such grotesque lines of humour—he related it moreover with so much wit, in such admirable language, and embellished and enforced it with such appropriate action, utterance, and emphasis—that it rivited, as you saw, the attention of all his auditors, and extorted laughter even from Turkish gravity,"

"But how came he to break off so suddenly?" said I.

"That," returned my friend, "is a part of the art of his profession, without which he could not live; just as he gets to a most interesting part of the story, when he has wound the imagination of his auditors up to the highest climax of expectation, he purposely breaks off to make them eager for the rest. He is sure to have them all next day, with additional numbers who come on their report, and he makes his terms to finish the story."

"Why then," interrupted I, "why did they who remained behind fall disputing?"

"That I will explain to you," said he. Just as he broke off, Cassem the miser (who, as far as I heard, seems as well drawn as Moliere's AVARE) having already suffered a thousand whimsical misfortunes and dilapidations of fortune, is brought before the cadi for digging in his garden, on the presumption that he was digging for treasure. As soon as the historian was gone, they first applauded him, and then began to discuss his story—which they one and all agreed in praising highly and when they came to talk of the probable issue of the sequel of it, there were almost as many opinions as there were men in company; each maintained his own, and they went to loggerheads as you saw about it— when the chance is a thousand to one, that not one of them was near the mark. One in particular surmised that Cassem would be married to the cadi's daughter; which gave great offence to some, and roused another of the company to declare, that he was well assured in his conscience that Cassem would be brought to the baſtinado or the ſtake, or elſe hanged, in the ſequel."

"And is it poſſible," ſaid I, "that a group of twenty or thirty rational beings can be ſo far bereft of all common ſenſe, as to diſpute upon the reſult of a contigency, which abſolutely depends on the arbitrary fancy of an acknowledged fabricator of falſehoods?"

"*C'eſt vrai*, Monſieur? and thereby they demonſtrate the power of the poet (for poet we may call him); and *entre nous*, I doubt whether it is not more rational, as well as more fair, to diſpute what the *denouement* ought to be before than after the inventor of the piece has diſpoſed of it, as is the practice with us. When he has once finiſhed his fable, you will find them all content, and the voice of criticiſm ſilent. Now in France or England, our critics lie *perdue*, in order to attack the poet, let him finiſh his performance how he may. But you will recollect, Monſieur, that in Turkey criticiſm is the honeſt ſpontaneous iſſue of the heart, and with us is a trade, where ſometimes lucre, ſometimes vanity, but oftener than both, envy and malice direct the deciſion, and diſpoſe to cavil and cenſure.

"But we will go again to-morrow," continued he, "probably he will be there to conclude or proceed further with his ſtory;" I agreed to this and we parted.

On the next day we went, and not ſeeing the orator in his place, lounged about the caravanſera, and going to another coffee-houſe found him declaiming with all his might. My friend told me that the ſtory he was now on was quite different from the former: however we watched his motions ſo effectually that we got the concluſion of the ſtory of Caſſem, which completely diſappointed the prognoſtics of the two conflicting Turkiſh critics; for Caſſem was neither baſtinadoed, ſtaked,

S

or hanged, nor married to the cadi's daughter, but lived to fee that extreme avarice was folly; and to be fenfible that to make the proper ufe of the goods of this life is to enjoy them.

LETTER XXXIV.

MY laſt letter has ſhewn you, that the conceptions of genius, though they may want the aid of the preſs to bring them in full and perfect diſcloſure to the world, will yet burſt through their bounds, and find ſome means of communication with mankind; for though the art of printing be unknown in Turkey, the emanations of ſuperior intellect and fancy find their way to the general ear through the medium of public declamation in coffee-houſes. This letter will ſerve to ſhew you that malverſation in office, public delinquency, and all thoſe crimes of the great, which with us are cognizable by no tribunal but that of the public preſs, are not altogether ſo exempt from the laſh and expoſure of the ſatiriſt in Turkey, as the want of that great palladium of freedom would diſpoſe us to believe; and that, incredible as it may appear, the magiſtrates are held up to ridicule in public exhibition, ſatiriſed with all the extravagant vulgarity of coarſe humour and unpoliſhed wit, and expoſed with all the bitter exaggerations of envenomed genius.

The French gentleman whom I mentioned to you in my laſt, as having procured me that pleaſant repaſt at the coffee-houſe, called on me a morning or two after that, and reminded me how highly I ſeemed to be entertained: ſaid, there were often to be ſeen, by walking about and going into public places, a variety of things, which however worthless and unentertaining in themselves, might, from the novelty of their appearance, and their unlikeliness to any thing seen in Europe, serve either to divert by their oddity, or promote the conception of new ideas in the mind: he therefore recommended it to me, with all the zeal of a person who took an interest in my happiness, to keep on my legs and in the streets while I remained at Aleppo.

You will conclude that I readily complied, and we sallied out directly in quest of adventure. We proceeded, therefore, to one of the before mentioned coffee-houses, where, as my friend observed to me, though there were no people of great rank, there was generally something to afford contemplation or amusement; and where, if nothing else occurred, the motley appearance of the company was sufficient to excite a variety of whimsical emotions, and suggest numberless ludicrous images to the imagination of an English or French man. As there was no orator at work declaiming, I had time to indulge myself with a more accurate view than I had before taken of the group that surrounded us: and surely never was ponderous gravity more ludicrously, or in more various forms depicted by any caricaturist in the world.—Here it was to be seen, in all its shadings, from the self-important nod of serious cogitation, down to the soporific aspect of stolid stupidity. Not a muscle was moved in way of mirth, not a face disgraced with a smile, and I could not help thinking all the time, that if every nation of the earth was to take some animal for its insignia, as the British assume the lion, and the Prussian the eagle, the Turks might be divided in their choice between the appropriate claims of the owl and the ass.

Soon after we entered, a band of what they called music, struck up a concert. And here again the notion of the owl and the ass struck me with increased force, as peculiarly presiding over their music: for no other combination of sounds that I know on earth, but the screeching of the one, and the braying of the other, could form any thing to resemble this concert, with which the auditory seemed vastly pleased, though I was obliged to betake myself to flight, in order to get relief from the torture it gave me. The Turks, however, as I retreated, honoured me with a few remarks, which as I did not understand, I could not precisely feel; my friend however told me, they were to the effect that we were Frangi Dumus (Frank Hog), and had no more ear than that filthy animal for music.

Come, said my friend, don't be discouraged!—But the music—the music! interrupted I.—Well then, said he, the music, or rather the sounds were execrable to be sure; they have at least served to establish this certainty, that there is nothing, however discordant or detestable, which habit will not reconcile us to. Doubt not, said he, that the best piece of Handel or Correlli, performed by the best band in Rome, would appear as ridiculous to them, as their concert did to us.

We visited many coffee-houses in the course of that day, in every one of which we found something to divert or disgust us; at length as we entered one, my friendly guide turning to me with satisfaction in his countenance, said " Here is something about to go forward that will please you better than the concert of music." What is it said I? A drama, returned he; a drama, to you most certainly of a new and extraordinary kind; and I do assure you that so zealous am I to procure you entertainment, I would rather than a couple of louis's you could understand what is going forward: your hearty mirth and laughter, added he, are sufficient to put one in spirits. He then directed my attention to a fellow who was busily employed in erecting a stage, which he accomplished in a time incredibly short. The light of the sun was completely excluded, and a puppet shew commenced, which gave great delight to all the audience, and ignorant as I was of the language, pleased me very much.

I was astonished when informed that one man only spoke for all the personages of the drama, for so artfully did he change his tone of voice, that I could have sworn there had been as many people to speak, as there were characters in the piece. The images were not actually puppets, commonly so called, but shadows done in the manner of Astley's *Ombres Chinoises*. They were, however, far inferior to his in execution and management, though the dialogue and incident evidently appeared even to me, to be executed with a degree of the *vis comica* far superior to any I ever saw in a thing of the kind in Europe; indeed so perfect was the whole, that though I knew not a word of the language, I comprehended clearly the plan of the piece, and many of the strokes of humour contained in the dialogues.—The plan was obviously taken from a story which I have read in some of the Eastern tales, I believe the Arabian Nights Entertainments, and it is founded on the law of the country, that a man may repudiate his wife twice, and take her back again; but in the event of a third divorce, cannot retake her to his marriage-bed, unless she be previously married and divorced by another man. To obviate which, husbands who repent having divorced their wives a third time, employ a man to marry them, and restore her back again; and he who does this office is called a *Hullah*.—In the piece before us, however, the Lady and the Hullah like each other so well, that they agree not to separate; the husband brings them both before the cadi to enforce a separation; and the scene before the cadi was as ludicrous, and as keen a satire upon those magistrates as can well be conceived, though of the low kind.

The piece was introduced with a grand nuptial procession, in which the master displayed the powers of his voice by uttering a variety of the most opposite tones in the whole gamut of the human voice; sometimes speaking, sometimes squeaking like a hurt child, sometimes hazzaing as a man, a woman, or a child; sometimes neighing like a horse, and sometimes interspersing it with other such sounds as commonly occur in crowds, in such a manner as astonished me: while the concomitant action of the images, grotesque beyond measure, kept up the laugh; horses kicking and throwing their riders, asses biting those near them, and kicking those behind them, who retire limping in the most ridiculous manner; while their great standing character in all pieces, KARA-GHUSE (the same as our Punch), raised a general roar of obstreperous mirth even from the Turks, with his whimsical action, of which I must say that, though nonsensical, though indecent, and sometimes even disgusting, it was on the whole the most finished composition of low ribaldry and fun that I ever beheld.

When they come before the cadi, he is seated in his divan of justice; but as soon as the complaint is opened and answered, he rises and comes forward between the contending parties: here he turns to one and demands in a terrific tone what he has to say, while the other puts cash in his hand behind, and in proportion as the cash is counted in, increases the terror of his voice; he then pockets the money, and again turns to the other, and demands what he has to offer, while in like manner he receives the bribes from his adversary and puts it in an opposite pocket: this alternate application lasts till the purses of both are exhausted, when, giving a great groan, he retires on one side to reckon the money of each from a pocket he has on either side, one called plaintiff, and the other defendant; when balancing them, he finds plaintiff better by one asper (or three-halfpence) than defendant, and pronounces his judgment accordingly. The defendant appeals to the bashaw; they go before him: KARA-GHUSE (Punch) however, takes the defendant aside, and in a dialogue, which my friend assured me was pointed, witty, and bitterly satirical, developes to him the whole system of magistratical injustice, advises him to bribe the bashaw, and declaring his zeal for all young people fond of amorous enjoyment (which he is at some pains to enlarge upon to the excess of indelicacy), offers him the aid of his purse. The advice is followed; the bribe is accepted; the cadi's decree is reversed, and himself disgraced, and the mob at once hustle him and bear the Hullah home to his bride with clamours of joy. Here again the master shewed his extraordinary powers, giving not only, as before, distinct and opposite tones of voice, but huddling a number of different sounds with such skill and rapidity together, that it was scarcely possible to resist the persuasion that they were the issue of a large and tumultuous crowd of men and animals. With this extravagant *melange* the curtain dropped, and the performance ended.

Returning home we conversed together on the subject of the piece, which I confess I could not get out of my head for some time. My friend explained to me, as well as he could recollect, a great part of the dialogue, and assured me, that the freedom of speech of Monsieur KARA-GHUSE had from time to time created a great deal of uneasiness, not only to private offending individuals, but to the magistracy itself—that no offender, however intrenched behind power, or enshrined in rank, could escape him—that bashaws, cadis, nay the Janissaries themselves, were often made the sport of his fury; that he was not more restrained in the effusions of obscenity which he uttered, than in his satire; that he was always well received and applauded, even venerated (as we venerate the liberty of the press) as a bold teller of truth, who with little mischief does a great deal of good, and often rouses the lethargic public mind to a sense of public dangers and injuries. He added, that in some cases the magistrate had been obliged to interfere; and the bashaw himself was seriously called upon at times to stop the licentious tongue of this champion of Freedom, KARA-GHUSE.

"Well then," said I, "it appears upon the whole that Monsieur KARA-GHUSE is a very great blackguard, but a very witty, and a very honest one."

"You have just hit it," said he; "and if Master Kara-ghuse was to take such liberties in France, Spain, Portugal, or Germany, all his wit, and honesty would not save him from punishment. In England you do not want him; every man there is a KARA-GHUSE, and every newspaper a puppet-shew."

"And yet," returned I, "we complain sadly of want of liberty!"

"That is natural," returned my sagacious Frenchman, "perfectly natural. Liberty is like money; the more we have of it, the more covetous we grow."

"Very true, Monsieur," said I, pleased with his compliment to our happy constitution, and to clinch his observation, gave a Latin quotation, which when a child I got out of Lilly's Grammar, "Crescit amor nummi, quantum ipsa pecunia crescit;" and then changing nummus for libertas, "Crescit amor libertatis, quantum ipsa libertas crescit."

"'Tis very well, Monsieur," said he; and to carry on your allusion, may we not say, that they who do not know when they have enough, are as dangerously wrong in the one case, as those who say we have too much, are in the other? The English complaining of the want of liberty, reminds me of the coffee-house orator's Lory of Cissem, who, wallowing in wealth, lost it all in the wild pursuit of more.—I hope however that they never will, like him, lose their stock in vain endeavours to increase it."

LETTER XXXV.

WHILE I was, in the manner I have already mentioned, endeavouring to pass away the time as cheerfully as possible, till a caravan was formed, or Company's dispatches were coming over land, of which I might avail myself; I found my situation in the house of Mr. ——— growing extremely critical. That gentleman, of whose good sense, and truly excellent disposition, I had too manifold proofs to call them in question, had, though fallen into the vale of years, married his lady at a very tender age. She was then young, beautiful, full of sensibility, and gifted with such natural endowments both of mind and person, accompanied with all those accomplishments which helped to dress them to advantage, that she might well be acquitted of vanity, even though fancy suggested to her she was fit to grace and confer happiness on a younger bed; while reflection on the obvious disparity of the match (which the cool temper of satiety possibly suggested to him) might perhaps have alarmed his mind to circumstances of probable danger, that, before wedlock, were all hid behind the deceptive veil of passion. Whether these were the private sentiments that influenced both or either of them, I cannot presume to determine, though I think it probable: for I was not long in the house till I plainly perceived they were on a very bad footing with each other, and in short that disagreement was become habitual to them. At first, that is to say, for a few days after my becoming an inmate of their house, decency enforced concealment, and the ebullitions of peevishness were stifled by the dictates of prudence; but the animosities of the connubial state are those which of all others are the most impatient under control; and as time, by producing familiarity, relaxed restraint, the pent-up passions began to force their way, and open bickering took place in my presence.

It is but barely doing justice to myself to say, that I felt the most poignant concern at seeing a couple, each so perfectly amiable in all other respects blasting the hours that should be given to harmony and love, in jarring reproach, and recrimination; and I would have given all I was worth that I had never had occasion to esteem them so much, or that I could give them that peace which seemed to have flown them for ever. Fain would I cast a veil over the whole transaction fain would I bury it even from myself, in oblivion: but it has been made by my enemies the subject of triumphant slander; and to do justice to myself, and disclaim the extent of guilt which they would impute to me, I am reluctantly obliged to avow the share I had, and declare how the matter really stood. I must speak the truth, and hope you will not conceive that I designedly lean too heavily upon any one, to ease myself of my share of the load.

Whatever domestic uneasiness may subsist between a married pair, the man, if prudent, will endeavour to conceal it; and the woman, if truly virtuous, will take care to do so: should great disparity of age (as in the present instance) be the case, the lady is more particularly bound to conceal any uneasiness, lest it should be attributed to that cause which people are in such cases too prone to suspect, dislike to her husband; and before young men, above all, she should be most exemplary, as she must well know that their natural vanity, combined with the leading idea of her aversion and infidelity to her husband, suggest ideas to them from whence their warm imaginations draw inferences of a nature too pleasing to be parted with, and too probable not to be put in practice, or at least attempted. Here then a woman at once lays herself fairly open to the assaults of illicit love. I think it will not be denied, that the woman who promulgates the disagreements between her and her husband, particularly if she suffers a young man to be privy to it, is either extremely ignorant, or intentionally vicious, or both.

That the lady I allude to may in some respect be acquitted of this imputation, I must tell you, that she was only eighteen years of age; her tender, inexperienced mind had not yet arrived to that maturity which gives sound judgment; and though of good natural talents, highly cultivated (for she spoke fluently English, French, Italian, Arabic, Persian, and the Greek and Turkish languages), she yet was simple, innocent, uninformed in the ways of the world, and incapable of reasoning from causes up to consequences. But unfortunately that simplicity is attended with as much mischief, though not guilt, as the wilful misconduct of the more experienced; it has the same baleful effects with the hearers, inspires the same confidence, emboldens with the same hopes, and leads to the same pernicious practices.

I have already mentioned, and will now remind you, that I was then young. Perhaps it was owing to a congeniality pointed out by our age, perhaps to a compassionate politeness amounting to tenderness, which I always disclosed on those unhappy occasions, joined perhaps to the ardent look of youth kindled by the imaginations to which this imprudent conduct insensibly gave birth, that the lady thought proper to take the very hazardous step of making a confidant of a young man and a soldier—and revealing to me the whole tale of her grievances, with a pathetic eloquence, that would have made an impression upon a much less susceptible heart than mine. I declare it most solemnly, that, though this extraordinary mark of confidence and esteem communicated to my heart strong sensations of unjustifiable pleasure; I so far got the better of myself at first, as to receive the whole with the same appearance of tranquility, as if I had been only a confidential female friend. I pitied, it is true;—I expressed my pity;—I advised, not treacherously but faithfully;—I laid such things as occured to me to be most likely to assuage and extinguish the flame of discord, and lead to an amicable adjustment; and I parted for that time with her to go to a self-approving pillow, where, while my fancy was inflamed and tickled by the flattering mark of regard shewn me by so all-accomplished a person, I had the soothing delightful consciousness of having, as far as I was able, done my duty, and escaped the corroding reflection of having violated the rights of hospitality.

Not an opportunity however afterwards offered, that the same unhappy point was not the subject of discussion, and unfortunately those opportunities but too frequently occurred; till at length we began to feel that they were the sweetest minutes of our lives, and were sought for with industrious avidity by both of us. No human resolution was sufficient to withstand such an unlucky concurrence of circumstances: from lamenting the grievances, we wished to remove them; from wishing, we proceeded to consider the means: and when we had got that length, the flight was not far to the extreme end—the execution of it. My passions hurried me before them, my expressions grew gradually more and more unguarded, our conversation became more interesting and warm; and though I felt and struggled to be guided by the strict principles of honour, and formed a thousand resolutions not to transgress the laws of hospitality, by injuring the man who had treated me with such kindness, the struggle became too severe for me—the desire of pleasing a lovely woman, who had reposed such unbounded confidence in me, and who seemed to expect and require of me to alleviate her misery, at length bore down all the oppositions suggested by reason and principle, and I agreed to become the instrument of her removal from this unhappy situation. We fell—but not intirely. There is one length to which no earthly consideration—no allurement however dazzling could tempt me—it is now the most cordial consolation to my mind; I never suffered myself to think of trespassing on the decorum of his house, nor did we in any single instance carry our intercourse to a direct violation of his bed. Though the transports of youthful passion hurried us into conversations and reflections on the subject of her determination to be separated from her husband, yet that passion was of too delicate a kind to sink into the brutal sordid indulgence of dishonourable stolen embraces. She wished for that separation, rather as a subterfuge from incessant diurnal misery, than as a prelude to any vicious or illicit enjoyment; and we looked with pleasure to the event, but we looked no further.

It is thus that, in the down-hill path of vice, we are hurried on step by step, fondly imagining that each successive object, which bounds our sight, will stop our headlong career; while alas! every step we advance gives additional rapidity to our descent: like the centripetal force of a projectile, our pace increases with uniformly accelerated motion—till disdaining all control, and breaking down every impediment that reason, morality, or honour throw in the way to rescue us or retard our ruin, we precipitate unexpectedly into the last gulph of vice and infamy.

Fortunately, however, an incident intervened in the present case, which arrested our progress down this hideous descent, and reserved us both I hope to conviction of our folly, and repentance of our error. And I have the consolation to reflect, that out of such a host of dangers and temptations as I was beset with, I have escaped without the actual perpetration of a deed, which would, had it happened, in all probability have embittered my life.

While we hugged ourselves in the security and secrecy of expressing our genuine sentiments, her husband discovered our wishes, and all at once took the necessary measures for preventing them. So that, overwhelmed with grief and shame, I directly formed the resolution to leave Aleppo, and proceed in the best manner I could on my destination.

Thus you see, my dear FREDERICK, was your father, by failing to resist the first impressions of an unlawful and dishonourable passion, insensibly led to the very brink of a precipice, the bare remembrance of which now makes him shudder with horror. The story, by means unnecessary for me to mention, took wind. The folly of some, the malice of others, and the unaccountable propensity to falsehood of more, trumpeted it about with many exaggerations to my injury, and I was held up as the deliberate seducer of innocence: but the whole transaction is exactly as I have stated it; and the disagreements previous to my arrival at Aleppo, which, in telling the story, they purposely left out, were of such public notoriety, that every European, even the consul himself, was fully acquainted with them. This is the consequence of a deviation from the strict rule of right. Treasure it up in your mind, my child, never to be forgotten; and let it operate as a caution to you, how you entangle

yourself in the snares of women: recollect that my escape was singularly fortunate, and the mere effect of accident; and flatter not yourself, that because accident served in one case it, will in another. Providence has, for the wisest of purposes, implanted in our nature a fondness for the fair sex; and so long as it is used prudently and virtuously, it constitutes the first happiness of life; but if on the contrary, it stimulates us to excess, impels to injure our fellow creature, or break in upon the repose of a family; it is our reproach, our shame, our curse, and very frequently our utter and irremediable ruin; add to this, that there is in the general character of women, a capriciousness, a levity, and a vanity, under the influence of which they sport with men, only to display their power, and evince the force of their charms, which make s the cultivation of their good graces in any way hazardous. To adopt the idea of an old epigram—
"There is no living with them, nor without them."

As your happiness, my dear boy, is the first object of my life, my efforts shall be turned to the guiding of your greener years from any premature impressions; and when reason and matured age fit you for the cultivation and enjoyment of female society, be it mine to direct your steps away from that class, who think rank a sufficient sanction for vice, who flare in all the bronze of aristocratic assurance, under a load of obloquy, beneath which the poorest peasant's wife would sink; who think that wealth and rank confer a right to commit excesses that would degrade the meanest of the canaille; and felicitate themselves with the reflection, that, under the protection of family or an infamous husband, they may indulge in enormities, for which the lowest of their sex are beating hemp in Bridewell.

LETTER XXXVI.

THE discovery to which I alluded in my last letter, surprised and grieved me very much; and indeed it astonished me the more, from the manner in which it was communicated.

One day I received a polite message from the British consul, saying, he wished to speak to me as soon as possible, upon a business of great consequence. I thought at first, that it might be some plan for my proceeding on my journey—perhaps Company's dispatches that had arrived to go over land; and at intervals, something like apprehensions of the true motive of his sending for me flew across my mind. I however went to him, when, after some little introductory conversation, he told me, that my host Mr. ——— had been with him that morning, laying before him a complaint of a most extraordinary and serious nature, of which, as it immediately concerned me, he thought himself bound to inform me, in order that I might either contradict so gross a calumny if it were untrue, or find means to avoid the obviously necessary result if founded in fact.

He then proceeded to relate to me, that Mr. ——— had informed him of a conspiracy having been meditated against his peace and honour, between his wife and the English gentleman whom he had entertained in his house; that their plan was nothing less than an elopement, and that he did not know how soon it might be carried into execution, if not timely prevented; and finally, that he had demanded the assistance of the consul and his interest with the Turkish magistrate to prevent it, by granting him an armed force for the protection of his house.

I was much surprised to find that conversations so very guarded as ours were discovered, and more so that the aggrieved person did not think proper to speak to myself, and charge me in person with the offence; never reflecting the while, that all my ideas were military, and his merely commercial: I was also much at a loss to conjecture how he came to make the discovery—but this I found afterwards he owed to a female servant, who had been improvidently intrusted by her mistress with the secret.

Finding, however, that by whatever means he became acquainted with the affair, it was a certain fact that he was apprised of it, I directly acknowledged the whole truth with the utmost candour to the consul; told him the affair step by step as it arose, assuring him (which I really thought to be the case) that pity for the lady's deplorable situation made me listen to such a measure; and that unlawful passion had so little to do with it, that in all our private conferences we had never transgressed the limits of purity; and that her person was, at least, respecting me, and I firmly believed all mankind, spotless and inviolate. I added, that great allowances were to be made for a young creature barely eighteen years of age, consigned by the wickedness of avaricious parents to the embraces of a man of sixty-five; who, amiable and worthy though he was, in social intercourse with the world (which I knew him to be), was yet in the most indispensable point of connubial felicity so utterly defective, as necessarily to create disgust and abhorrence in a youthful mind. I remarked to him, that, in the forming of laws, it as plainly appeared on their face, who made them amongst the English, as it does on the face of the Gentoo laws, that they were made by the Bramins: for, as by the latter the penalty of a few puns* of couries (not value a shilling) is annexed to the perpetration of a crime, for which those of another class loose their lives ; so, among us, it appears that our laws are made by the aged, the decrepid, the sensual, and the rich. Else it could never happen that there were in the same code, laws to punish marriage between the young and vigorous, and enable the brutality of a parent to take its full scope, and consign, as in the present instance, youth, beauty, health, and every personal attraction, to the arms of age, infirmity, and impotence. And I concluded by saying, that all parties aiding in such an unnatural confederacy should be punished.

The consul fairly acknowledged there was too much truth in what I had said ; but remarked withal, that it was rather a hazardous experiment, and he was sure it would be an endless one, to correct all the abuses to which the fallibility of man, and his incompetency to form any thing perfect, necessarily left society and their laws liable—that the law was written, and it was the duty of every individual to obey it—and that in cases of adultery, the offence could be justified on no solid grounds whatever, for, independent of the feelings of the husband, which perhaps were more poignant in old age than youth, the injury to his family was not to be got over, in probably giving to him an heir no way a-kin to him. " It would be right, I think," said he, " to stop such disproportionate matches ; yet, once made, they should be as religiously observed inviolate as those of love, among which we almost as frequently, as in those of compulsion, see instances of infidelity. If you doubt this," said he, " read the records of Doctors' Commons?"

---

* Couries, a kind of small shells used in India, as a circulating medium in place of coin, in value much below the smallest copper coin—a Pun is a certain number of them.

I agreed to the justice of what he said, at the same time assured him, that my intentions went no farther than wishing the lady to be rescued from her thraldom, which I told him was dreadful.—" I am sure," said the consul, " that Mr. Campbell thinks so, because I am convinced he would not otherwise say so. But may not," said he, smiling, " may not Mr. C. have deceived himself? these are things in which the passions are strangely apt to hoodwink the understanding. However," continued he, breaking off pleasantly, " I must give you all the comfort that truth will allow me to do: I am sure that the poor lady is condemned to great wretchedness; partly from my own observation, partly from public report, and partly from her own mouth: for you must know she has several times complained to me of her husband's peevishness and tyranny; and even besought me to use my influence and authority to relieve her from her misery. Mr. ———," continued he, " is a man whom on all other accounts I esteem, and value highly. In this instance he has erred, and I cannot pity him, even though he suffers all the torments of jealousy: and as there are laws for punishing with death premature intercourse with the sex, I cannot see, any more than you, why the sacrificing youth to extreme old age should not be equally punished, for I am sure it is equally unnatural, and still more injurious to a state. These are my sentiments," continued he; " but let not this declaration induce you to think that I the less disapprove of your intermeddling. You have allowed me the privilege of a friend, and I will not suffer it to be made an empty one. You were more culpable than many young men would be; first, because you are married, and should, upon the common principle of doing as you would be done by, have refrained; and next, because you were enjoying the sweets of hospitality in his house, and should have dashed from his lips, rather than held to them, the deepest cup of bitterness."

"But, my dear sir," said I, "I do not attempt to justify—I only endeavour to mitigate the matter, and you will recollect that the very circumstance which in one point of view aggravates, in another alleviates the fault: the living in his house afforded those interviews and exposed me to those temptations under which I was near sinking—I should never have sought them: but he must be more or less than man, that could have resisted them: and though I have a high sense of Mr. Consul's strict honour and virtue, as well as prudence, he must excuse me, though I doubt whether he could himself have resisted so long and so effectually as I did. I am sure there are many who will censure, that could not."

The consul smiled, and, turning the discourse from its direct line, observed, that it was absolutely necessary I should desist, else he would be obliged to use his influence and power to protect Mr. ——.

In answer to this, I gave him my honour in the first place, that I would proceed no farther in the business; and that, on the contrary, I was determined to set out upon my journey to India directly, if means could be contrived for my conveyance; adding, that I should consider it as a great favour, in addition to those I had already received at his hands, if he would contrive some means to set me forward in my route.

To this he answered, that as the making up of a caravan would be extravagantly expensive, he knew no means that were not attended with certain hardship and eventual danger; but finding me determined at almost any danger or hazard to set off, he proposed to send for a man who knew some source in that way, and when he came would talk farther on the business; and in the mean time, recommended great circumspection to me while I

DEPARTURE FROM ALEPPO.

continued at Mr. ———'s house, to which I very solemnly pledged my word.

Being now constrained by every consideration, as well of prudence and decency as of inclination, to leave Aleppo immediately; I determined that no common impediments should stop me, and waited with impatience the arrival of the person on whom the consul rested his hopes of dispatching me.

He came in the evening, and after a conference with the consul he introduced him to me, and acquainted me that he was a Tartar, and one of the vast number of that description who are employed by the Turkish state in carrying dispatches from court to the various viceroys and bashaws, and interchangeably between them again; that they were men on whose fidelity the utmost reliance could be had; and that this man, who had an excellent character, had agreed to take me to Bagdad, provided I would submit to the disguise of a Tartar.

The agreement between us I entirely submitted to the discretion of the consul, who had the goodness to settle it thus:—The Tartar was to deliver me safe at Bagdad; to supply me and my servant, who acted as interpreter, with an ample sufficiency of provisions and horses on the road; to exchange my horse for me as often as I pleased, and to go at such a rate, whether faster or slower, as I thought proper: for this he was to receive one hundred pounds; and I further promised, as an encouragement to him, that if he acted to my satisfaction, I would, on our arrival at Bagdad, add a douceur of twenty pounds.

The next day he came, and I had a distinct view of this my new fellow traveller and supposed master, for in several places, I was to pass for his slave. He was one of those striking *character* figures that a painter would like to take a sketch of—and methought Tartar was written legibly in every lineament of his countenance and person.—He was tall, muscular, and bony—his figure bespoke great hardihood, strength, and activity—nor could the trowsers which he wore conceal the Herculean texture of his limbs—his shoulders were expanded to an enormous breadth—he was unincumbered with flesh, or indeed rather extremely lean—his forehead, though partly concealed beneath his turban, was very high—his nose large, hooked, sharp, and prominent—a pair of small, fierce, black, penetrating eyes, barely separated by the nose, and a formidable pair of mustachios, which he carefully flecked with pomatum into a point resembling an awlblade, and which moved like the whiskers of a purring cat, with every word he spoke, gave a whimsical ferocity to the countenance, beyond the reach of description, and rendered him altogether as discouraging a confidental friend, as ever a Christian trusted his life to since Mahomet first set up the trade of a prophet. He surveyed me with great attention—opened his mouth two or three times like a gasping pike, as if to speak—stroaked his whiskers as often—and at last pronounced that he would undertake to conduct me; adding, in allusion to my black hair and dark complexion, that I looked more like a native, than any Frank he had ever seen. He ordered me to cut my hair quite short, to provide myself with the Tartar dress and cap, in the fashion of his own; and saying he would call on me in proper time, departed.

Thus equipped, we set out, not without great pain and regret on my part; pain at leaving a most beautiful young woman, whom I pitied and esteemed, subject to the resentment of a husband, at once jealous from nature, peevish from habit, and enraged from her open and unequivocal demonstrations of hatred and regret at having been betrayed by situation into such a very serious dilemma.

After my departure from Aleppo, this affair was represented in a variety of unfavourable lights to the different new comers from England; and as a story is that commodity which of all others honest people do not love to steal any thing from, in its passage though their hands, it found its way in various forms (none of them however tending to soften it) to many of my friends and connections, those from whom of all others I wished to conceal it. Labouring under such calumnies, it cannot be considered as a violation of decorum, or unnecessary infraction upon delicacy, if I state the truth, in order, though I cannot acquit myself of censurable conduct, at least not silently to submit to unlimited calumny, and charges of crimes which I hope I have too much honour and integrity to commit.

I must add, that previous to my departure the consul did every thing that it was possible for him to do, conducive to my safety and accomodation on the road, which as we were obliged to go to the city of Diarbeker, a great length out of our way, he observed would be long, dreary, fatiguing, and hazardous; he procured me from others, and gave me himself, a number of letters, and at parting desired me to comfort myself with the reflection, that when I arrived at my journey's end, I should have to boast, that I went to India by a route never travelled by an European before.

LETTER XXXVII.

As I became familiarised to my Tartar guide I found his character disclose much better traits than his first appearance bespoke, and I began insensibility to think him a very entertaining fellow: perceiving that I was very low spirited and thoughtful, he exhibited manifest marks of compassion; and taking it into his head that I was actually removed for ever from my friends and my family, he spoke in a style of regret and feeling, that did great honor to his heart: and to say the truth, he did every thing in his power to alleviate my feelings, conversing with me either by means of the interpreter, or in broken lingua franca; supplying all my wants cheerfully and abundantly; changing horses with me as often as I pleased, and going slow or golloping forward just as best suited my inclination or humour.

The first object he seemed to have in view on our journey, was to impress me with a notion of his consequence and authority, as a messenger belonging to the Sultan. As all those men are employed by the first magistrates in the country, and are, as it were, the links of communication between them, they think themselves of great importance in the state; while the great men whose business they are employed in, make them feel the weight of authority, and treat them with the greatest contempt: hence they become habitually servile to their superiors, and by natural consequence insolent and overbearing to their inferiors, or those who being in their power they conceive to be so. As carriers of dispaches, their power and authority wherever they go is in some points undisputed; and they can compel a supply of provisions, horses, and attendants, wherever it suits their occasions; nor dare any man resist their right to take the horse from under him to proceed on the Emperor's business, be the owner's occasion ever so pressing.

My feelings, which I can tell you were altogether of the most unpleasant kind, served as a stimulus to my mind, and increased my anxiety to get forward; I therefore pushed on as fast as the horses, which were in general excellent, could carry me: and as we halted at a number of stages to get fresh horses and provisions, my Tartar guide had frequent opportunities of indulging his self-importance, and displaying his great authority and power. As soon as he stopped at a caravansera, he immediately called lustily about him in the name of the Sultan, demanding with an imperious and menacing tone of voice, fresh horses, victuals, &c. on the instant. The terror of this great man operated like magic; nothing could exceed the activity of the men, the briskness of the women, and the terror of the children; for the caravanseras are continually attended by numbers of the very lowest classes of the people; but no quickness of preparation, no effort or industry could satisfy my gentleman; he would shew me his power in a still more striking point of view, and fall belabouring them with his whip, and kicking them with all his might. I must confess I was much hurt at this extravagant abuse of upstart power, and was two or three times on the point of interfering; but fortunately, recollected that it would neither be in character, nor have any good effect, and that if I presumed to speak, my guide would be obliged in my defence to give me a flogging in order to prevent suspicion.

This inconsiderate tyranny and cruelty, I had afterwards reason to believe, was by no means a part of his natural disposition; but vanity, to which so many among us in Europe fall victims, urged him to excesses, which I dare say his heart privately condemned.

It was on the fifth or sixth day (I cannot precisely say which) after our leaving Aleppo, that we got to the city of Diarbeker, the capital of the province of that name, having passed over an extent of country of between three and four hundred miles, most of it blessed with the greatest fertility, producing, in the few cultivated parts, grain, fruits of various kinds, and silk in great variety and abundance, and abounding with as rich pastures as

U

I ever beheld, covered with numerous herds and flocks. The air was charmingly temperate in the day-time, but, to my feeling, extremely cold at night.

Yet notwithstanding the extreme fertility of this country, the bad administration of government, conspiring with the indolence of the inhabitants, leaves it unpopulous and uncultivated. Diarbeker, proper, called also Mesopotamia, from its lying between the two famous rivers Tigris and Euphrates, and by Moses called PADAN ARAM, that is to say —" The fruitful Syria ;" abounds with corn, wine, oil, fruits, and all the necessaries of life. It is supposed to be the seat of the Earthly Paradise, and all geographers agree that it was there the descendants of Noah first settled after the flood.

Insignificant as those circumstances may appear to mere calculators of profit and loss, it cannot be denied that they have a powerful and pleasing effect on the refined imagination. To be treading that ground where Abraham trod ; where Nahor the father of Rebecca lived ; and where Laban, to whom Jacob fled to avoid his brother Esau's resentment, and whom he served fourteen years for the love he bore to Rachel, was to me a circumstance productive of delightful sensations. How finely has that giant of the pen, Johnson, justified those sensations in his Tour to the Highlands of Scotland and Western Islands ;—describing his emotions on visiting the famous island of Iona, or Colombkill, he says—" We were now treading that illustrious island which was once the luminary of the Caledonian regions, whence savage clans and roving barbarians derived the benefits of knowledge, and blessings of religion." To abstract the mind from all local emotion, would be impossible if it were endeavoured, and would be foolish if it were possible. Whatever withdraws us from the power of our senses—whatever makes the past, the distant, or the future, predominate over the present, advances us in the dignity of thinking beings. Far from me, and from my friends, be such frigid philosophy, as may conduct us indifferent and unmoved over any ground which has been dignified by wisdom, bravery, or virtue!—that man is little to be envied whose patriotism would not gain force upon the Plain of Marathon, or whose piety would not grow warmer among the ruins of Iona."

The city of Diarbeker itself is situated in a delightful plain on the banks of the river Tigris, and nearly at its head; it is one of the richest, most trading, strong, and populous cities in Asiatic Turkey; and is adorned with many piazzas and market places in the Turkish style, and a large magnificent mosque, formerly a Christian church; for Christianity flourished over this country so late as the sixth century. There is even now a sect, whose patriarch still resides here: and they shew on the road near the town, a chapel where the holy man Job is said to be buried. This city is supplied amply with water by a canal cut from the Tigris, and has many caravanseras on both sides of the river.

Few countries in the world exceed that about this city for natural richness and beauty:—the bread and wine are excellent—the fruit beyond conception delicious—and my friend the Tartar took care, under pretence of supercilious *hauteur*, to tear in pieces a couple of fowls, and hand me now a leg, now a wing, till I made the most delicious repast I ever remember to have eat in my life.

It is computed that there are resident in this city no less than twenty thousand Christian inhabitants, some of whom are of the Church of Rome;—and perhaps it is owing to that mixture, that the fair sex have more freedom, and the men more politeness and affability, than those of any other city in the empire:—the chief busineſs there, is making that fine leather commonly called Turkey leather.

Figure to yourſelf, my dear FREDERICK, my Tartar guide, who was an admirable actor, ſitting at a caravanſera in ſtate at his dinner, devouring excellent fowls, choice pillaws, and delicious fruit, in as great pomp as a baſhaw; and in order to keep up the ſemblance of authority over me, to favour my diſguiſe, handing to me, who ſat at humble diſtance, a part of his proviſions. You may form to yourſelf an idea of the ſcene; but all the efforts of imagination muſt fall ſhort of the manner, the figure, the words, the looks, and the actions of the Tartar; ſometimes affecting contemptuous pity, ſometimes ſupercilious arrogance; ſometimes brutal ſterneſs, and ſometimes the gentle blandiſhments of conſcious ſuperiority; and all in ſuch a maſterly ſtile of performance, that I doubt whether Garrick himſelf, with all his powers of countenance, could outdo him. Critical though my ſituation was, and much as I was harraſſed with the corroſions of mental pain, the extravagant action and ludicrous pompoſity of this man frequently overbore my prudence, and compelled me to laugh incontinently and loudly;—on all ſuch occaſions he would put his hands a-kimbo, draw up his eyebrows to his turban, ſcrew down the corners of his mouth in the moſt rueful manner, and give a loud whew! with his eyes fixed in a ſtare at me, till entirely overcome with laughter, and ready to ſink under it, I clipped my face between my hands, and, as well as I could, bowed in token of ſorrow and ſubmiſſion; when, threatning me vehemently, and at the ſame time uttering a lamentable expreſſion of doubt that he was afraid he had had an idiot impoſed on him, he would buſtle about, direct the horſes to be got ready, and order me to get on horſeback, with many denunciations of ſevere treatment, and a thouſand flouriſhes of his whip over my head.

As I have rode along musing upon the contemptible stratagems to which I was reduced, in order to get through this country, for no other reason but because I was a Christian, I could not help reflecting with sorrow on the melancholy effects of superstition, and regretting that that place, which in the times of primitive simplicity was called the Terrestrial Paradise; that place where GOD first planted man after the flood; where the god-like Abraham and the holy Job breathed the pure air of piety and simplicity; that place which from all those circumstances ought to be considered above all others as the universal inheritance of mankind, should now be cut off from all but a horde of senseless bigots, barbarous fanatics, and inflexible tyrants. And I could not help considering with melancholy concern, the blindness and infatuation of men, who, less earnest to accommodate themselves than injure others, shut out their fellow-creatures from that which they themselves will not use, and, while they suffer millions of the richest acres in the universe to be untilled, and spend their sweetness in the desert air, with wicked jealousy, and envy more than diabolical, begrudge to others the little spot on which they stand, and chase them as they would a ravening tiger from their country.

LETTER XXXVIII.

As we advanced towards the southward and eastward, in our way from Diarbeker towards Bagdad, I found the air become sensibly warmer, and observed that the disposition of the people grew more and more brutal. My guide's conduct (for he knew them well) became proportionately artful, and my manners were of course to grow so much the humbler. I observed, however, that his authority continued the same, and that he seemed to exert it with greater rigour; not in severity or chastisement, but in exacting implicit obedience. Yet still he evidently acted with great caution and circumspection; for, in some districts, he either avoided the little villages by a circuitous route, or dashed through them at a very quick pace, while the gaping multitude considered us as on a dispatch of haste and importance—in others, he entered the towns without reserve, and left it to chance to decide whether we should be discovered or not. At some caravanseras he treated me with affected negligence, at others he made me eat with him and drink wine, of which, in some places, he himself drank copiously, and at others as scrupulously refrained from. And sometimes we lay at night out in the open air, rather than enter a town; on which occasions I found the weather as piercing cold as it was distressfully hot in the day time. Bred, as the man was, a mixture of slave and tyrant, I can suppose some parts of this conduct to arise from caprice; but, as he was naturally kind, as many of those aberrations from the usual mode of travelling were attended with hardship and inconvenience to himself, and as my servant and the other Tartar were clearly of opinion he was right, I am rather disposed to believe that he, on the whole, acted from principles of sound sense and policy.

He frequently advised me against indulging in laughter; said it was unmanly, indecorous, inconsistent with the gravity becoming a wise man, and withal dangerous.

One evening we came to a caravansera much fatigued, the day being extremely hot, and we having rode very hard—whether it was caprice or fatigue, or the suggestion of policy that moved him,

I cannot say, but he was certainly more disposed to play the tyrant than I had ever before seen him. He flogged the men who took the horses, kicked every one he met, made the house ring with his enormous voice; directed supper to be got ready, ate growling, and finding fault with every thing; and under pretence of disliking the ingredients of an excellent pillaw, handed it over to me, saying, "Here, Jimmel (the name he called me), here, take this filth, and cram it down thy coarse throat, it is only fit for a Frank"—I took it with best air of humility I could assume; and tearing the meat with my fingers, which I also used instead of a spoon to eat the rice, swallowed it eagerly; he watching me all the time attentively. When I had finished it, I gave him a hint in the Frank language, that I should like to wash it down with some wine; but he did not, or rather would not understand me.

Supper done, he ordered a servant to attend him with some water, and directed him to wash his feet; while that operation was performing, he continued menacing every one about him. My servant, who sat next me and behind him, interpreted every thing he said. "Yes, ye slaves," said he, as he lolled back upon his cushion, "yes, I will make the best of you wash my feet; for who shall refuse to wash the feet of him, who represents the Sultan of the World, the Son of Mahomet, the Messenger of the Lord?" The poor fellow proceeded in his humble office, and only interrupted him by saying, "Blessed be my Lord the Sultan, and glory be to the Lord our God, and Mahomet his prophet." "Yes, yes," continued my Tartar, "bless God and the prophet, and pray for his servant our Sultan, and all who represent him like me, that slaves of your description are permitted to live: nay, thou shalt wash this Frank's feet:" then turning to me with an air of magisterial tenderness, "Jimmel," said he, "hold forth thy feet, and let them be washed by this disciple of Ali—I say, hold forth thy feet."

Scarcely able to refrain from laughter at this Bombardinian of the East, and his pompous manner of issuing his orders, I drew up my trowsers and took off my boots—the man brought fresh water, and fell to rubbing my feet with great good will and humility; yet evidently felt so much hurt at the humiliation, that I was sorry for it, and would rather have dispensed with the washing, though it was a luxury.

In the midst of this operation, the Tartar, who was reclining on his cushion, smoking, rose up, and stalking two or three times across the room, with the most ludicrous air of self-conceit and importance, took his tobacco pipe from his mouth, brandished it in ostentatious parade, and in the tone and manner rather of one that was raving than of a man in his sober senses, burst out with an emphatical expression of satisfaction, and said, "This it is to be protected by a great man: Mussulmen salam to him and wash his feet."

The extravagance of this sentiment, the absurdity of its application, and the consequential solemnity of his action and countenance while he spoke, altogether rushed upon me with such impetuous force, that I could not resist it, and, in spite of every effort to restrain myself, burst into an immoderate fit of laughter.

Had I the pencil of Hogarth, the pen of Shakespeare, or the powers of a Garrick, I might attempt to give some idea of his countenance, when, turning, he beheld me convulsed with laughter. I might attempt it, I say, but I could not do it justice. Such a combination of ludicrous expression I never beheld: it was indeed an epitome of all the lower order of human passions. Fury predominated, but it was risible fury—it was fury that rather grinned than frowned; though under it were to be seen shame and mortification, sorrow and resentment, pride and degradation, silly bashfulness and decayed importance. For some time he stood transfixed to the spot, his eyes glistening like those of a rat in a trap; his pointed whiskers moving with the contortions of his lips, and his mouth every now and then opening like the beak of a wounded hawk. To utter his sensations he was unable; and he continued in this state, not only till my laughter was abated, but till I had time to reflect and be seriously concerned.

At length, without saying a sentence, he wheeled about, threw off his slippers, drew on his boots, vociferated till he brought all the people of the caravansera about him, and ordered horses to be ready instantly. As orders from such a person were not likely to be disobeyed, the horses were got ready. I saw that I must either proceed, or come to an open rupture with him; so recollecting that I was myself in fault, that a dispute might be fatal, and that at all events it was only the humour of the moment, I drew on my boots too, and was ready to go, though I was much fitter for a twelve hours' nap than for an hour's travelling on horseback.

We mounted immediately, and it was my good fortune to have the best horse. He let out upon the gallop, the moon shining as bright almost as day; I put forward my horse, and kept rather before him, which vexed him so, that he beat the poor animal he rode on most unmercifully. At length after about eight or ten miles riding, he called a halt—dismounted, and said he would rest there all night. I saw it was all resentment; but knowing that it would be in vain to remonstrate, I dismounted too; and, judging that the best way to mortify him in return, was to comply with affected approbation, turned to my servant and told him (knowing that it would go from him to the Tartar) that I was delighted with the beauty of the night; remarking at the same time, that lying in the sweet salubrious air was far preferable to being confined in the sultry filth of a caravansera.

As soon as this was communicated to the Tartar, he remarked, that the open air was the fittest place for the beasts of the forest, and therefore suitable to a Frank; but for his part, he had much rather repose on a cushion, which he should have done, had it not been for my accursed risible faculties.

Here the conversation rested, and we fell asleep. In a few hours he awoke us, and we set forward: after some pause, he began in the following manner, which was interpreted to me, as he spoke, by my servant:

" Surely God made laughter for the derision and shame of mankind, and gave it to the Franks and the monkies; for the one ha, ha, ha's, and the other he, he, he's, and both are malicious, mischievous, and good for nothing but to fret and tantalize all that come across them."

Here he paused, as waiting for something to be said: however, I remained silent. At length, he continued: " Not but that, with all their laughter, they have the wisdom to take special care of themselves; for half a dozen monkies, will he, he, he, and empty a whole orchard of its fruit in the reckoning of a hundred; and a Frank will ha, ha, ha, and eat you up pillaws and poultry like a wolf, and drink up wine with the same moderation that a camel drinks up water."

I thought I should have choaked with smothered laughter: I would not however interrupt him, and so contrived to keep it to myself: he proceded to apothegmatize:

" But with all their he, he, he's, and ha, ha, ha's, it sometimes turns out that they are caught: the monkey is seized in a trap and caged or knocked in the head, and the Frank is put in jail, and baſtinadoed or hanged; and then the tune is changed, and it is Oh, ho, ho!" Here he began to mimic crying ſo admirably, and at the ſame time ſo ridiculouſly; that I burſt out laughing again.

"Obſerve, Jimmel," ſaid he haſtily, "obſerve! you can't refrain! But by our holy prophet," ſaid he ſeriouſly, "it may end as I ſaid: ſo look to yourſelf, and avoid laughter in caravanſeras, or we part; for there are places, and that was one of them laſt night, where ſuſpicion would ruin you. And if you loſt your life, what ſhould I ſay for myſelf on my return to Aleppo? Eh, what ſhould I ſay for myſelf? Ha ha, ha! would not do. No, no, they would not believe it, and I ſhould loſe my character."

"Why don't you laugh yourſelf?" ſaid I.

"Very ſeldom, or rather never," returned he; "at leaſt I would not in time of danger. No, no, none but Chriſtians and monkies makes a practice of laughing--Turks and Tartars are wiſer." I promiſed him, that I would in future take more care; and, by way of appeaſing him with a little flattery, ſaid, that he played his part ſo admirably, it was impoſſible to reſiſt the impulſe. But he anſwered, with a grave face, that his action in that caſe was of too ſerious nature to be made a ſubject of merriment—and adviſed me to believe it ſo.

LETTER XXXIX.

THE ſolicitude of my guide for my ſafety was the earneſtneſs of a man of buſineſs zealous to diſcharge with the utmoſt punctuality the duty he had undertaken; and I muſt obſerve to you, that the whole of his conduct evinced a precision and punctually of dealing rarely found in our intercourse with mankind. Previous to leaving Aleppo, he had undertaken to convey me safe—he was, as you may already perceive, indefatigable and unremitting in his endeavours to do so; he had promised to supply me with food—so he did, in the most ample manner; he promised to go as I pleased fast or slow—so he did; he promised to change horses with me, as often as I thought proper to desire—he did so. But beyond this, he seemed to carry his care of me no farther than to any bale of goods he might have in his charge. He was bound to deliver me safe, in good order and condition, at Bagdad: so much he was determined to do, and no more did he think of. I had got letters to the bashaws of some of the towns through which we were to pass: but as the delivery of a letter is, according to the custom of that country always accompanied with a present, I thought it better to decline delivering them, except when necessity compelled—though the state of the country was so unsettled, that we often had occasion for a guard.

As soon as the remembrance of the laughing affair was a little decayed, the Tartar began to relax into good humour, and to talk with his usual vehemence; for he was always, according to the flow of his spirits, either sullenly silent or extravagantly loquacious. His tongue might be considered as a thermometer, by which the warmth or coldness of his temper might be calculated, and the extremes, of garrulity and taciturnity were the indices. His conversation, however, was very circumscribed, and consisted chiefly of stories of himself and his horse, the amazing journeys he made, and the feats of manhood he performed. One circumstance I must in justice mention, as I think it marks strongly the habitual delicacy and modesty of this people. Although he frequently lamented my banishment from my family, and although we were for eighteen days continually conversing on a variety of occasions that might lead to the subject, he never once talked of women; never, in all his pity for my situation, glanced even remotely at the possibility of my getting a substitute in that way; never hinted that he thought of them himself. On seeing women, coming to the wells, they remined me of some of the stories in the Old Testament. I mentioned it, but it went no farther; for whenever the subject was started, he threw cold water on it.

That he conceived me to be in some respects a parcel of property, I have good reason to believe: for I observed that at some caravanseras the people collected round me, and regarded me with strong symptoms of surprise and pity; some viewed me with commiseration, some with contempt; but not one creature, however wretched or abject, seemed to envy my situation.

I was the more confirmed in this opinion by an incident that happened between Diarbeker and Mosul. One morning I was unusually overcome with the fatigues of the preceding day: the Tartar called me, summoned me to horse; and finding that I gave no answer, nor shewed any token of awaking, he lifted me in his arms bodily from my couch (such was his strength that he did it without any difficulty), carried me out without the least ceremony, and, before I was so completely awake as to be sensible of my situation, had me fixed upon a horse ready to depart.

A transaction so very singular, you may well conclude, surprised me at the time, and would not readily be forgotten: such a crowd of strange, confused, and incongruous thoughts and sensations as occurred to me, I never before experienced: they were painful, they were surprising—but I was in such a state that I could not afterwards analyse them. The chief reflection that arose from it was,

X

that human sentiment must be in a deplorable state of degradation indeed, when such a circumstance could occur from the notion that a man was as much an asset or piece of property, could be transferred by the same means, and moved in the same unfeeling manner, as any portion of inert matter that makes up a bale of merchandize. Of the truth of this position I had soon after a melancholy proof, in an incident which, though lamentable, was attended with such ludicrous circumstances, that even now I never think of it without smiling—smiling, as I did then, with a heart bleeding with pity.

One morning I was awakened before day-break with a bustle in the caravansera where we lodged. I conjectured that the Tartar was preparing to get forward, and rose in order to lose no time. I was so far right in my conjectures: the horses were ready, and I came out to mount, and was very much surprised to perceive several horses before me loaded with something which stood erect from their backs, and which I had barely light to discern were not men. I concluded that they were bales of merchandize packed in a particular form, and asked no questions till full day-light disclosed to me that they were human creatures tied up in sacks, and fastened astride on the horses' backs. There was a strange union of horror and oddity in the conception, that struck me at once with a mixed emotion of indignation, pity, and mirth.—The former however got the better, and I asked my servant with some warmth what it meant—He said that the sacks contained some young women whom the Tartar had bought.—"Good God!" said I, "is it possible that he can have bought wretched females to treat them with so little tenderness?" "He has bought them," returned my servant, "in the way of traffic, not for pleasure."

"Suppose he has," said I, "suppose even they were men, not to mention young women, how can he imagine that they will survive this? Tied up and sweltered in a sack—fastened cross-legs, on a horse, and driven at such an amazing rate (for by this time we had set forward, and another Tartar was whipping the horses up all the time, and driving them on)—how is it possible they can survive? They must be smothered—they must be shattered to pieces—they must be stripped, excoriated, and tortured to death!"

"If I might presume to advise," said he, "I would say that you had better make no remarks upon it: it would only get them perhaps worse treated, and raise his anger against you."

To conclude, I took his advice, and kept my mind to myself. The unfortunate women were in this manner carried fifty miles, at the end of which their tender-hearted purchaser disposed of them in some way of keeping till his return; when I suppose they were to be carried back in sacks astride upon horses, all the way to Aleppo, there to be sold to the highest bidder.

To us, my FREDERICK, who live in a country where an hour's detention in a house against our will is punished as unlawful imprisonment, and who feel and value the rich treasure of liberty above all earthly blessings, the bare idea of slavery appears horrible; when the miseries of slavery are sharpened by cruelty, our indignation burns at the offence: but such a complicated piece of enormity as that I have mentioned, almost transcends belief, and indignation is lost in amazement. There are but few men, even in our bracing climate, whom fifty miles riding would not shake to pieces, and torture almost to death. No woman would think of it. But when to that is superadded, first the compulsion—then the sorry and at best painful equipage of the horses—the tender persons, unaccustomed to riding, of the women—the smothering heat of the fack---and above all the horrid climate, burning with an almost vertical heat (vertical at least compared with our oblique sun)---it will be allowed to be a wonder, almost approaching to a miracle, that they survived one half of their journey. The wonder-working hand of Omnipotence alone could bring them through it; and when I asked in the evening whether they were dying or dead, and was told that they were not only alive but in perfect health, I could not help repeating, that most beautiful expression put into the mouth of Maria by the inimitable Sterne, " God tempers the wind to the side of the shorn lamb."

This affair tended to prejudice me strongly against my Tartar guide, and I was for some time that I could not look upon him without horror: but at length my resentment abated; and reason, resuming her seat of cool decision, told me, that though it was a crime and a grievous one, he was not so responsible for it as those who, knowing better, authorised it by their concurrence, gave it the sanction of law, and made it familiarly practised; he only did that which he had been even from his mother's breast instructed to do, and should therefore not be judged by those rules which a Briton would lay down for the government of such cases.

A Briton!—Hold! Have I not now been uttering a most severe satire upon the British nation? Yes! imputing to men a virtue which they want, is the worst kind of satire—I meant it not at the time, but will not retract what I have written— Britons deserve the lash of satire! They deserve a worse lash: for the traffic in human bodies still stands a bloody brand of infamy on her great national councils. Their brother's blood! the blood of millions of murdered Africans, like that of Abel, cries to Heaven against them, and will not, I fear, cry in vain.

Great God!—What a horrible thought!—what an indelible stigma! that a legislator shall, in the cold blood of commerce, make a calculation of the probable profit upon human lives—put commercial expediency in the balance against murder—and make convenience the excuse for crime!—Why, the robber may do so!—But shall Britons, generous Britons, who boastful claim precedence of the world in freedom, humanity, and justice—shall they look on and see inferior nations spurning from them with horror the debasing traffic; and stimulated by avarice, or misled by wicked policy, retain the blot that other states have wiped away, and live at once the curse of one part, and the scorn of the rest of mankind?—Forbid it mercy! Forbid it Heaven!—And oh! may that virtuous man, who, disdaining the malignant taunts of the base and interested, boldly steps forth the advocate of man and of his country, and session after session springs from the couch of repose which opulence presents him, to break the fetters and the scourges which improbity and avarice have forged for our fellow creatures—may he succeed and bear down all his opposers! and may the justice of his country make his triumph and his glory as certain and complete here, as the justice of that Being, under whose direction he acts, will doubtless make them hereafter!

LETTER XL.

FROM the considerations I have already pretty fully mentioned, my mind was by no means at ease. The incessant travelling for so many days, at the rate of seventy-five miles a day, to be continued I knew not how long, increased my anxiety: and the apprehensions of accident, interruption, and above all sickness, intercepting me on my way, haunted my imagination with all its terrors. I was besides approaching fast to that region where the winds strike all living things that draw them in instantly dead: and conceiving that the more expeditious I was in getting over the journey, the greater chance I had of escaping those mischiefs; I pushed heartily forward, and urged the Tartar till he at last expressed his astonishment and approbation; paid me the compliment to say, that I was almost equal to himself for enduring fatigue; and concluded with a very sagacious surmise, that in all probability I had been myself a carrier of dispatches among the Frank governments.

One day after we had rode about four miles from a caravansera, at which we had changed our cattle, I found that a most execrable bad horse had fallen to my lot: he was stiff, feeble, and foundered; in consequence of which he stumbled very much, and I every minute expected that he would fall and roll over me. I therefore proposed to the guide to exchange with me; a favour he had hitherto never refused, and for which I was the more anxious, as the beast he rode was of the very best kind. To my utter astonishment he peremptorily refused: and as this had been a day of unusual taciturnity on his part, I attributed his refusal to peevishness and ill temper, and was resolved not to let the matter rest there. I therefore desired the interpreter to inform him, that as he had at Aleppo agreed to change horses with me as often as I pleased, I should consider our agreement infringed upon if he did not comply, and would write to the Consul at Aleppo to that effect.

As soon as this was conveyed to him, he seemed strongly agitated by anger; yet endeavoured to conceal his emotions under affected contempt and derision, which produced from him one of the most singular grins that ever yet marred the human physiognomy. At length he broke forth:

"You will write to Aleppo, will you? Foolish Frank! they will not believe you! By Mahomet, it would be well done to hear the complaint of a wandering Frank against Hassan Artaz---Hassan the faithful and the just, who for ten years and more has been the messenger of an emperor, and the friend and confidant of cadis, bashaws, and viceroys, and never yet was called so much as liar! Who, think you, poor misguided one! who, think you, would belive that I broke my promise?"

"Why do you not then," said I, interrupting him, "why do you not perform it by changing horses, when you are convinced in your conscience (if you have any) that it was part of your agreement?"---"Once for all I tell you," interrupted he, "I will not give up this horse. There is not," said he gasconadingly, "there is not a Mussulman that ever wore a beard, not to talk of a wretched Frank, that should get this horse from under me; I would not yield him to the commander of the faithful this minute, were he in your place: I would not, I tell you Frank---and I have my own reasons for it."

"I dare say you have," returned I; "love of your ease, and fear of your bones."

At hearing this, he grew quite outrageous---called MAHOMET and ALLA to witness that he did not know what it was to fear any thing---declared that he was convinced that some infernal spirit had that day got possession of me---and indeed seemed well disposed to go to logger-heads. At length observing that I looked at him with sneering contemptuous defiance, he rode up along side of me--- I thought it was to strike, and prepared to defend myself. I was however mistaken; he snatched the reins out of my hand, and caught hold of them collected close at the horse's jaw; then fell flogging my horse and spurring his own, till he got them both in full speed; nor did he stop there, but continued to belabour mine with his whip, and to spur his own, driving headlong over every impediment that came in our way, till I really thought he had run mad, or designed to kill me. Several times I was on the point of striking him with my whip, in order to knock him off his horse---but as often patience providentially came to my assistance, and whispered to me to forbear and see it out. Mean time I considered myself as being in some danger; and yet such was the power he had over the cattle, that I found it impossible to stop him: so resigning the event to the direction of Providence, I suffered him without a further effort to proceed; I calling him every opprobrious name I could think of in lingua Franca, and he grinning, and calling me Dumus, Jihash, Burhl (i. e. hog, ass, mule), in rapid and impetuous vehemence of tone and utterance.

He continued this for a length of I dare say some miles, over an uncultivated tract, here and there intersected with channels formed by rills of water in the periodical rains; thickly set with low furze, ferns, and other dwarf bushes, and broken up and down into little hills. His horse carried him clean over all: and though mine was every minute stumbling and nearly down, yet with a dexterity inexpressible, and a vigour altogether amazing, he kept him up by the bridle, and I may say *carried* him gallantly over every thing. I was astonished very much at all this, and towards the end as much pleased as astonished; which he perceiving, cried out frequently and triumphantly, " O, la Frangi! Heh! Heh! Frangi!" and at last drawing in the horses, stopping short, and looking me full in the face, exclaimed in lingua Franca, " Que dice, Frangi---Que dice?"

For some time I was incapable of making him any answer, but continued surveying him from head to foot as the most extraordinary savage I had ever beheld; while he stroked his whiskers with great self-complacency and composure, and nodded his head every now and then, as much as to say, Ay, ay, it is so! look at me! am not I a very capital fellow?---" A capital fellow indeed you are," said I, " but I wish I was well out of your confounded clutches."

We alighted on the brow of a small hill, whence was to be seen a full and uninterrupted prospect of the country all round. The interpreter coming up, he called to him and desired him to explain to me carefully the meaning of what he was about to say; which I will give you as nearly as I can in his own words, as they were translated by the linguist:

" You see those mountains yonder," said he, pointing to the east; " those are in the province of *Kurdestan*, inhabited by a vile race of robbers called Jesides, who pay homage to a God of their own called Jesid (Jesus), and worship the Devil from fear. They live by plunder, and often descend from those mountains, cross the Tigris which runs between them and us, and plunder and ravage this country in bands of great number and formidable strength, carrying away into slavery all they can catch, and killing all who resist them. This country therefore, for some distance round us, is very dangerous to travellers, whose only safety lies in flight. Now it was our misfortune this morning to get a very bad horse, for which, please ALLA (stroking his whiskers), some one shall receive the bastinado. Should we meet with a band of those Curds, what could we do but fly? And if you, Frangi, rode this horse, and I that, we could never escape: for I doubt you could not keep him up from falling under me, as I did under you: I should therefore come down and be taken—you would lose your guide, and miss your way, and all of us be undone. Besides," continued he, "there are many villages here where people live, who, if they only suspected you were a Frank, would follow and sacrifice you if they could to MAHOMET, and where of course you must run for it."

As soon as the interpreter had explained this to me, "Well," continued the Tartar, "what does he say now to it?" Then turning to me, and tossing up his head—"Que dice, Frangi?"

"Why, I say," returned I, "that you have spoken good sense and sound reason; and I am obliged to you."

This, when interpreted fully, operated most pleasingly upon him; his features relaxed into a broad look of satisfaction, and he said:—"I will do every thing I can to make you easy and contented: and when I am obstinate, don't resist—for be assured I have reason for it; and above all things avoid laughing in my presence. But we shall reach Mosul by and bye, and probably then we may have no more rides." For I expected to get down the river Tigris from Mosul to Bagdad, and had told him so, and he encouraged me with the expectation.

That night we came to a caravansera which lay at some distance from a village. Here the Tartar, pleased with himself for the conduct of the day, and pleased with me for my approbation of it, ordered a most admirable supper; and not only, as was very common with him, rejected the best dish in order to present it to me, but also selected for me the choicest bits of those upon the table. He then ordered wine, observing that the fatigue of a government messenger demanded indulgence; and using a salvo of my suggestion on a former occasion, viz. that the Prophet would not be offended with travellers more than with the sick for taking it as it were *medicinally.*

We accordingly had wine, and admirable it was, though by no means equal to that we drank at the city of Diarbeker. I took little however, and the Tartar was much surprised at my abstemiousness; remarking, that he never saw a Frank before that was not a downright hog when he got the cup to his lips. My taking it in small portions, while he drank it as we do table beer, particularly astonished him. Before he lay down on his couch, he gave orders for horses, threatening the people with severe castigition if they gave bad ones; holding up as an example the person that gave us the stumbling horse that day, who he declared should be bastinadoed as soon as he returned, if there was a cadi within ten leagues of him; and I dare to say that he kept his word most religiously.

The next morning we had excellent cattle; fear produced wonders among them, and we set forward just as the sun rose. As we entered the first village, I was somewhat alarmed by perceiving my guide draw up his horse—deliberate—mutter to himself—and seem rather uneasy while he viewed a crowd that was up the street before us; some of whom I perceived to be agitated with some extraordinary motions of the body, while one man stood in the middle, rolling his body into a variety of strange contortions.—The Tartar, for a minute or two, seemed to be debating within himself whether he should proceed or turn about: at length putting me on his left hand, he set forward at full speed, leaving the crowd on his right, who, seeing the rapidity of our pace, flew on one side, and let us pass. We soon however heard shouting behind us, and could hear plainly the words, "Chiaour! Frangi Cucu!" and looking back, perceived several ragged men like savages pursuing us, lifting stones occasionally, and casting them after us with all their might. The speed of our horses at last got us out of both sight and hearing; and I plainly perceived, and was for the first time convinced, that my guide's conduct was directed by sound sense, spirit, good faith, and integrity.

LETTER XLI.

THE extraordinary occurrence which I mentioned in my last letter required explanation, and my Tartar friend was not backward in giving it; for he loved exceedingly to hear himself talk, and, on any subject within the compass of his knowledge, was shrewd, perspicuous, and even naturally eloquent: he had moreover on that occasion acted the part of a skilful general; and as I applauded his prudence and address, he was extremely kind and communicative, and gave me a full account of that affair, his motives, his deliberations, and the urgency of the case; and, in short, every thing that could elucidate the circumstance, or aggrandize his own importance. It would be a pity to take it out of his own words: I shall therefore relate them to you, as I had them through the medium of our linguist, for they made an impression on my memory not easily to be erased.

"You must know," said he, ". that there are spread over the face of this great and glorious empire a number of dervises of different kinds---*holy men*, who renounce the enjoyments and pleasures of the world to converse with Mahomet and worship Alla. Some of those are very good men, indeed saints, and never do any thing bad; preaching and praying, without hurting any thing, even a rat or a snake; nay, they would not hurt a Christian. There are others again, of whom I have heard our bashaws and effendis, and even the Maazeen, declare that they are forbid by the Koran; and yet the common people (the lower sort you know have no sense) reverence and worship them—they are called *Santons;* live by themselves, sometimes under ground like rabbits, and sometimes in the thickets and woods. They go where they please, take the best seat in any man's house, cram themselves with meat and drink, and yet none resist them; for some will not, and others dare not. Nay, they often pollute women in the open streets—and they never set their eyes on a Christian or a Frank, that they will not kill, if possible. For my part, I think that they ought to be hanged, every one of them that had a head to be hanged by—or rather staked—for no punishment is too great for them; but I dare not say so in that town—if I did, I should be stoned to death by the rabble.

"As soon as I perceived the crowd, and the rascals dancing, I knew that they were santons, and was sure that they would stop us in order to extract money from us; in which case they would most probably have discovered you—for they have the eyes of the devil. Nothing then could save your life; the crowd would join them, and your brains would have been beat out with stones. I had a mind to turn back and go round the town, but that might have caused suspicion, and got us perhaps intercepted; so I determined to push by them boldly, which I did, you can testify, like a brave man. You saw enough yourself, to convince you of the danger you have escaped, and of my wisdom and valour; let me therefore entreat you to be entirely guided by me, and above all things avoid that accursed propensity to laughter."

Since I first formed the resolution of writing this account of my journey, I have been at some pains to dip into the best histories of that country, and I find that in every instance my Tartar guide's information was correct. Those santons, as well as other classes of dervises and sheihs, travel about the country, and levy contributions on the inhabitants: some are really what they pretend to be, and are as pure and as pious as the monks of the primitive Christian church; but the santons are monsters, who exist only by the barbarous credulity and more than savage ignorance of the lower order of the people—though reprobated, and indeed, execrated, by the better sort of Turks. They affect to be dementated (which with the Mahomedans is the greatest mark of sanctity), and under cover of that madness commit every excess and enormity, not merely with impunity, but with applause. Such is the melancholy state of degradation, to which the weight of superstition's chains bends the mind of man! It is no long since I had a very pleasing discussion of this extraordinary subject, with a gentleman of my acquaintance, for whose veracity I have great respect. Superstition and credulity very naturally led us a consideration of the Turkish religion, and I expressed my satisfaction, that the worst excrescences of the Christian schisms could not be compared with the Turkish faith in their dervises. He said, that he agreed it did not go quite the length of the santons; but he related to me a conversation between him and a Roman catholic, not more than twenty-four miles from the enlightened city of Dublin, which surprised me much.

"I was," said he, "when a youth, very free in censuring all religions, and chiefly Popery; for, being bred among Roman catholics, I had the greater opportunity of seeing their absurdities, which I treasured up as so much gain, without ever taking into account their many virtues, of which they have their share. One day I was on a party of pleasure, at a place called ———, and in presence of a poor country fellow ridiculed the priesthood, attributing to them many vices, and particularly fornication and adultery. The man resisted me, and declared it was impossible, Then I suppose, said I, if a priest and a woman were locked up in a room together for a year, and the woman in a week after coming forth was brought to bed of a child, you would not believe it to be the priest's. No, said he, I would not. Then how comes the child? I don't know, replied he—any way but by him. In short, he would believe in self-impregnation, or preternatural visitation, rather than allow a priest to be capable of fornication."

"But," said I, "you supposed a case—if the fellow was shrewd enough to say, no such case could at all happen, he would have put you down; that was what he meant, though he knew not how to go about expressing it."

The difficulties and hazards of the journey, which seemed to thicken upon us as we advanced, made me pant for a speedy conclusion to it; and the adventure of the last day opened more clearly to my view the dangers we had to encounter, which were still likely to increase as we got to the eastward and southward, where the fury of bigotry raged without remorse; where the greater distance from the seat of government made the populace more lawless, and the magistrate more corrupt and tyrannical; where the total seclusion from all well ordered society rendered the manners barbarous; where strangers were seldom seen, and when seen fleeced and persecuted; and where particularly I had reason to believe, scarcely any Englishman had ever set his foot; and above all, where the very winds that blew were charged with destruction, and carried instant death upon their wings. I therefore earnestly longed to reach Mosul, where the probability was, I should get at least the more comfortable and commodious conveyance of water carriage, and where I might refresh myself completely, after the fatigues of so many days journey; and, if there was occasion, claim a guard and protection, having along with me a letter to the bashaw, which I might withhold or deliver, just as best suited my inclination or convenience.

I could not help viewing with a sad and melancholy eye my present state; wandering, I may say alone, unaccommodated and wretched, through an inhospitable region, and more inhospitable people; where danger beset me in a thousand forms, and every step I took, I took in hazard of my life; and comparing it with those scenes of opulence and comfort which I had once experienced, where every lawful wish met with its accomplishment; where every necessity was supplied, and every difficulty obviated; where tender love and attachment anticipated every desire; and soothed every care: where the mutual endearments and reciprocal accommodations of tender relatives, wife, children, faithful friends, and kindly intimates gave a zest to life, made me feel that my existence was of interest to others as well as to myself, and communicated a conscious importance which the isolated, solitary, selfish man can never feel: I could not help looking back with grief and mortification, to think that I once possessed those blessings, and should perhaps possess them no more; but, on the contrary, might perish unknown, unheeded, and unlamented, in an unknown corner of the wilds of an unknown hostile country, without one friend to solace or to cheer me, or tell to those who loved or took share in my concerns, the place where I lay, or the particulars of my fate.

Nor in this dismal train of reflections was Aleppo forgotten. It made the great connecting link between my former happiness and present misery; it was, as it were, the door through which I passed when I took my last farewell of comfort: when it closed and shut me out, the prospect was indeed gloomy; nor did I after feel one happy sensation,

BIGOTRY.

uuless the convulsive transports of a laugh, and the boisterous fleeting mirth arising from the singularities of my guide, which, as the surge raised by the tempest above its proper height lifts up the shattered bark only to cast it on the beach and leave it ship-wrecked, elevated my spirits for the moment beyond their proper pitch, to retire quickly, and leave them in the horrors of ten times deeper melancholy.

Perceiving how much cast down I was, my friendly Tartar began to rally me: "Jimmel," said he, "the santons have frightened you:—but don't be afraid—HASSAN ARTAZ is no boy: he can bring you through greater difficulties than those, should they befall us."

"But how comes it," said I, "Hassan, that you, who have so much power at the caravanseras, have not power to resist those rascally santons, or the mobs of a village?"

"Why, as to the mob," said he, "if I was by myself, or had only a true Believer with me, I would make them fly before me like the dust before the wind. As to the santons, no one can resist them: the Great, who hate them, are obliged to show them respect: and the bashaw of Aleppo, nay the Commander of the Faithful himself, could not save you, if one of them called on the mob to stone you, or tear you to pieces. However, be of good cheer; for, please ALLA, I will deliver you safe and sound to the Coja at Bagdad: besides, we shall very soon be at Mosul from whence we will go down by water, which will be very pleasant: and the chief danger then will be in fair fighting, which is better than being cut off by santons.— Should there be occasion," said he, looking most ferociously and brandishing his whip—"should we be attacked by Curds or Robbers, you shall see— you shall see, Jimmel—Oh! holy Prophet, how I'll fight!".

LETTER XLII.

IT was early in the evening when the pointed turrets of the city of Mosul opened on our view, and communicated no very unpleasant sensations to my heart. I found myself on Scripture ground; and could not help feeling some portion of the pride of the traveller, when I reflected that I was now within sight of Nineveh, renowned in Holy Writ.---The city is seated in a very barren sandy plain, on the banks of the river Tigris, embellished with the united gifts of Pomona, Ceres, and Flora. The external view of the town is much in its favour, being encompassed with stately walls of solid stone, over which the steeples or minarets of other lofty buildings are seen with increased effect. Here I first saw a large caravan encamped, halting on its march from the Gulph of Persia to Armenia; and it certainly made a most noble appearance, filling the eye with a multitude of grand objects, all uniting to form one magnificent whole.

But though the outside be so beautiful, the inside is most detestable: the heat is so intense, that in the middle of the day there is no stirring out; and even at night the walls of the houses are so heated by the day's sun, as to produce a disagreeable heat to the body at a foot or even a yard distance from them. However, I entered it with spirits, because I considered it as the last stage of the worst part of my pilgrimage. But, alas! I was disappointed in my expectation; for the Tigris was dried up by the intensity of the heat, and an unusually long drought; and I was obliged to take the matter with a patient shrug, and accommodate my mind to a journey on horseback, which, though not so long as that I had already made, was likely to be equally dangerous, and which therefore demanded a full exertion of fortitude and resolution.----There are a thousand latent energies in every man, which only want the powerful voice of necessity to call them out : and now drawn to the top of my bent, I prepared my mind to set out in the morning, with as much cheerfulness as if the hopes of water carriage to Bagdad had never once occured to my mind.

It was still the hot season of the year, and we were to travel through that country, over which the horrid wind I have before mentioned sweeps its consuming blasts : it is called by the Turks samiel, is mentioned by holy Job under the name of the East Wind, and extends its ravages all the way from the extreme end of the Gulph of Cambaya up to Mosul; it carries along with it fleaks of fire, like threads of silk; instantly strikes dead those that breathe it, and consumes them inwardly to ashes; the flesh soon becoming black as a coal, and dropping off from the bones. Philosophers consider it as a kind of electric fire, proceeding from the sulphureous or nitrous exhalations which are kindled by the agitation of the winds. The only possible means of escape from its fatal effects, is to fall flat on the ground, and thereby prevent the drawing it in: to do this, however, it is necessary first to see it, which is not always practicable.

But besides this, the ordinary heat of the climate is extremely dangerous to the blood and lungs, and even to the skin, which it blisters and peels away from the flesh, affecting the eyes so much that travellers are obliged to wear a transparent covering over them to keep the heat off.

That night, Hassan said, that as we must proceed to Bagdad on horseback, he would stay the next at Mosul to refresh us; which I objected to: he then spoke of the succeeding part of the journey as a thing of nothing: we had already come near nine hundred miles, and had not above five to go: besides, as the weather was warmer, we would travel more in the night, and lie-by in the day-time, in places with which he was well acquainted.

In short, the poor fellow seemed to take an interest in my safety, and to wish to alleviate the pains of my mind; and he always concluded with a remonstrance against laughing, which from frequently hearing I now understood even in his own language.—" Don't laugh, Jimmel, don't laugh," he would say with great solemnity.—By the bye, I observed, that when he was well disposed to me he always called me Jimmel (a name which I presume he constructed, with my servant's assistance, from the resemblance of sound between Campbel and Camel, Jimmel being the Turkish for that animal); and when angry, he called me Frangi, with all its gradations of Turkish abuse, Dumus, Cucu, &c.

That evening, as we sat in the caravansera, a man entered and spoke to Hassan, who seemed to pay great attention to what he was saying.---He was a well made man---below the middle size---and had that kind of countenance which bespeaks shrewdness, ingenuity, and mirth. At length he retired; and soon after Hassan bade us rise and follow him: he went into a sort of public room, where a number of people were collected, sitting as is the custom in coffee-houses on low stools. Hassan pointed to me to sit down, which I did: then placing the Interpreter near us, he sat himself: and straight I perceived the little man, who had just been speaking to him, step forth from the crowd and begin to pronounce a sort of prologue, which I neither understood nor wished to understand: it appeared from his cadences to be metrical, and seemed, by the little impression it made on his auditors, to have nothing particular to recommend it. At length, however, he paused, and, hemming several times to clear his pipes, begin again to hold forth. " He is going to tell a story," said the Interpreter. The attention of all was fixed upon him, and he proceeded with a modulation of tones, a variety of action, and an energy of expression, that I think I have never heard or seen excelled: his action indeed was singularly admirable; and I could perceive that he was occasionally speaking in the tones of a man and a woman: in which latter character he gave a picture of whining ludicrous distress, that moved the risible muscles of all the company. I looked at Hassan, and he was grinning as merrily as could any monkey or Frank in Asia. The Linguist occasionally interpreted what the story-teller was saying; and I soon began to suspect that it was a story I had more than once read in the Arabian Nights, though altered, and in some measure dramatized by the speaker. I looked several times archly at Hassan, and he returned my glance, as much as to say, You see I don't laugh at all this. At length, however, the orator came to a part where he was to mimic a poor little hunch-back (for I now discovered it to be the story of little Hunch-back) choking with a bone: he threw up his back; squeezed till all the blood in his body seemed collected in his face, his eyes rolled in their sockets, his knees knocked, he twisted and folded his body, putting his fore-finger, and thumb into his throat, and pulling with all his might, as if to pull something out: at length he grew weaker, stretched his arms down, and his fingers back, like those of a person straggling---kicked, fell, quivered, and died. It is impossible for any description to do justice to the perfection of his acting; and what rendered it the more extraordinary was, that though it was a scene of death, and well acted death, he continued to render it so ludicrous in circumstances, as to suspend the audience between a laugh and cry. They did not remain long so; for he suddenly bounced up, and began the most doleful lamentation of a woman, and exhibited such a scene of burlesque distress as I never witnessed. All burst out in torrents of laughter, Hassan as well as the rest---I alone remained purposely serious; and the orator, according to custom, broke off in the middle of an interesting scene.

When we returned to the caravansera, I rallied the Tartar on the score of his laughter: he growled, and said, " who could avoid it? Why did not you laugh as you were wont?"—" Because," said I, " he did not act as comically as you."—" No," returned he, " but because Franks and monkies only laugh for mischief, and where they ought not. No, Jimmel, you will never see me laugh at mischief."—" What," said I, " not at a poor man's being choked to death!"—" Nay," said he, " I seldom laugh, Yet I could not avoid it then." That very hour, however, a puppet-show was exhibited in the same room, and my grave guide laughed till the tears ran down his cheeks, and his voice sunk into a whining treble. *Kara ghuse* was certainly extravagantly comical, though filthy; and frightened a cadi with a whole troop of Janissaries, by letting fly at them a shot or two—*a parte post*———

The next day we set out well mounted, and pushed on with renovated spirits towards Bagdad.— Hassan could no more have the assurance to censure laughing and, as I was little disposed to do it in time of danger, we were likely to agree well. In short, we began to like one another's company; and if I brought him to be a greater laugher than he used to be, he gave himself the credit of having made me much more serious than I had been before—I profited by his instructions.

It would be an effort as idle and fruitless on my part, as unentertaining and uninteresting on yours, to attempt to give you a regular detail of our progress from Mosul to Bagdad; the same general cautions were observed, with the same occasional relaxations. Hassan still continued to treat me with a repetition of himself and his horse, his own feats and his horse's feats; to be silent when ill-tempered, and loquacious when gay; to flog the attendants at the caravanseras; order the best horses, and eat the best victuals, and to give me the best of both; and finally we had our fallings out and fallings in again: but I had not the mortification of seeing any more women tied in sacks on horse's backs, and excoriated with a ride of fifty miles a day.

As we rode along we overtook several times straggling callenders, a kind of Mahomedan monks, who profess poverty and great sanctity; they were dressed all in rags, covered with filth, carried a gourd, by way of bottle, for water—I presume sometimes for wine too—and bore in their hands a long pole decorated with rags, and pieces of cloth of various colours. They are supposed by the vulgar to have supernatural powers: but Hassan, who seemed to have caught all his ideas from his betters, expressed no sort of opinion of them; he *salam'd* to them and gave them money, however. It was extraordinary enough, that they were all in one story—all were going on a pilgrimage to Mecca—or, as they call it, *Hadje*.

As soon as ever we got out of their sight and hearing, Hassan shook his head, and repeated " Hadje, Hadje!" several times doubtingly, and grinned, as he was accustomed to do when he was displeased, without being able to manifest anger. " Hadje!" he would cry, " Hadje, Hadje!" I asked him what he meant; and he said, that these fellows were no more going to Mecca than I was. " I have a thousand and a thousand times," said he, " met callenders on the road, and always found them facing towards Mecca. If I am going southward, I always overtake them; if northward, I meet them; and all the time they are going wherever their bufinefs carries them. I overtook," continued he, " one of them one day, and I gave him alms and paffed him by; he was coming he faid, after me, towards Mecca: but I halted on purpofe for a day, and he never paffed; and a merchant arriving at the fame caravanfera informed me, he had met the very fame fellow four leagues farther northward; who had anfwered him with the fame ftory, and ftill had his face turned towards the fouth."

Fifty years ago, no man in Turkey would have dared to hold his language; but every day's experience evinces that the light of reafon fpreads its rays full through the world—even through Turkey; and furnifhes a well founded hope, that in another half century every monkifh impoftor (I mean real impoftors,) whether they be Mahomedan monks, or Chriftian monks, will be chafed from fociety, and forced to apply to honeft means for fubfiftence.

END OF PART II.

JOURNEY TO INDIA, &c.

PART III.

LETTER XLIII.

My Dear Frederick,

AFTER passing through an immense tract of country, distinguished by nothing that could serve even as a circumstance to mark and remember our daily journeys, but which I observed to grow manifestly worse, both in soil and climate, as we proceeded Southward, we came in sight of the famous city of Bagdad, on the seventh day from that on which we left Mosul, and on the eighteenth from that of my departure from Aleppo; in which eighteen days we had rode fourteen hundred miles, partly through a route which no European, I have reason to believe, ever took before.

On entering the city, I desired my guide to conduct me to the house of a Merchant, to whom I had got letters of credit and introduction. He took me accordingly through the windings of several streets, and at last stopped at the door of an Armenian Merchant, or *Coja*, where he made me alight, and come in. I was received with great politeness; and, on producing my letter, found that he was not the person to whom it was directed: I accordingly made a suitable apology, and was for retiring to find the house of the proper person, for which purpose the Armenian offered me a servant, when, to my great astonishment, my Tartar interfered; said that it was to this Merchant he brought all his goods, and that I must remain where I was; at the same time ordering the Armenian, in a peremptory tone, to take charge of me, and use me well. It was in vain that the Armenian endeavoured to explain to him the nature of the business, and that I insisted I must go to the other Merchant—HASSAN was peremptory, and declared that I should not. It was so extremely *outre* and ridiculous, that I could not be angry; and the good Armenian uniting his voice with that of the Tartar, and entreating me to favour him with my company, I acquiesced, and indeed remained in his house all the time I was at Bagdad. This was proof positive, if any other than I already had was wanting, that he considered me merely as a piece of merchandise, which he was bound (according to the language of Merchants) to deliver in good order and condition.

I had undertaken, before leaving Aleppo, to give the guide, if he acted conformably to my wishes, and behaved well, twenty pounds over and above the hundred provided by the agreement: I therefore sent for him, to settle finally, and part. He had heard that I was a person different from what he had supposed me to be: but it did not alter his conduct, as might be expected, or make him stoop to cringing; he still spoke with the same honest, bold familiarity; and when I gave him the promised twenty pounds, he never hinted, cringed for, or even looked as if he expected more: but when we came to part, the feelings he disclosed, and those I myself felt, convinced me, that Man is not naturally that brute which prejudice has made him; and, when left to his own operations, the human heart would be uniformly kindly, affectionate, and sympathetic: the poor, rough, unpolished Turk, betrayed the strongest marks of sensibility, and I myself once more felt the uneasiness of parting.

I think this is the proper place to give you my opinion of the Turks, while the recollection of honest Hassan is fresh in my mind; and I cannot do it better than by quoting the words of an excellent French Writer——

"The Turks (says M. du Loir) are naturally a good people, which is not to be ascribed to the climate; for the Greeks born in the same climate have very different dispositions, and retain only the bad qualities of their ancestors, viz. roguery, treachery, and vanity. The Turks, on the contrary, priding themselves on their integrity and modesty, are distinguished in general by an open, ingenuous simplicity of manners; courtiers only excepted, who, in Turkey, as every where else, are the slaves of ambition and avarice."

The name of Bagdad has been so renowned in Eastern story, and is the scene of so many of those bewitching tales which we find translated, or pretended to be translated, from the Arabic and Persian, that I felt great pleasure in seeing it, and conceived myself to be at the very fountain-head of marvellous adventure and romance. Fraught with this idea, I was impatient to go forth into the town; and notwithstanding the weather was beyond conception hot, I paraded a number of streets: but never did I, in the course of my life, see a place so calculated to belie the opinion one would form of it from the eastern tales. It appeared to me to be among the most disagreeable cities of the world, and has no one circumstance that I could discover to recommend it: the heat is so great, that in the Summer-time the inhabitants are forced to keep their markets in the night, and to lie all night in the open air, on the terraces of their houses.

The Armenian with whom I resided, did every thing in his power to render the place agreeable to me; and I shall always retain a lively sense of his goodness and hospitality: he was not only generous and polite, but well informed, and pleasing in conversation. I took occasion to express to him the disappointment I felt at finding Bagdad so very different from what I expected; and told him that I had, when a youth, learned to think highly of it, or rather romantically, from reading Eastern tales. This led to a conversation on the Arabian Nights Entertainments, a copy of which he had in the Arabic, and produced it: he then shewed me, with great triumph, a French translation of them, printed at Paris, which he had read, and declared that the translation was nothing at all in comparison with the original. I believe he was well qualified to judge, for he was a perfect master of the French language.

We talked of the Eastern tale of the Glass Man, who, in a reverie, increases his stock till he gets so rich as, in imagination, to marry the Cadi's daughter, &c. &c. and in kicking his wife, kicks all his glasses about, and destroys the whole of his visionary fortune. I praised the humour of it much —" Sir," said he, " there is nothing in it that may not be experienced frequently in actual life: those waking dreams are the usual concomitants of opium: a man who has accustomed himself to the pernicious practice of eating opium, is constantly subject to them. I have, in the course of my time, found a thousand of those dreamers holding forth in the plenitude of imaginary power. I have seen a common porter become Cadi, and order the bastinado. I have seen a wretched tailor raised by the effects of opium to the office of Aga of the Janissaries, deposing the Sultan, and ordering the bowſtring to all about him. I have ſeen ſome indulging in the blandiſhments of love with Princeſſes, and others wallowing in the wealth of Golconda. But the moſt extraordinary viſionary of this kind I ever met with, was one who imagined himſelf tranſlated to Paradiſe, co-equal to Mahomet, and ſitting by the ſide of that prophet, arguing with him in defence of the uſe of wine and opium: he argued moſt ingeniouſly, liſtened in ſilence to the ſuppoſed arguments of his adverſary, anſwered them, replied, rejoined, and ſtill argued on—till, growing at laſt angry, he ſwore that he was as good a prophet as him, did not care a fig for him, and called him fool and falſe prophet. A Turk who was preſent, in the fulneſs of his zeal, laid a ſtick very heavily acroſs his ſhoulders, and put an end to the viſion: and never did I ſee a wretch ſo abject, ſo forlorn, or ſo miſerably deſponding; he put his forehead to the ground, which he wet with his tears, crying, Mercy, Mahomet! mercy, holy Prophet! mercy, Alla!—nor could he find relief (ſuch is the ruin of opium) till he got a freſh ſupply of it in his mouth, which ſoon gave him a temporary reſpite from the horrors of his ſituation."

Unqueſtionably, Bagdad was once a great city, of flouriſhing commerce; but the Sultan Amurath the Fourth, when he made himſelf maſter of it, put the richeſt Merchants ſettled there to death; and it has ever ſince gradually declined. About two days journey from it, lie the ruins of the once famous city of Babylon. I was much diſpoſed to go to ſee it, and thence drop down the Euphrates to Baſſora: but my Armenian hoſt told me there was nothing in it to recompenſe a perſon for half the trouble; for, of that magnificent city, which was ſixty miles in circumference, which was encompaſſed with walls eighty-ſeven feet in thickneſs, and three hundred and fifty in height, nothing was to be ſeen but the bare foundations of some great edifices. The Tower of Belus, and the Palace of Nebuchadnezzar, lie with the rest in undistinguished ruin. The greatest curiosities, then, were, in the first place, the ruins of a building said to be the famed Tower of Babel, which appeared to have been half a league in compass; and the remains of a vast bridge over the Euphrates, where it is half a league broad.

I was not more anxious to arrive at the city of Bagdad than I was to leave it; and having written letters, and put them in a way of being forwarded to Europe, I took leave of my friendly hospitable Armenian, and, with a thousand acknowledgments for his kindness, set out on horseback to a place on the Tigris, where I embarked in a boat, in order to proceed to Bassora. This river, known since the first records of human existence by Geographers, is remarkable for its rapidity, whence, PLINY says, it has the name of Tigris, (in the Median language, a dart); and for its extraordinary course, which is in many places under ground, rises in Armenia, sinks into the earth near mount Taurus, and runs under a mountain—then rising at the other side, follows its course through the lake Thespites—again sinks frequently under ground, and continues hid at one time for a space of twenty-five miles; where, once more emerging, it glides along with a very rapid stream, meets the Euphrates at a place called Korna, passes through Bassora, and falls into the Persian Gulph.

As the boat in which I took my passage had no convenience for excluding the violence of the sun, except an awning, I suffered extremely from the heat. The River itself was grand; but the banks, and contiguous country, contained nothing to attract notice—no object to diversify the dreary, deserted aspect of the scene—nothing to afford room for reflection, or give birth to a new idea. I do not remember to have ever passed through such a

ARRIVAL AT BASSORA.

vast extent of country, so uniformly dull and uninteresting. The only thing that served to keep the mind alive, was the apprehension of robbers, who, in great numbers, hover over this river, and plunder passengers. We had taken care, on leaving Bagdad, to be well provided with fire-arms; and they did us yeomen's service—for we were frequently attacked by robbers with a view to plunder, but found that a shot or two dispersed and sent them off in consternation. One night, however, in passing a creek, we perceived several boats issuing from it, in great order, and in a manner that evinced method and premeditation: we silently prepared for their reception, and were completely ready to meet them warmly, while they thought us quite unprepared, and unconscious of their approach: they first endeavoured to board us by surprise: wishing rather to frighten than to kill them, we began by firing over their heads; on which they set up the most horrible shouts, and rushed on with a tumultuous rapidity, making the most terrible noise in order to intimidate us: they were by this time quite near us; we therefore took aim at them, and let fly, and immediately perceived them in great confusion, some of the boats losing their helm, and falling with the stream on the others: at last we saw them sheer off, and they gave us no farther trouble.

LETTER XLIV.

AFTER eight or ten as disagreeable days as I remember to have spent in my life, weakened with incessant watching, harassed with bodily fatigue, and melted with the excessive heat of the sun, I arrived at the city of Baſſora, where I was received with the utmoſt hoſpitality by Mr. LA-TOUCHE, the Company's Reſident from Bombay, who did every thing poſſible for my accomodation, and procured me every inſtruction reſpecting my further progreſs.

This city, as well as Bagdad, is famous in marvellous ſtory. The country about it is conſidered by the natives as the beſt ſpot in Aſia, though the burning winds annoy and frequently deſtroy travellers, overwhelming them with mountains of hot ſand, driven like waves of the ſea, before the tempeſt out of the neighbouring deſerts. It carries on a great trade, and is inhabited by vaſt numbers of Chriſtians and Jews. The Engliſh and Dutch have factories here, ss well for the purpoſe of commerce, as the tranſit of diſpatches, by way of Damaſcus and Aleppo, to Europe. The Richeſt merchandiſe of India and Europe are brought here in caravans; and its opulence is greatly increaſed by the caravans of Pilgrims, who paſs through it on their way to Mecca, and pay great duties, bartering for many rich commodities. The horſes of this place are celebrated for their ſuperior excellence: it is ſaid that they will run thirty hours without meat or drink—I doubt the fact, and ſhould be ſorry to ſee ſo inhuman an experiment tried.

One comfortable circumſtance attending Baſſora is, that at night the ſtreets may be walked with perfect ſafety at all hours. It is ſubject to an Arab Prince, who is tributary to the Turk, and whoſe revenue is very great, as well from the above-mentioned cauſes, as becauſe he gives full liberty to all Nations to come and trade to his capital.

From Baſſora I took my paſſage in a date-boat going to Muſkat, expecting to get from thence a ſpeedy paſſage to Bombay: but the boat ſprung a leak at ſea, and we were obliged to run into Buſheer, where I was very hoſpitably received and entertained by Mr. GALLEY, the Company's Resident.

There really seemed to be an unusual fatality attending me throughout the whole of my journey. You will recollect, in the first instance, I was prevented, by the war with France, from going by the direct route which I should otherwise have taken, and obliged to pass through the Low Countries and Germany—In the next place, at Venice I was disappointed in obtaining a passage to Latachæa; and, immediately on the heels of that, lost my servant at Trieste, by sending him for letters to Venice—Afterwards, when I had gone to Alexandria with expectation of travelling through Egypt, and viewing that interesting part of the world, I found myself prevented by the unhappy circumstances of the country—the plague raging in Alexandria, and all the roads being blocked up by an incursion of the Arabs. Thus mortified and disappointed, I turned about, in order to make my way in another direction; and arriving at Cyprus, found, to my infinite surprise and regret, that an epidemic disease, little short of the plague, prevailed there, and swept off the inhabitants in great numbers: when, after surmounting all those obstacles, I arrived at Aleppo, the first information I got was, that the caravan was gone, and that it would be a long time before another would be ready; and my departure from Aleppo was attended with circumstances no less inauspicious than my entrance—At Mosul I experienced another disappointment, by the river's being dried up, and rendered impracticable by boats—My passage from Bassora to Muskat was impeded by the vessel springing a leak—And now, when at last I hoped to get from Busheer to Bombay, I was stopped by the intelligence that the Gulph was blocked up by French privateers, insomuch as no vessel could hope to escape. I was therefore obliged to remain at

Busheer, till a Company's frigate, commanded by Captain HARDY, and soon expected should afford me an opportunity of proceeding to Bombay. Time, however, brought that period about; and I took my passage, and arrived safe at Bombay, where I soon after embarked on board a Portuguese vessel, being the only conveyance that offered for me to proceed to Madras: she was first bound to Goa, and we arrived safely at that island, where I was received with great politeness, and treated with the most friendly attention, by Mr. HENSHAW, the English Resident.

Goa belongs to the Portuguese: the Viceroy of the Nation lives there in great pomp. It was once the scene of the most abominable cruelties, exercised by that flagitious people on the natives, under pretended zeal for Christianity—I had read the Abbé RAYNAL's glowing description of it; and as I trod the ground, my frame trembled at the thoughts of the massacres perpetrated there.

I was impatient to get from Goa, and yet I looked forward to my departure with a secret uneasiness, for which I was entirely unable to account—I wished to proceed, and yet some secret foreboding whispered to my heart that I was on the verge of calamity: so powerful was it, and so obstinate, that I could neither reason away its admonitions, nor resist its impressions; and something incessantly told me, in as plain language as if a human being spoke, that I should suffer a dreadful misfortune. As I had all my life been an enemy to superstition, I felt my spirit insulted, and my understanding degraded, by the involuntary victory it I allowed to this impression—I combated it with reason, with ridicule, with self-contempt —all in vain: in spite of me, I became the very slave of gloomy presentiment; and in order to get the succedaneous aid of a friend's reason, as well as to be prepared, I communicated the state of my

ARRIVAL AT BASSORA.

feelings to Mr. Henshaw. In vain he endeavoured to cheer me: all he could do was to give me his counsel; in consequence of which I actually settled all my affairs up to that day, made my will, left it with Mr. Henshaw, and, full of dreadful forebodings of shipwreck, went on board a Portuguese snow bound to Madras.

It was now the eighteenth day of May when we sailed from Goa. The hemisphere had been for some days overcast with clouds: some light showers of rain had fallen; and you may conclude that it did not tend to raise my spirits, or free me from ominous apprehensions, to hear that those circumstances indicated an approaching gale of wind. I observed, moreover, that the vessel was much too deep in the water, being greatly overloaded—that she was in many respects defective, and, as the seamen say, ill-found, and in short very unfit to encounter a gale of wind of any violence. I scorned, however, to yield to those united impressions, and determined to proceed.

On the nineteenth, the sky was obscured by immense fleeces of clouds, surcharged with inflammable matter; and in the evening, the rain fell in torrents, the firmament darkened apace, sudden night came on, and the horrors of extreme darkness were rendered still more horrible by the peals of thunder which rent the air, and the frequent flashes of lightning, which served only to shew us the horror of our situation, and leave us in increased darkness: mean-time the wind became more violent, blowing on the shore; and a heavy sea, raised by its force, united with it to make our state more formidable.

By day-light on the morning of the twentieth, the gale had encreased to a furious tempest; and the sea, keeping pace with it, ran mountain-high; and as it kept invariably to the same point, the Captain and Officers became seriously alarmed, and almost persuaded that the South-West Monsoon had set in, which, if it were so, would render it absolutely impossible for us to weather the coast. All that day, however, we kept as close as the violence of the weather would allow us to the wind; but the sea canted her head so to leeward, that she made more lee than head-way; and the rigging was so strained with the work that we had little hope of keeping off the shore, unless the wind changed, of which there was not now the smallest probability. During the night there was no intermission of the storm: many of the sails flew into ribbons; some of the rigging was carried away; and such exertions were made, that, before morning, every stick that could possibly be struck was down upon the deck.

About seven o'clock on the morning of the twenty-first, I was alarmed by an unusual noise upon the deck, and running up, perceived that every remaining sail in the vessel, the fore-sail alone excepted, was totally carried away. The sight was horrible; and the whole vessel presented a spectacle as dreadful to the feelings as mortifying to human pride. Fear had produced, not only all the helplessness of despondency, but all the mischievous freaks of insanity. In one place stood the Captain, raving, stamping, and tearing his hair in handfuls from his head—here some of the crew were cast upon their knees, clapping their hands, and praying, with all the extravagance of horror painted in their faces—there, others were flogging their images with all their might, calling upon them to allay the storm. One of our passengers, who was Purser of an English East-Indiaman, had got hold of a case-bottle of rum, and, with an air of distraction and deep despair imprinted in his face, was stalking about in his shirt. I perceived him to be on the point of serving it about, in large tumblers, to the few undismayed people; and well convinced, that, so far from alleviating, it would sharpen the horrors of

ARRIVAL AT BASSORA.

their mind, I went forward, and with much difficulty prevented him.

Having accomplished this point, I applied myself to the Captain, and endeavoured to bring him back (if possible) to his recollection, and to a sense of what he owed to his duty as a commander, and to his dignity as a man: I exhorted him to encourage the sailors by his example; and strove to raise his spirits, by saying that the storm did not appear to me by any means so terrible as some I had before experienced.

While I was thus employed, we shipped a sea on the starboard side, which I really thought would have sent us down. The vessel seemed to sink beneath its weight, shivered, and remained motionless—it was a moment of critical suspense: fancy made me think I felt her gradually descending—I gave myself up as gone, and summoned all my fortitude to bear approaching death with becoming manhood.

Just at this crisis, the water, which rushed with incredible force through all parts of the vessel, brought out floating, and nearly suffocated, another English passenger, who was endeavouring to take a little repose in a small cabin boarded off from the deck: he was a very stout young man, and full of true spirit. Finding that the vessel was not, as I had thought, going immediately down, he joined me in exhorting the captain to his duty: we persuaded him to throw the guns overboard, as well as a number of trunks and packages with which the vessel was much encumbered; and with some little exertion, we got the pumps set agoing.

Here I will stop, knowing the warm sensibility of my FREDERICK's mind; and, convinced that his sympathetic heart will go hand-in-hand with his Father's suffering's, I will not overcharge it with grief by an immediate continuation of the business, but defer it to another Letter.

LETTER XLV.

THE name of the English passenger, whom I mentioned to you in my last Letter as assisting me in getting the Captain and Mariners to do their duty, was HALL. He was a young man of a most amiable disposition, and with it possessed all that manly spirit that gives presence of mind in exigences of danger. He and I having, with great difficulty, got some hands to stick to the pumps, stood at the wheel, at once to assist the men, and prevent them from quitting it ; and, although hopeless, determined that no effort practicable on our parts should be wanting to the preservation of the vessel. The water, however, gained upon the pumps, notwithstanding every effort ; and it evidently appeared that we could not keep her long above water.

At ten o'clock the wind seemed to increase, and amounted to a downright hurricane : the sky was so entirely obscured with black clouds, and the rain fell so thick, that objects were not discernable from the wheel to the ship's head. Soon the pumps were choaked, and could no longer be worked : then dismay seized on all—nothing but unutterable despair, silent anguish, and horror, wrought up to frenzy, was to be seen ; not a single soul was capable of an effort to be useful—all seemed more desirous to extinguish their calamities by embracing death, than willing, by a painful exertion, to avoid it.

At about eleven o'clock we could plainly distinguish a dreadful roaring noise, resembling that of waves rolling against rocks ; but the darkness of the day, and the accompanying rains, prevented us from seeing any distance; and if they were rocks, we might be actually dashed to pieces on them before we could perceive them. At twelve o'clock, however, the weather cleared up a little, and both the wind and the sea seemed to have abated: the very expansion of the prospect round the ship was exhilerating; and as the weather grew better, and the sea less furious, the senses of the people returned, and the general stupefaction began to decrease.

The weather continuing to clear up, we in some time discovered breakers and large rocks without side of us; so that it appeared we must have passed quite close to them, and were now fairly hemmed in between them and the land.

In this very critical juncture, the Captain, entirely contrary to my opinion, adopted the dangerous resolution of letting go an anchor, to bring her up with her head to the sea: But, though no seaman, my common sense told me that she could never ride it out, but must directly go down. The event nearly justified my judgment: for she had scarcely been at anchor before an enormous sea rolling over her, overwhelmed and filled her with water, and every one on board concluded that she was certainly sinking—On the instant, a Lascar, with a presence of mind worthy an old English mariner, took an axe, ran forward, and cut the cable.

On finding herself free, the vessel again floated, and made an effort to right herself; but she was almost completely water-logged, and heeled to larboard so much that the gunnel lay under water. We then endeavoured to steer as fast as we could for the land, which we knew could not be at any great distance, though we were unable to discover it through the hazy weather: the foresail was loosened; by great efforts in bailing, she righted a little, her gunnel was got above water, and we scudded as well as we could before the wind, which still blew hard on shore; and at about two o'clock the land appeared at a small distance a head.

The love of life countervails all other considerations in the mind of man. The uncertainty we were under with regard to the shore before us, which we had reason to believe was part of Hyder Alli's dominions, where we should meet with the most rigorous treatment, if not ultimate death, was forgotten in the joyful hope of saving life; and we scudded towards the shore in all the exulting transports of people just snatched from the jaws of death.

This gleam of happiness continued not long: a tremendous sea rolling after us, broke over our stern, tore every thing before it, stove in the steerage, carried away the rudder, shivered the wheel to pieces, and tore up the very ring-bolts of the deck—conveyed the men who stood at the wheel forward, and swept them overboard. I was standing, at the time, near the wheel, and fortunately had hold of the taffarel, which enabled me to resist in part the weight of the wave. I was, however, swept off my feet, and dashed against the mainmast. The jerk from the taffarel, which I held very tenaciously, seemed as if it would have dislocated my arms: however, it broke the impetus of my motion, and in all probability saved me from being dashed to pieces against the mast.

I floundered about in the water at the foot of the mast, till at length I got on my feet, and seized a rope, which I held in a state of great embarrassment, dubious what I should do to extricate myself. At this instant I perceived that Mr. Hall had got upon the capstern, and was waving his hand to me to follow his example: this I wished to do, though it was an enterprise of some risk and difficulty; for, if I lost the hold I had, a single motion of the vessel, or a full wave, would certainly carry me overboard. I made a bold push, however, and fortunately accomplished it. Having attained this station, I could the better survey the wreck, and saw that the water was nearly breast-high on the quarter-deck, (for the vessel was deep-waisted); and I perceived the unfortunate English Purser standing where the water was most shallow, as if watching with patient expectation its rising, and awaiting death: I called to him to come to us, but he shook his head in despair, and said, in a lamentable tone, "It is all over with us! God have mercy upon us!"—then seated himself with seeming composure on a chair which happened to be rolling about in the wreck of the deck, and in a few minutes afterwards was washed into the sea along with it, where he was speedily released from a state ten thousand times worse than death.

During this universal wreck of things, the horror I was in could not prevent me from observing a very curious circumstance, which at any other time would have excited laughter, though now it produced no other emotion than surprise—We happened to be in part laden with mangoes, of which the island of Goa is known to produce the finest in the world; some of them lay in baskets on the poop; a little black boy, in the moment of greatest danger, had got seated by them, devouring them voraciously, and crying all the time most bitterly at the horrors of his situation!

The vessel now got completely water-logged; and Mr. HALL and I were employed in forming conjectural calculations how many minutes she could keep above water, and consoling one another on the unfortunate circumstances under which we met, lamenting that fate had thus brought us acquainted only to make us witnesses of each other's misery, and then to see one another no more.

A a 2

As the larboard side of the vessel was gradually going down, the deck, and of course the capstern, became too nearly perpendicular for us to continue on it: we therefore foresaw the necessity of quitting it, and got upon the starboard side, holding fast by the gunnel, and allowing our bodies and legs to yield to the sea as it broke over us. Thus we continued for some time: at length the severity of the labour so entirely exhausted our strength and spirits, that our best hope seemed to be a speedy conclusion to our painful death; and we began to have serious intentions of letting go our hold, and yielding ourselves up at once to the fury of the waves.

The vessel, which all this time drifted with the sea and wind, gradually approximated the shore, and at length struck the ground, which for an instant revived our almost departed hopes; but we soon found that it did not in the smallest degree better our situation—Again I began to yield to utter despair—again I thought of letting go my hold, and sinking at once: It is impossible thought I ever to escape—why, then, prolong, for a few minutes, a painful existence that must at last be given up? Yet, yet, the all-subduing love of life suggested, that many things apparently impossible had come to pass; and I said to myself, If life is to be lost, why not lose it in a glorious struggle? Should I survive it by accident, life will be rendered doubly sweet to me, and I still more worthy of it by persevering fortitude.

While I was employed in this train of reflection, I perceived some of the people collecting together, talking, and holding a consultation—It immediately occurred to me, that they were devising some plan for escaping from the wreck, and getting on shore: and, so natural is it for man to cling to his fellow-creature for support in difficult or dangerous exigences, I proposed to Mr. HALL to join them, and take a share in the execution of the plan—observing to him at the same time, that I was determined at all events to quit the vessel, and trust to the protection and guidance of a superintending Providence for the rest.

LETTER XLVI.

As prodigality of life is, in some cases, the excess of virtue and courage—so there are others in which it is vice, meanness and cowardice. True courage is, according to the circumstances under which it is to operate, as rigidly tenacious and vigilant of life in one case, as it is indifferent and regardless in another; and I think it is a very strange contradiction in the human heart (although it often happens), that a man who has the most unbounded courage, in seeking death even in the cannon's mouth, shall yet want the necessary resolution to make exertions to save his life in cases of ordinary danger. The unfortunate English Purser could not collect courage sufficient to make an effort to save himself; and yet I think it probable that he would have faced a battery of artillery, or exposed himself to a pistol-shot, if occasion required, as soon as any other man. Thus it appears at first view: but may not this seeming incongruity be explained by saying, that personal courage and fortitude are different qualities of the mind and body, and depend upon the exercise of entirely different functions?

Be that as it may, I argued with myself, in the height of my calamitous situation, upon the subject of fortitude and dejection, courage and cowardice; and, notwithstanding the serious aspect of affairs, found myself listening to the suggestions of pride: What a paltry thing to yield, while strength is left to struggle! Vanity herself had her hint, and whispered, " Should I escape by an effort of my own, what a glorious theme of exultation!" There were, I confess, transitory images in my mind, which, co-operating with the natural attachment to self-preservation, made me persevere, and resolve to do so, while one vestige of hope was left for the mind to dwell on.

Observing, as I told you before, the people consulting together, and resolving to join them, I made an effort to get to the lee shrouds, where they were standing, or rather clinging; but before I could accomplish it, I lost my hold, fell down the hatchway (the gratings having been carried away with the long-boat), and was for some minutes entangled there amongst a heap of packages, which the violent fluctuations of the water had collected on the lee side. As the vessel moved with the sea, and the water flowed in, the packages and I were rolled together—sometimes one, sometimes another, uppermost; so that I began to be apprehensive I should not be able to extricate myself: by the merest accident, however, I grasped something that lay in my way, made a vigorous spring, and gained the lee shrouds. Mr. HALL, who followed me, in seizing the shrouds, came thump against me with such violence that I could scarcely retain my hold of the rigging. Compelled by the perilous situation in which I stood, I called out to him for GOD's sake to keep off, for that I was rendered quite breathless and worn out: he generously endeavoured to make way for me, and, in doing so, unfortunately lost his hold, and went down under the ship's side. Never, never shall I forget my sensations at this melancholy incident—I would have given millions of worlds that I could have recalled the words which made him move; my mind was wound up to the laſt pitch of anguiſh : I may truly ſay, that this was the moſt bitter of all the bitter moments of my life, compared with which the other circumſtances of the ſhipwreck ſeemed leſſened—for I had inſenſibly acquired an unuſual eſteem and warm attachment for him, and was doubtful whether, after being even the innocent occaſion of his falling, I ought to take further pains to preſerve my own life. All thoſe ſenſations were paſſing with the rapidity of lightning through my thoughts, when, as much to my aſtoniſhment as to my joy, I ſaw him borne by a returning wave, and thrown among the very packages from which I had but juſt before, with ſuch labour and difficulty, extricated myſelf—In the end he proved equally fortunate, but after a much longer and harder ſtruggle, and after ſuſtaining much more injury.

I once more changed my ſtation, and made my way to the poop, where I found myſelf rather more ſheltered—I earneſtly wiſhed Mr. HALL to be with me, whatever might be my ultimate fate—and beckoned to him to come to me ; but he only anſwered by ſhaking his head, in a feeble, deſponding manner—ſtaring at the ſame time wildly about him : even his ſpirit was ſubdued ; and deſpair, I perceived, had begun to take poſſeſſion of his mind.

Being a little more at eaſe in my new ſtation than I had been before, I had more time to deliberate, and more power to judge. I recollected, that, according to the courſe of time, the day was far gone, and the night quickly approaching : I reflected, that for any enterprize whatſoever, day was much preferable to night ; and above all I conſidered, that the veſſel could not hold long together—I therefore thought, that the beſt mode I could adopt would be, to take to the water with the firſt boyant thing I could ſee ; and, as the wind and water both seemed to run to the shore. to take my chance in that way of reaching it. In pursuance of this resolution, I tore off my shirt, having before that thrown off the other parts of my dress—I looked at my sleeve buttons, in which was set the hair of my departed children—and, by an involuntary act of the imagination, asked myself the question, " Shall I be happy enough to meet them where I am now about to go?—Shall those dear last remains, too, become a prey to the devouring deep?"—In that instant, reason, suspended by the horrors of the scene, gave way to instinct; and I rolled my shirt up, and very carefully thrust it into a hole between decks, with the wild hopes that the sleeve buttons might yet escape untouched. Watching my opportunity, I saw a log of wood floating near the vessel, and, waving my hand to Mr. HALL as a last adieu, jumped after it. Here, again, I was doomed to aggravated hardships—I had scarcely touched the log when a great sea snatched it from my hold: still as it came near me, I grasped at it ineffectually, till at last it was completely carried away, but not before it had cut and battered and bruised me in several places, and in a manner that at any other time I should have thought dreadful.

Death seemed inevitable, and all that occured to me now to do, was to accept it, and get out of its pangs as speedily as possible; for, though I knew how to swim, the tremendous surf rendered swimming useless, and all hope from it would have been rediculous. I therefore began to swallow as much water as possible; yet, still rising by the the boyant principle of the waves to the surface, my former thoughts began to recur; and whether it was that, or natural instinct, which survived the temporary impressions of despair, I know not—but I endeavoured to swim, which I had not done long, when I again discovered the log of wood I had lost floating near me, and with some difficulty caught it;

hardly had it been an instant in my hands, when, by the same unlucky means, I lost it again. I had often heard it said in Scotland, that if a man will throw himself flat on his back in the water, lie quite straight and stiff, and suffer himself to sink till the water gets into his ears, he will continue to float so for ever; this occured to me now, and I determined to try the experiment; so I threw myself on my back in the manner I have described and left myself to the disposal of providence: nor was it long till I found the truth of the saying—for I floated with hardly an effort, and began for the first time to conceive something like hopes of preservation.

After lying in this manner, committed to the direction of the tides, I soon saw the vessel—saw that it was at a considerable distance behind me. Liveliest hope began to play about my heart, and joy fluttered with a thousand gay fancies in my mind: I began to form the favourable conclusion, that the tide was carrying me rapidly to land from the vessel, and that I should soon once more touch *terra firma*.

This expectation was a cordial that revived my exhausted spirits: I took courage, and left myself still to the same all directing Power that had hitherto preserved me, scarcely doubting that I should soon reach the land. Nor was I mistaken; for, in a short time more, without effort or exertion, and without once turning from off my back, I found myself strike against the sandy beach. Overjoyed, as you may well suppose, to the highest pitch of transport at my providential deliverance, I made a convulsive spring, and ran up a little distance on the shore; but was so weak and worn down by fatigue, and so unable to clear my stomach of the salt water with which it was loaded, that I suddenly grew deadly sick, and apprehended that I had only exchanged one death for another; and in a minute or two fainted away.

LETTER XLVII.

THAT admirable man and sagacious penetrating philosopher, Dr. FRANKLIN, has left us, among innumerable instructions for the conduct of human life, and for remedying many of the grievances of it, directions for going a voyage at sea, and has particularly enforced the folly of quitting ships hastily, and yielding one's self up to despair. I am convinced, that nine tenths of the people who perish by shipwreck, perish from the want of presence of mind, and sufficient fortitude to bear them out. The unhappy purser, who sat deliberately in a chair, and suffered himself, without a struggle, to be carried overboard, is an instance in point. The feeble conduct of the captain and crew is another. Had he, instead of tearing of his hair, raving, and acting the part of a bedlamite, encouraged his men, and taken vigorous measures in time; and had they, instead of whimpering prayers on their knees, and whipping their images, made all clear, and prepared for the worst; in short, had they, according to the moral of the old fable, put their shoulder to the wheel, instead of calling on Hercules, it is not impossible but the vessel might have been saved.

As for my part, the joy of escaping immediate death made me blind to the other miseries of my situation. Naked, moneyless and friendless, upon an unknown, and probably inhospitable coast, what reasonable cause had I to rejoice? Perhaps the reverse. But that remains to be seen.

How long I continued in the swoon into which I had fallen, it is impossible for me to tell; but, when I recovered, I found myself surrounded by a guard of armed soldiers, sepoys, and pikemen. I knew them immediately to be the troops of HYDER ALLI, and almost wished myself back into the waves again. Looking round, I saw that the people and effects that had been saved from the wreck were collected all together along with me.

In this state we remained till it was dark. A Lascar* belonging to the vessel, perceiving that my nakedness gave me great concern, tore into two a piece of cloth which he had tied round his waist, and gave me one part of it, which afforded a short apron. This simple act of a poor, uninformed black man, whom christian charity would call an idolator, methought had more of the true and essential spirit of charity in it, than half the ostentatious, parading newspaper public charities of London—the slough of purse-proud vanity, and unwieldy bloathed wealth. Of all the acts of beneficence that I ever met with, it struck me the most forcibly: it had kindness, dis-interestedness and delicacy for its basis; and I have never since thought of it without wishing that I could meet the man, to reward him for his beneficence with a subsistence for life. The lower order of people of a certain country, I know, would think a man in such circumstances as I was then in, a fitter object of pleasantry than pity.

The vast quantity of salt water I had swallowed, still made me deadly sick in the stomach: however, after some time, I threw it up, and got great relief. I had hardly felt the comfortable effects of this, before I was ordered to march: nine of us, all Lascars except myself, were conveyed to a village at a few miles distance on the sea-side, where we were for the night put into a square place, walled round, open to the inclemency of the wea-

---

* Natives of India, employed sometimes as sailors, sometimes for inferior offices in the army, such as pitching tents, drawing guns, &c.

ther above and below, and filled with large logs of wood; it blew most violently, and the rain fell in torrents—while not one smooth plank could be found on which to stretch our fatigued and wasted bodies. Thus, naked, sick, exhausted with fatigue and fasting, drenched with wet, and unable to lie down, our misery might be supposed to be incapable of increase. But, alas! where are the bounds which we can set to human woe?—Thirst, that most dreadful of pains, occasioned by the drenching with salt water, seized us: we begged, we entreated, we clamoured for water; but the inhuman wretches, deaf to the groans and screeches of their fellow-creatures, (for some grew delirious with the agony of thirst), refused them even the cheap and miserable indulgence of a drop of water!

The influence of the mind upon the body has been much insisted on by philosophers and physicians, and I believe will be admitted by all wise men. I was myself in this instance, a striking proof of it; for, though I had swallowed and thrown up so much salt water, though my thirst had exceeded any thing I had ever before felt—yet, finding that water was not to be had or expected, I composed my mind to do without it, diverted my thoughts from it by the contemplation of the many other evils which beset me, and passed the night without that horrible agony experienced by the others.

Indeed, a night of more exquisite horror cannot be imagined. The thoughts of being a prisoner to HYDER ALLI, was, of itself, sufficient to render me completely unhappy: but my utter want of clothes almost put me beside myself; and lying exposed to the open air, where I was glad to sit close to the Lascars to receive a little heat from their bodies, and to hold open my mouth in order to catch a drop of the descending rain, was a state that might be considered as the highest refinement upon misery.

About four o'clock in the morning, a little cold rice was brought us to eat, and water was dug out of a hole near the spot for us; but as all things in this life are good or bad merely relatively, this wretched fare was some refreshment to us. I was then removed to the ruins of a toddy-hut,* separated from the rest, and a guard set over me. Here I had full room for reflection, and could "meditate e'en to madness." The whole of my situation appeared before me with all its aggravating circumstances of horror; and to any one who considers it, I believe it will appear that it was hardly possible to fill the bitter cup of calamity fuller. Oh! what were my thoughts! My family bereft of him on whose efforts they were in a great measure to depend for support and protection—you, then a little innocent cherub, appeared to my distracted imagination twining round your mother's neck, and, in infant clamour, calling your father—while he, in a dreadful captivity, compared with which even a cruel death were mercy, lay wasting, naked and forlorn, perishing with the inclemency of the weather, wanting even food fit for his support, and exposed to the scourge of every petty tyrant that barbarous power might employ to guard him!— Such were my reflections: they were in reason well founded; for there was no probability of my being ever released, as my captivity was unlikely to be known to my country, or by my friends.

In this state I was, when, to my utter astonishment, and to my no less joy, the amiable companion of my shipwreck, Mr. HALL, appeared before me. I scarcely knew how to think his appearance reality, as I understood that the Lascars then along with

* A small temporary hut, where *toddy* (a liquor extracted from the cocoa-nut tree) is sold.

me were all that were saved from the wreck; and he was, at the time I parted from him, so exhausted both in body and mind, that I thought he would be the last who could escape. He, however, shook me by the hand; and, sitting down, told me that he had given me up for lost, and remained with the vessel until the tide, having ebbed, left her almost dry—that, immediately on getting ashore, and being taken prisoner, he made inquiries about me, and heard that I had been saved—that, finding this, his joy was such as to make him almost forget his own misfortunes—and, exerting all his entreaties not to be separated from me, they had been so far indulgent to him, and had brought him to me, that we might be companions in bondage. He added, that out of eleven Europeans and fifty-six Lascars who were on board, only he and 1 of the former, and fourteen of the latter, were saved from the wreck, the rest having been drowned in the attempt, excepting some who, overcome with terror, anguish and anxiety, and exhausted with fatigue, had bid a formal adieu to their companions, let go their hold, and calmly and voluntarily given themselves up to the deep.

I here took occasion to remark to him, what I have already said to you, that thousands lose their lives for want of perseverance, fortitude, and courage to preserve them—Had the English Purser collected courage enough to hold fast till the tide ebbed, he might have been safe on shore as we were, as he was superior to either of us in bodily strength.

"Ah! my friend!" said he, shaking his head despondingly—"is he worse where he is? I doubt whether death is not far preferable to our present prospects."

"Come, come," said I, perceiving he was melancholy, though I myself laboured under all the horrors he expressed—"come, let us not think; all will yet be well: I foresee it will; and you must known I have something of the prophet in my nature—perhaps the second sight." I then told him my presentiments on leaving Goa, which much astonished him.—Still more when I acquainted him with the formal acts I had done in consequence thereof, by Mr. HENSHAW's advice, and with his privity.

In fact, our joy at meeting was reciprocally great, and in some respect cheered us for the time under all our miseries in hand, and the dreary prospect of those yet to come.

Perceiving that he stood as much in need of relief as I did when the Lascar relieved me by dividing his cloth, I took mine off, tore it in two, and gave him half of it: you may well conceive our misery from this, if other circumstances were wanting, that such a thing as a rag of linen, not worth six pence, was a very material accommodation to us both.

LETTER XLVIII.

YOUR letter, occasioned by the account of my shipwreck and subsequent disaster, gave me, my amiable boy! as great pleasure as those disasters gave me pain. Your account, too, of JOHN's bursting into tears on the reading of it to him, had almost a similar effect upon myself: and I trust in the Almighty disposer of events, that that excellent turn of mind will be so fashioned by the education I give you, as to make it the source of boundless gratification and true greatness (by which I mean goodness) here, and of never-fading felicity hereafter. You say you cannot account for it, but you found more happiness at my escape, than misery at my misfortunes. I hail that circumstance as the strongest mark of perfect excellence of disposition. A great moral philosopher has laid it down as a maxim, that it is the surer mark of a good heart to sympathise with joy than with sorrow; and this instance only comes in aid of that opinion of you which my fond hopes have always nourished.

At the same time I must declare to you, that my pleasure at escaping shipwreck was by no means as great as the agony my mind underwent as the prospect now before me was poignant. I have already said, and indeed with truth, that I should have with much greater pleasure embraced death: I, who had been already some years in India, and had opportunities of hearing, as well from my father as from other officers in the service, what the disposition of the tyrant in whose power I had now fallen was, knew too well the horrors of my situation to feel any thing like hope. The unmerciful disposition of HYDER, and all those in authority under him, and the cruel policy of the Eastern chiefs, making the life of any one, particularly a British prisoner, at the best a precarious tenure, I did not know the moment when death might be inflicted upon me with perhaps a thousand aggravating circumstances: and at all events, the affairs which demanded my presence in India so very importunately as to urge me to all the fatigues and hardships of a passage over land, were, of themselves, sufficient to make my mind uneasy; but the abject state of want and nakedness in which it seemed I was likely to remain, struck a deep and damp horror to my heart, and almost unman'd me.

Mr. HALL and I, however, endeavoured with all our might to stem the headlong torrent of our fate—Melancholy preyed deeply and openly upon him, while I concealed mine, and endeavoured to cheer the sinking spirits of that noble youth, who, I perceived was the prey rather of extreme sensibility than feebleness of mind. All the horrors of shivering nakedness, though, to a mind delicate like his, and a person reared in the lap of luxury, sufficiently goading, appeared as nothing when compared with one loss he had sustained in the depredations with which shipwreck is constantly followed up. In the cruel suspense between life and death, which I have already described, previous to my getting on shore, this amiable young man had secured and treasured next his heart, as the inseperable companion of his fate, a miniature portrait of a young lady; it hung round his neck, and was, by the unfeeling villains who seized him on his landing, taken away. This cruel deprivation was an incessant corrosive to his mind—the copious source of anguish to his heart—the hourly theme of the most pathetic, afflicting exclamations. "Had I," he would cry, "oh! had I had but the good fortune to have gone to the bottom while yet it hung about my neck; I should have been happy: but now, separated from the heavenly original, and bereft of the precious image, what is life? what would be life were I yet sure of it? What pleasure, what common content, has the world left for me? None—oh! none, none! Never shall this heart again know comfort!"

I did every thing I could to console him, and, as far as I could, prevent him from dwelling on those gloomy subjects. Our conversations were interesting and pathetic; but, alas! the picture, at every pause, chased away the slight impressions of the preceding converse: no sufferings of the body could countervail that loss—no consolation mitigate it; and amidst the horrid reflections which unparalleled calamity imposed upon his mind, the loss of that one dear relic rose paramount to all—and as every thought began, so it ended, with the picture.

For some days we lay in this place, exposed to the weather, without even the slender comfort of a little straw to cover the ground beneath us—our food, boiled rice, served very sparingly twice a-day by an old woman, who just threw a handful or more of it to each upon a very dirty board, which we devoured with those spoons nature gave us.

At the end of that time, we, and, along with us, the Lascars, were ordered to proceed into the country, and drove on foot to a considerable distance, in order to render up an account of ourselves to persons belonging to government, authorised to take it. It was advanced in the morning when we moved, without receiving any sort of sustenance; and were marched in that wasting climate eight hours, without breaking our fast; during which time we were exposed alternately to the scorching heat of the sun and heavy torrents of rain, which raised painful blisters on our skin: we had often to stand exposed to the weather, or to lie down, under the pressure of fatigue and weakness, on the bare ground; then wait an hour, or more, at the door of some insolent, unfeeling monster, until he finished his dinner, or took his afternoon's nap; and when this was over, drove forward with wanton barbarity by the people who attended us.

You, my FREDERICK! who only know the mild and merciful disposition of the people of Great Britain, where government, religion, and long habit, have reduced charity and benevolence so completely to a system that they seem to be innate principles of the mind, can have no conception of a people who will not only look upon the worst human afflictions with indifference, but take a savage delight in the miseries of their fellow-creatures, even where no possible advantage can be reaped from their inhumanity, and where the only reward they can propose to themselves for their cruelty is the pleasure of contemplating human sufferings.

Such, sorry am I to say it, is the disposition of some parts of the East Indies that I have been in; and although those parts under the dominion of Great Britain owe their emancipation from the most galling yokes to the English—and though, under their auspices, they live in a state of greater happiness than ever they did, and greater freedom even than Britons themselves—yet such is the wicked ingratitude of many of them, such the inflexible animosity arising from a contradictory religion, that the death or suffering of an Englishman, or any misfortune that may befal him, often serves only as matter of sport or amusement. to them. It would be well if it rested there---but unfortunately they are worse again; for in general they have the like coldness and indifference, or indeed, to speak more properly, the like aversion, to each others good; and the same diabolical principles of selfishness and treachery pervade the greater number in those vast regions, almost boundless in extent, and almost matchless in fertility.

Two days after this, we were moved again, and marched up the country by a long and circuitious route, in which we underwent every hardship that cruelty could inflict, or human fortitude endure—now blistered with the heat, now drenched with the rain, and now chilled with the night damps—destitute of any place but the bare earth to rest or lay our heads on, with only a scanty pittance of boiled rice for our support—often without water to quench our thirst, and constantly goaded by the guards, who pricked us with their bayonets every now and then, at once to evince their power, entertain the spectators, and mortify us. We arrived at Hydernagur, the metropolis of the province of Biddanore—a fort of considereble strength, mounting upwards of seventy guns, containing a large garrison of men, and possessed of immense wealth.

It was about two o'clock in the morning when we arrived at Biddanore: the day was extremely hot, and we were kept out under the full heat of that broiling sun till six o'clock in the evening, before we were admitted to an audience of the Jemadar, or governor of the place, without having a mouthful of victuals offered to us after the fatiguing march of the morning.

While we stood in this forlorn state, a vast concourse of people collected about, and viewed us with curiosity. Looking round through those who stood nearest, I observed some men gazing at me with strong marks of emotion, and a mixture of wonder and concern pourtrayed in their countenances. Surprised to see such symptoms of humanity in a Mysorian Indian, I looked at them with more scrutinizing attention, and thought that their faces were familiar to me. Catching my eye, they looked at me significantly, as though they would express their regard and respect for me, if they dared; and I then began to recollect that they were formerly privates in my regiment of cavalry, and were then prisoners at large with HYDER.

I was not less surprised that those poor fellows should recognise me in my present miserable fallen state, than affected at the sympathetic feeling they disclosed. I returned their look with a private nod of recognition; but, seeing that they were afraid to speak to me, and fearing I might injure them by disclosing our acquaintance, I forbore any thing more. The guilty souls of despotic governments are perpetually alive to suspicion: every look alarms them; and alarm or suspicion never fails to be followed up with proscription or death.

Men, when in the fullness of power and pride of office, very seldom give themselves time to reflect upon the instability of human greatness, and the uncertainty of earthly contingencies. When, invested with alll the trappings of authority, I commanded the regiment to which those poor fellows belonged, I would have thought that he spoke wildly indeed who would have alledged that it was possible I could ever become an object of their pity—that I should stand naked and degraded before them, and they be afraid to acknowledge me; but, though I should have thought so then, it was yet some comfort to me, when that unfortunate event did come to pass, to reflect, that, when in power, I made such use of it as to excite emotions in their bosoms of affection and respect. Did the tyrant and overbearing insolent chiefs consider this, and govern themselves by its instructions, they would go into the field with the consoling reflection, that no gun would be levelled at their head except that of the common enemy—a thing that does not always happen.

LETTER XLIX.

HAD we been made prisoners of war in battle against an enemy, there is no law of nature or nations, no rule of reason or principle of equity, that could palliate such treatment as that which we now received: but, - cast by misfortune and ship-wreck on their shore, we were entitled to solace and protection. The worst wretches who hang out false beacons on the western coasts of England, to allure ships to their destruction, would not be cruel without temptation; and, if they did not expect to gain some profit by it, would rather decline knocking their fellow-creatures in the head: but those barbarians, without any profit but what a malignant heart derives from the miseries of others, or any pleasure but what proceeds from their pain, exercised upon us the most wanton cruelty. Compared with such treatmen, instant death would have been an act of mercy to us; and we should have had reason to bless the hand that inflicted it.

Mortifications of one sort or other—the incessant torturing of the mind on the rack of suspense—the injuries to the animal system, occasioned by constant exposure to the weather, and the want of food—all conspired to reduce me to the dimensions and feebleness of a skeleton. I had grown daily weaker and weaker, and was now nearly exhausted, and quite faint; while, on the other hand, my amiable companion in affliction was reduced by a dysentery, which attacked him soon after our shipwreck, and which the torments of his mind, the want of medicine and comfortable food, and, above all, the alternate violent changes from profuse perspiration in walking to chilling cold at night, had increased to such an alarming degree, that he was obliged to be carried the two last days journey:—In this state, we appeared to each other as two spectres hanging over the brink of the grave: and in truth, perceiving the rapid progress he was making to his dissolution, I was affected to a degree, that, while it really exasperated my own worn-down state, deprived me of all attention to the rapid decline I was falling into, and almost entirely engrossed my care. In my progress through life, I have had occasion to try several men, and have found among them many who were every thing that a good heart could wish to find: but this young gentleman had at once so much suavity and spirit—such gentleness and fortitude—his sufferings (those of his mind, as well as those of his body) were so exquisite, and he bore them with such meekness, tempered by such uninterrupted good humour, and concealed and managed with so much delicacy, that I do not transgress the bounds of truth when I say I never met one who so entirely interested my feelings, and attached my friendship so unalterably, upon principles of instinctive impulse, as well as reason. Impelled by the irresistible claims he had upon my approbation and esteem, I entered with all the warmth of a brother into his sufferings, and can assert with truth that they constituted the severest trials I underwent during my whole imprisonment.

While we stood in the court, waiting to be brought before the Jemadar, we presented a spectacle that would have wrung pity, one would think, from the heart of a tiger, if a tiger was endued with reflection. At length we were summoned to appear before him, and brought into his presence. I had made up my mind for the occasion—determined to deport myself in a manly, candid manner—and to let no consideration whatsoever lead me to any thing disgraceful to my real character, or unworthy my situation in life; and, finally, had prepared myself to meet, without shrinking, whatever misfortunes might yet be in store for me, or whatever cruelties the barbarous disposition or wicked policy of the Tyrant might think proper to inflict.

On entering, we found the Jemadar in full Durbar.* He was then occupied with the reading of dispatches, and in transacting other public business. We were placed directly opposite to him, where we stood for near an hour, during which time he never cast his eyes towards us: but when at last he had concluded the business, in which he was engaged, and deigned to look at us, we were ordered to prostrate ourselves before him: the Lascars immediately obeyed the order, and threw themselves on the ground; but I contented myself with making a talam, in which poor Mr. HALL, who knew not the Eastern manner as I did, followed my example.

* Court.

As soon as this ceremony was over, the Jemadar (who was no other man than the famous HYAT SAHIB that has made some noise in the history of that war) began to question me. He desired to know, who I was?—what my profession was?—what was the cause and manner of my approaching the country of HYDER ALLI?—To all those questions I gave answers that seemed to satisfy him. He then asked me, what news I had brought with me from Europe?—inquired into the state of the army, and number of recruits dispatched in the ships of that season—was minute and circumstantial in his questions respecting the nature and success of the war in Europe—and examined me closely, touching the resources of the East India Company. I saw his drift, and was cautious and circumspect in my answers, and at the same time contrived to speak with an air of candour that in some sort satisfied him.

Having exhausted his whole string of questions, he turned the discourse to another subject—no less than his great and puissant Lord and Master, HYDER, of whom he had endeavoured to impress me with a great, if not terrible idea—amplifying his power, his wealth, and the extent and opulence of his dominions—and describing to me, in the most exaggerated terms, the number of his troops—his military talents—his vast, and, according to his account, unrivalled genius—his amazing abilities in conquering and governing Nations—and, above all, his many amiable qualities, and splendid endowments of heart, no less than understanding.

Having thus, with equal zeal and fidelity, endeavoured to impress me with veneration for his Lord and Master, and for that purpose attributed to him every perfection that may be supposed to be divided among all the Kings and Generals that have lived since the birth of CHRIST, and given each their due, he turned to the English Government, and endeavoured to demonstrate to me the folly and inutility of our attempting to resist his progress, which he compared to that of the sea, to a tempest, to a torrent, to a lion's pace and fury—to every thing that an Eastern imagination could suggest as a figure proper to exemplify grandeur and irresistible power. He then vaunted of his Sovereign's successes over the English, some of which I had not heard of before, and did not believe; and concluded by assuring me, that it was Hyder's determination to drive all Europeans from Indostan, which he averred he could not fail to do, considering the weakness of the one, and boundless power of the other. This part of Hyat Sahib's discourse is well worth your remembering, as it will serve to make a very diverting contrast with his subsequent conduct.

After having expended near half an hour in this manner, he called upon me to come over near him, and caused me to seat myself upon a mat with a pillow to lean upon—encouraged me, by every means he could, by the most gentle accents, and the most soothing, mollifying language, to speak to him without the least reserve—exhorted me to tell him the truth in every thing we spoke of—and hinted to me, that my falling into his hands might turn out the most fortunate event of my life.

I was at a loss to what motive to attribute all those singular marks of indulgence; but found that he had learned whose son I was, and knew my father by reputation from the prisoners, our Sepoys, who were now prisoners at large here: and as rank and office are the chief recommendation in the East, as well as elsewhere, or rather much more than any where else, the sagacious Hyat Sahib found many claims to esteem and humanity in me as the son of a Colonel Campbell, which he never would have found in me had I been the son of a plain humble farmer or tradesman in England.

After a full hour's audience, in which Hyat Sahib treated me with distinguished marks of his favour, considering my situation, he dismissed me with the ceremony of beetle-nut,* rose-water, and other compliments, which are in that country held as the strongest marks of politeness, respect, and good-will.

Leaving the Durbar, I was led to the inner fort or citadel: and the officious zeal of those about me, unwilling to let me remain ignorant of that which they conceived to be a most fortunate turn in my affairs, gave the *coup de grace* to my miseries as I went along, by congratulating me on the favourable opinion which the Jemadar had formed of me, and intimating at the same time that I would soon be honoured with a respectable command in Hyder's service.

If I was miserable before, this intimation entirely destroyed the last remnant of peace or hope. I was determined to die a thousand deaths sooner than serve any State hostile to Great Britain—but still more a Tyrant, whose country, nature and principles I detested, and could never think of without the greatest horror; and I judged, that if such an offer should be made, and I refused it; my life would fall a sacrifice to their rage and disappointment, or at least I should live a life of imprisonment, and never more behold country, family, friends, connections, or any thing that I valued in life.

That night the Jemadar sent me an excellent supper, of not less than six dishes, from his own table; and although I had been so long famishing with the want of wholesome food, the idea of being enlisted in the service of Hyder struck me with such horror, that I lost all appetite, and was scarcely able to eat a mouthful. Mr. Hall and I, however,

---

* An aromatic nut which the East Indians chew; it is warm and astringent, and considered by them a great restorative.

were seperated from the Lascars, who were released and forced to work.

Notwithstanding the favourable intentions manifested towards me by the Jemader, as I have already mentioned, no mark of it whatsoever appeared in our lodging. This consisted of a small place, exactly the size of our length and breadth, in the zig-zag of one of the gates of the citadel: it was open in front, but covered with a kind of a shed on the top; and a number of other prisoners were about us: each of us was allowed a mat and pillow, and this formed the whole of our local accommodations. Upon my remarking it, we were told, that in conformity to the custom of the Circar,* we must be treated so for some time, but that our accommodations would afterwards be extended, and made more agreeable to our wishes: even this was better than our situation since we landed.

In addition to this luxury, we were allowed to the value of four pence halfpenny a day for our maintenance; and a guard of Sepoys was put over us and a few more prisoners, one of whom was directed to go and purchase our victuals, and do such offices for us.

This guard was changed every week—a strong mark of the suspicious and wary tempers of those people, who could fear intrigues and cabals between wretched prisoners like us and their soldiers.

In two or three days after this, HYAT SAHIB sent for me, treated me with great kindness, gave me some tea, and furnished me with two or three shirts, an old coat, and two pairs of breeches, which were stripped from the dead bodies that were thrown ashore from the wreck—every thing that was saved from it being sent to Biddanore. At this interview he treated me with great respect—gave me, besides the articles already mentioned,

* Country or Province.

thirty rupees—and, upon my going away, told me that in a few days a very flattering proposal would be made to me, and that my situation would be rendered not only comfortable, but enviable.

It is impossible for me to express to you, my dear FREDERICK! the horror I felt at the idea of this intended proposal—for I knew but too well what it meant. It was the source of bitter misery to my mind: nevertheless, I determined to resist every effort that should be made, whether blandishment, intreaty, or menace—to lay down my life itself, though in obscurity, with honour—and to carry along with me, go where I would, the consciousness of having done my duty.

I have in the course of my life met with many people, who, under the plausible pretext of liberality and greatness of mind, have called themselves citizens of the world, and declared that the country where they lived, be that what country it might, was their's, and demanded their allegiance and protection: but I have always shrewdly suspected, that such men act from a consciousness of being outcasts of their own country---and, scorned and rejected by their fellow-citizens, would retaliate by affecting to deny their natural attachment. There are men who neither love father, mother, sister, brother, or connection: such, however, are, thank GOD! very thinly sown in this world; but, except it be a few such unnatural people, I am convinced that there is no one whose heart does not confess the patriotic passion, and burn with a flame, more or less ardent, of love for his country. My predilections that way are naturally strong, and I am now happy to reflect that I evinced them by the most unequivocal proofs: had I not, I were indeed, in my own opinion, fit for any punishment, however ignominious: and to all such as lift their arms against their country, as to Parricides, I will say, in the words of the poet,

" Never pray more—abandon all remorse:
" On horrors head, horrors accumulate;
" Do deeds to make Heaven weep—all earth amaz'd;
" For nothing can'st thou to damnation add,
" Greater than that."

LETTER L.

ON the evening of that day on which the Jemadar HYAT SAHIB had honoured me with an audience, given me clothes and money, and informed me that a proposal, which he called flattering, would be made to me, I was sent for to attend, not at the Durbar, but at the house of a man high in office. As I expected to meet HYAT SAHIB himself, and trembled at the thoughts of his expected proposition, I was surprised, and indeed pleased, to find that it was with one of his people only I was to have a conference. This man, whose name I now forget, received me with great kindness, encouraged me, made me sit down with him, and began to speak of HYAT SAHIB, whom he extolled to the skies, as a person endowed with every great and amiable quality; informing me at the same time, that he was possessed of the friendship and confidence of his master, HYDER ALLI, in a greater degree than any other person—TIPPOO SAHIB, his own son, not excepted: he then gave me the private history of HYAT---saying, that he was born a Gentoo prince, of one of the provinces of the Malabar coast, which had fallen beneath the irresistible arms of HYDER, and had been by him annexed to the vast Mysorean Empire. HYAT, he said, was then only a boy of eleven or twelve years of age, of a most promising genius, and a quickness of mind unusually met with in one of those tender years. HYDER, who was in all respects a man of unrivalled penetration, thought he saw in the boy that which, if properly cultivated, would turn out of vast use to a state; and as, in all Mahomedan governments, unconnected, isolated boys, oft-times slaves, are bred up in the seraglio to succeed to the great offices of the state, HYDER adopted the boy, had him made a Mahomedan, and, in fact, treated him as if he had been the issue of his own loins, and brought him up with all the affection and tenderness of a fond parent. I am the more particular in stating this part of HYAT's history to you, as some respectable historians, deceived by erroneous report, have said that he was the illegitimate offspring of HYDER. The sultan, however, was not disappointed in the expectations he had formed; for HYAT SAHIB had, in zeal, fidelity and attachment, as well as in intellectual faculties and talents for governing, even surpassed the warmest hopes of his master.

Having given me this concise account of the Jemadar, he proceeded to inform me, that the Arcot Sepoys, whom I have before mentioned to you, had discovered to HYAT SAHIB who I was, given him a full account of my family, and informed him that I had commanded a regiment of cavalry in the service of the Nabob of Arcot, together with a corps of infantry and artillery attached to it. In consequence of this report, HYAT SAHIB, he said, had interested himself very warmly in my favour, and expressed an anxious desire to render me a service.

Thus far the discourse pleased me. Nothing was said in it to give me alarm; on the contrary, I indulged a hope, that, knowing my rank, and the rank of my father, he would no longer entertain a hope of my entering into the service of HYDER, and for the time I was to be imprisoned, treat me with suitable indulgence. But I flattered myself too soon; or, as the old saying is, "reckoned without my host."

HISTORY OF HYAT SAHIB.

When he had finished his history of HYAT SAHIB, which he overcharged with fulsome panegyric, he told me, with a face full of that triumphant importance which one who thinks he is conferring a great favour generally assumes, that it was the intention of HYAT SAHIB, for and on behalf of his master the Sultan, to give me the command of five thousand men—an offer which he supposed I could not think of declining, and therefore expected no other answer but a profusion of thanks, and strong manifestations of joy on my part.

It is not possible for me to describe to you my dismay at this formal proposal, or pourtray to you the various emotions that took possession of my breast. Resentment had its share—the pride of the soldier, not unaccompanied with the pride of family and rank, while it urged me to spurn from me such a base accommodation, made me consider the offer as a great insult. I therefore paused à little, to suppress my feelings; and then told him my firm resolution, never to accept of such a proposal; and upon his expressing great astonishment at my declining a station so fraught with advantage, I laid down, in the best manner I could, my reasons; and I must say, that he listened to all the objections I started with great patience; but, in the conclusion, said he had little doubt of finding means to overcome my reluctance.

He dismissed me for the present, and I returned to my prison, where I related to my companion, Mr. HALL, every thing that passed between us: we canvassed the matter fully, and he agreed with me, that it was likely to turn out a most dreadful and cruel persecution. It was on this occasion that I first felt the truth of the principle, that persecution never fails to be subversive of its own end, and to promote that which it is intended to destroy. There is, in the human mind, an innate abhorrence of compulsion; and persecution always gives new strength and elasticity to the soul: and at last, when strained to its utmost extent, makes man surmount difficulties which at first seem to be beyond the reach of humanity.

Piqued by the idea of persecution, I began to feel a degree of enthusiasm which I was before a stranger to: I looked forward, with a kind of gloomy pleasure, to the miseries that brutal tyranny might inflict upon me, even to death itself; and already began to indulge the exultation of martyrdom. "No," said I, "my dear HALL! never will I tarnish the character of a British soldier—never will I disgrace my blood or my profession—never shall an act of mine sully the pure fame of my revered father—never shall any sufferings of mine, however poignant, or worldly advantage, however seductive, tempt me to do that which his noble spirit would regard with horror or contempt. I may, and I foresee I must be miserable; but I never will be base or degenerate!" Indeed, I had wrought myself up to such a pitch of firmness, that I am persuaded the most exquisite and refined cruelties which the ingenuity of an Iroquois Indian could have inflicted on my body, would have been utterly incapable of bending the stubborn temper of my mind.

The place in which we were lodged was situated in a way not very favourable to our feelings. Just within sight of it, the commandant of the citadel held a court---by him yclep'd a court of justice---where the most shocking, barbarous cruelties were hourly exercised—most of them for the purpose of extorting money, and compelling the discovery of hidden, or suppositious hidden treasures. Indeed, five sixths of those who suffered were of this description; and the process pursued was as artful as barbarous: they first began with caresses, then proceeded to examination and cross-examination, thence to threats, thence to punishment, and finally, to the most cruel tortures.

HISTORY OF HYAT SAHIB.

Directly opposite to us, was imprisoned an unfortunate person, who had for years been a close captive, and the sport and subject of those enormities. He was a man once of the highest rank in the country where now he was a prisoner: for a series of years he had been govenor and sole manager of the whole province of Biddanore. This was during the reign of the last Rana, or Queen, whose family had been sovereigns of the country for time immemorial, till HYDER made a conquest of, and annexed it to his other usurpations. Unfortunately for him, he was supposed to have amassed and secreted enormous treasures, in consequence of which he had already undergone the fiery ordeal of torture several times. He was supposed to have produced, from first to last, about fifteen lacks of pagodas; and then, in the course of eighteen months, was degraded gradually, from the high respect in which he was at first held, down to a most abject state---threatened, flogged, punished in a variety of ways, and, finally, put to the most cruel tortures. I myself saw him treated with the highest degree of respect, and afterwards brought to the lowest stage of misery and humiliation. One thing, however, I must not forget, is the fortitude with which he and all of them bore their punishment: it was truly heroic---indeed, beyond all belief. Nothing could surpass it, except the skill and inventive ingenuity which the barbarians exhibited in striking out new modes of torture. My soul sickened with horror at the sight: the amiable HALL could worse support it than his own miseries, and lost all that fortitude, in his feeling for others' misfortunes, which he displayed in so unbounded a share in his own: and often, very often, we found the rigour and severity of our own situation utterly forgotten in our anguish and sympathy for the sufferings of others. Never shall I forget it: never shall I think without horror of the accursed policy and wicked tyranny of the Eastern governments, where every sense of humanity is extinguished, and man, more merciless than the tyger, riots in the blood of his fellow-creatures without cause.

Mr. HALL, notwithstanding the various sufferings both of mind and body which he had undergone, began to recruit, and get a little better; and this circumstance, of itself, diffused a flow of spirits over me that contributed to my support. We consoled each other by every means we could devise—sometimes indulging in all the luxury of woe—sometimes rallying each other, and, with ill-dissembled sprightliness, calling on the goddess EUPHROSYNE to come with her "*quirps and cranks, and wreathed smiles:*" but, alas! the mountain nymph, sweet LIBERTY, was far away, and the goddess shunned our abode. We however began to conceive that we might form a system for our relief, and by a methodical arrangement, entrench ourselves from the assaults of grief: to this end, we formed several resolutions, and entered into certain engagements—such as, never to repine at our fate, *if we could*—to draw consolation from the more dreadful lot of others, *if we could;*—and to encourage hope—hope that comes to all; and, on the whole, to confine our conversation as much as possible to subjects of an agreeable nature: but these, like many other rules which we lay down for the conduct of life, were often broken by necessity, and left us to regret the fallibility of all human precautionary systems.

The youth and strength of Mr. HALL was to the full as adequate as mine to the support of any personal hardship: his intellectual powers were excellent, his temper incomparable, and his fortitude unparalleled; yet could I see, that something more than appeared upon the surface wrought within him, and gnawed his heart with hidden pain. United as we were by sentiment, as well as by parity of suffering, I felt for him too deeply, not to have an interesting curiosity to know what it was that preyed upon his mind: we had been, months together, fellow-sufferers; and I thought myself not without some claim to his confidence—I told him so, and desired him to impart to me his story; which he, with his accustomed suavity and condescension, agreed to—assuring me that it was not such a story as could requite the trouble of hearing it, or interest any one but himself, or some very warm friend indeed: such, however, he added, he took me to be; and, as such, would tell it to me. I think it, however, worth relating, and will give it to you in his own words; and, though it be very short, must defer the relation to another letter.

LETTER LI.

Mr. HALL having, as I told you in my last, obligingly agreed to favour me with a relation of his story, I now give it to you as nearly in his own words as I can remember them. He proceeded thus:

"Although you are now, my dear friend! a witness to my being the most perfectly wretched of all created beings, yet the time is not long past when fortune smiled upon and gave me promise of as much happiness as Man in this wretched vale of tears is allowed by his circumscribed nature to hope for. I have seen the time, when each revolving sun rose to usher me to a day of joy, and set to consign me to a night of undisturbed repose—when the bounties of Nature, and the productions of Art, were poured with the profusion of fond paternal affection into my lap—when troops of friends hailed my rising prospects—when health and peace made this person their uninterrupted abode—and when the most benignant love that ever blessed a mortal filled up the measure of my bliss. Yes, CAMPBELL! it was once my happiness, though now, alas! the source of poignant misery, to be blessed with the best parents that ever watched over the welfare of a child—with friends, too, who loved me, and whom my heart cherished—and—O God! do I think of her, and yet retain my senses—with the affections of a young lady, than whom providence, in the fullness of its power and bounty to mankind, never formed one more lovely, one more angelic in person, more heavenly in disposition, more rich in intellectual endowments. Alas! my friend, will you, can you pardon those warm ebullitions of a fond passion? will you for a moment enter into my feelings, and make allowance for those transports? But how can you? Your friendship and pity may indeed induce you to excuse this interruption; but, to sympathise truly, and feel as I feel, you must have known the charming girl herself.

"My father, though he did not move in the very first walk of life, held the rank of a Gentleman by birth and education, and was respectable, not only as a man of considerable property, but as a person who knew how to turn the gifts of fortune to their best account: he was generous without prodigality, and charitable without ostentation: he was allowed by all who knew him to be the most tender of husbands—the most zealous and sincere of friends; and I can bear witness to his being the best of parents. As long as I can remember to have been able to make a remark, the tenderness of both my father and mother knew no bounds: I seemed to occupy all their thoughts, all their attention; and in a few years, as I thank God I never made an unsuitable return for their affection, it increased to such a degree, that their existence seemed to hang upon mine.

"To make so much of a child so beloved as his natural talents would allow, no expence was spared in my education: from childhood, every instruction that money could purchase, and every allurement to learn, that fondness could suggest, were bestowed upon me: while my beloved father tracing the advances I made with the magnifying eye of affection, would hang over me in rapture, and enjoy by anticipation the fame and honours that, overweening fondness suggested to him, must one day surround me. These prejudices, my dear friend! arising from the excess of natural affection, are excuseable, if not amiable, and deserve a better fate than disappointment. Alas! my honoured father, you little knew—and, oh! may you never know, what sort of fame, what sort of honours, await your child! May the anguish he endures, and his most calamitious fate, never reach your ears!—for, too well I know, 'twould give a deadly wrench to your heart, and precipitate you untimely to your grave.

"Thus years rolled on; during which, time seemed to have added new wings to his flight, so quickly did they pass. Unmarked by any of those sinister events that parcel out the time in weary stages to the unfortunate, it slid on unperceived; and an enlargement in my size, and an increase of knowledge, were all I had to inform me that eighteen years had passed away.

It was at this time that I first found the smooth current of my tranquility interrupted, and the tide of my feelings swelled and agitated, by the accession of new streams of sensation—In short I became a slave to the delicious pains of Love; and, after having borne them in concealment for a long time, at length collected courage to declare it. Frankness and candour were among the virtues of my beloved: she listened to the protestations of affection, and, rising above the little arts of her sex, avowed a reciprocal attachment. The measure of my bliss seemed now to be full; the purity of my passion was such, that the thoughts of the grosser animal desires never once occured; and happy in loving, and being beloved, we passed our time in all the innocent blandishments which truly virtuous love inspires, without our imagination roaming even for an instant into the wilds of sensuality.

"As I was to inherit a genteel, independent fortune, my father proposed to breed me up to a learned profession—the Law; rather to invigorate and exercise my intellects, and as a step to rank in the state, than for mere lucrative purposes. I was put to one of the universities, with an allowance suited to his intentions towards me; and was immediately to have been sent to travel for my further improvement, when an unforeseen accident happened, which immediately crushed all my fathers views, dashed the cup of happiness from my lips, and brought me ultimately to that deplorable state in which you have now the misfortune to be joined along with me.

"It was but a few months antecedent to my embarking for the eastern world, that my father, whom I had for some time with sorrow observed thoughtful, studious and melancholy, took me into his study, and, seizing my hand, and looking earnestly into my face, while his countenance betrayed the violent agitation of his mind, asked me emphatically, if I thought I had fortitude to bear the greatest possible calamity? I was horror-struck at his emotion, accompanied by such a question— but replied, I hoped I had. He then asked me if I had affection enough for him to forgive him if he was the cause of it? I answered, that the idea connected with the word *forgiveness*, was that which I could never be brought by any earthly circumstance to apply to my father; but begged him at once to disclose the worst to me—as, be it what it might, my misery could not surpass what I then felt from the mysterious manner in which he then spoke.

"He then told me that he was an undone man—that he had, with the very best intentions, and with the view of aggrandizing me, engaged in great and important speculations, which, had they succeeded, would have given us a princely fortune—but, having turned out, unfortunately, the reverse, had left him little above beggary. He added, that he had not the resolution to communicate his losses to me, until necessity compelled him to tell me all the truth.

"Although this was a severe shock to me, I endeavoured to conceal my feelings from my father, on whose account, more than on my own, I was affected, and pretended to make as light of it as so very important a misfortune would justify; and I had the happiness to perceive that the worthy man took some comfort from my supposed indifference. I conjured him not to let so very trivial a thing as the loss of property, which could be repaired, break in on his peace of mind or health; which could not; and observed to him, that we had all of us still enough—for that my private property (which I possessed independent of him, and which a relation left me) would amply supply all our necessities.

"Having thus endeavoured to accommodate my unhappy father's feelings to his losses, I had yet to accommodate my own; and began to revolve in my mind what was likely to ensue from, and what step was most proper to be taken, in this dreadful change of circumstances. That which lay nearest my heart first occurred;—you will readily guess that I mean my love; to involve her I loved more, far more, than my life, in the misfortunes of my family, was too horrible a consideration to be outweighed even by the dread of losing her. I knew not what to do, and I thought upon it till I became almost enfrenzied—In this state I went to her, and unfolded the whole state of our concerns, together with my resolution not to involve her in our ruin;—when---can you believe it?---the lovely girl insisted on making my fate indissolubly her's---not, as she said, that she had the smallest apprehension lapse of time or change of circumstance could make an alteration in our affection, but that she wished to give my mind that repose which I might derive from security. This I would by no means accede to; and, for the present, we contented ourselves with mutual vows of eternal fidelity.

" As soon as I thought my father's mind fit for such a conversation, I opened to him a plan I had formed of coming to India, to advance my fortune. His understanding approved of it, but his heart dissented; and he said, that to part with me would give the finishing stroke to his misfortunes; but, as my interest was tolerably good, I represented to him the great likelihood I had of success; and at last, with some difficulty, he consented.

" My next step was to acquaint Miss ——— with my resolution. I purposely pass over a meeting which no power of language can describe!—then how can I?—Oh! CAMPBELL, the remembrance of it gnaws me like a vulture here," (and he put his hand upon his heart, while the tears rolled down his cheeks), " and will soon, soon bring me to my end.

" Not to detain you with vain efforts to describe all our feelings, I will confine myself to telling you that after having made every necessary preparation, and divided with my much honoured parents the little property I possessed, I set sail for India, in a state of mind compared with which the horrors of annihilation would have been enviable: the chaos in my thoughts made me insensible to every object but one; and I brooded with a sort of stupid, gloomy indulgence, over the portrait of Miss ———, which hung round my neck, and was my inseparable companion, till the people who seized me as I came ashore plundered me of it, and thereby deprived me of the last refuge for comfort I had left. Oh! monsters! barbarians! had you glutted your savage fury by dissevering my limbs, one after another, from my body, it would have been mercy, compared with depriving me of that little image of her I love! But it is all over, and I shall soon sink into the grave, and never more be blessed with the view of those heavenly features, till we meet in that region where all tears are wiped away, and where, I trust, we shall be joined together for endless ages, in eternal, never-fading bliss!"

LETTER LII.

"ON the day succeeding that on which the agent of HYAT SAHIB had held the discourse with me, mentioned in my last letter but one, I was again sent for, and brought to the same person, who asked me, whether I had duly considered of the important offer made me by HYAT SAHIB, and of the consequences likely to result from a refusal? and he apprised me at the same time, that the command of five thousand men was an honour which the first Rajahs in the Mysorean dominions would grasp at with transport. I told him I was well convinced of the honour such a command would confer on any man but an Englishman, whose country being the object of HYDER's incessant hostility, would make the acceptance of it infamy—that although I knew there were but too many Englishmen apostates to their country, I hoped there were but few to be found in India willing to accept of any emoluments, however great, or any temptations, however specious, to fly from the standard of their country, and rally round that of its bitterest enemy---that, for my own part, being of a name ever foremost in the ranks of loyalty and patriotism, and of a family that had hitherto detracted nothing from the honours of that name, such an act of apostacy would be peculiarly infamous in me, and I could view it in no better light than traitorous and parricidal---that, independent of all those claims, which were of themselves sufficient to deter me, I felt within myself a principle, perhaps innate, perhaps inspired by military habit, that forbade my acceding---and, finally, appealed to the good sense of HYAT SAHIB, whether a man who in such circumstances had betrayed his country, and sacrificed her interests to his own convenience, was such a person as confidence could properly be put in.

Notwithstanding these, and a thousand other remonstrances, which I cannot immediately recollect, but which the hazards of my situation suggested, he still continued to press me, and used every argument, every persuasion, that ingenuity could dictate, or hints of punishment enforce, to shake my purpose—but in vain: attachment to country and family rose paramount to all other considerations; and I gave a peremptory, decisive refusal.

Circumstanced as I was, it was impossible for me to keep an accurate journal of the various incidents that passed, or vicissitudes of thought that occurred, during the period of my imprisonment. Indeed, I was scarcely conscious of the length of my captivity, and could not, till I was released, determine exactly how long it had continued. You must therefore content yourself to be told in general terms, that I was repeatedly urged on the subject by fair persuasives: they then had recourse to menace; then they withheld the daily pittance allowed for my support; and at length proceeded to coercion, tying a rope round my neck, and hoisting me up to a tree. All this, however, I bore firmly: if it had any effect, it was to confirm me in my resolution, and call in policy to the aid of honour's dictates. Every man of feeling or reason must allow, that it was better to die, than live a life of subjection to tyranny so truly diabolical.

Mr. HALL and I, thus drove to the brink of extinction, yet consoled ourselves with the reflection, that those whom most we loved were not sharing our unhappy fate, and were fortunately ignorant of our sufferings; and as I enjoyed perfect good health, hope yet lived within me.

There is a spring, an elasticity, in every man's mind, of which the owner is rarely, very rarely conscious, because fortunately the occasions seldom occur in which it can be brought to the proof, for, as lassitude is the necessary forerunner of refreshment, so is extreme dejection to the most vigorous exercise of our fortitude. So I found it: as the horrors of my situation thickened round me, I felt my spirits increase; my resolution became more firm, my hopes more sanguine---I even began to look forward, and form projects for the future: whole hours amusement, every day and every night, arose from the contemplation of my beloved boy; I in imagination traced his growth, directed his rising sentiments, formed plans for his future success and prosperity, and indulged by anticipation in all the enjoyment which I now trust I shall yet have in his ripened manhood.

Thus we continued for many months, during which no alteration whatsoever took place in our treatment or situation. We heard a thousand contradictory reports of victories gained over the English, and again of some successes on their part: they, however, desisted to press me into their service. The only relief from our sufferings lay in the resources of our own minds, and in our mutual endevours to please and console one another: the circumstances of aggravation were the necessity of daily bearing witness to the most barbarous punishments he inflicted upon wretched individuals under the semblance of justice, and the occasional deprivation of our food, either by the fraud of the sepoys who attended us, or the caprice or cruelty of their superiors. It is but justice, however, to say, that they were not all alike: some overflowed with mercy, charity, and the milk of human kindness; while others, again, were almost as bad men as the sovereigns they served. We were not allowed the use of pen, ink, or paper; and very seldom could afford ourselves the luxury of shaving, or clean linen: nor were we at all sheltered from the inclemency of the weather, till at length a little room was built for us of mud, which being small and damp, rendered our situation worse than it was before.

The prisoner whom I have already mentioned, as having, in the time of the former sovereign, held the first office in Bidanore, still continued opposite to me; and he and I at length began to understand each other, and found means, by looks, signs and gestures, to exchange thoughts, and hold an intercourse of sentiments together. From the circumstance of his being a native, and better skilled in the language than me, he had much better intelligence than I could possibly have, and he was always eager to convey to me any circumstance or news that he thought might be agreeable: some messages also passed between us, by means of the sepoys who had alternately been his guard and mine —for our guards were changed every week.

Projects and hopes of a new kind now began to intrude themselves on my thoughts; and I conceived a design, which I flattered myself was not entirely impracticable to effect an escape, and even a revolt in the place. A variety of circumstances concurred to persuade me, that the tyranny of HYDER, and his servant HYAT SAHIB, was abhorred, though none dared to give vent to their sentiments. I thought I could observe, that the native prisoner opposite to me was privately beloved, and might, from the recollection of his former dignities, have considerable influence in the place. Several Arcot sepoys and their officers (some of them belonging to my own regiment) were also prisoners at large; and withal I recollected, that difficulties apparently more stupendous had been overcome by Englishmen—having often heard it asserted, that there was not a prison in the known world out of which a British subject had not made his escape.

Fraught with those conceptions, I attempted to sound the officers of the Arcot Sepoys, whether it were not possible for us to effect our escape? So ardent is the flame of liberty in all men's breasts, so great is the detestation of human nature to slavery, that I perceived a manifest willingness in the people about us to join me in an attempt to procure our liberty, or bring about a revolt in the garrison. My heart beat high with the hope; and I began to flatter myself, that, the day was not far removed when we should not only bid defiance to our tyrants, but even make them repent the day on which we were cast ashore on their coast.

Having thus distantly sounded all who I thought were likely to concur, upon the practicability of the attempt, and found them, as I conceived, disposed to take share in it, it yet remained to consider of the *quomodo*—and, after having formed the general outlines of a plan, to lick it into shape. The first of these was a critical consideration: the second required address and management, and was likely to be impeded by the vigilance of the people about, who would not fail to remark, and take the alarm, from any unusual intercourse or discourse between us; and without a mutual communication of thoughts, and full deliberation by all parties concerned, as well as knowledge of the fort and its different gates, nothing could, with any prospect of success, be determined---nothing, without the most imminent hazard, be attempted. I therefore held various councils with my own mind, and with Mr. HALL, on the subject---most of which were abortive, without at all discouraging us.

At last I began to think of sounding the Bidanore prisoner, *ci-devant* governor of the place; and determined, if possible, to bring him into our consultations, as I had before hoped to make him a party in the execution of the project: but while I was settling all this much to my own satisfaction, an event occured which extinguished all my hopes in that way—of which you shall have an account in my next letter.

LETTER LIII.

WHETHER the plan which I mentioned in my last was discovered or not, or from what other motive it arose, I have not to this day been able to decide; but so it was, that while my sanguine mind was overflowing with the hope of carrying my project for an escape into effect, Mr. HALL and I were one day unexpectedly loaded with irons, and fastened together, leg by leg, by one bolt. This, as nearly as I can compute, was four or five months before my release. Of all the circumstances of my life, it has made the strongest impression upon my mind: it unexpectedly and suddenly broke down the most pleasing fabric my imagination had ever built. The surprise occasioned by the appearance of the irons, and the precautionary manner in which it was undertaken, was indeed great: still more was I surprised to observe, that the person who was employed to see this put in execution, manifested unusual emotions, seemed much affected, and even shed tears as he looked on: and while the suddenness and cautionary mode of doing it convinced me that some resistance on our part was apprehended, the sorrow which the officer who superintended it disclosed, portended in my mind a fatal, or at least a very serious issue.

Unfortunately, poor Mr. HALL had for some time been afflicted with a return of his dreadful disorder, the dysentery; and our being shackled together increased an unconquerable mortification of feelings which we had before undergone, from a delicacy of nature that would have done honour to the most modest virgin, be her sensibility ever so exquisite, or her delicacy ever so extreme—And here, my dear FREDERICK! I cannot let slip this opportunity of remarking to you, that the man, as well as the woman, who would render himself truly amiable in the eyes of his fellow-creatures, should cultivate delicacy and modesty, as the most captivating of all the moral virtues: from them, heroism derives additional lustre—wit, ten-fold force—religion and morality, the charms of persuasion—and every personal action of the man, irresistible dignity and winning grace. From this unlucky event, I received a temporary depression; and the rapidly increasing illness of poor HALL rendered my situation more than ever calamitous; when, again, my spirits, eagerly prone to grasp at every thing that gave a momentary hope of support, were a little recruited by confused rumours of the

English army having made a descent on the Malabar coast: and so powerful is the influence of mind on the animal system, that Mr. HALL enjoyed from the report a momentary alleviation of his malady; but, having no medical assistance, nor even sufficient sustenance to further the favourable operations of nature, he relapsed again; the disease fell upon him with redoubled fury: a very scanty portion of boiled rice, with a more scanty morsel of stinking salt fish or putrid flesh, was a very inadequate support for me, who, though emaciated, was in health —and very improper medicine for a person labouring under a malady such as Mr. HALL's, which required comfort, good medical skill, and delicate nutritious food. The tea which HYAT SAHIB had given me was expended; and we were not allowed to be shaved from the hour we were put in irons, an indulgence of that kind being forbidden by the barbarous rules of the prison: and, to refine upon our tortures sleep, "the balm of hurt minds," was not allowed us uninterrupted; for, in conformity to another regulation, we were disturbed every half hour by a noise something resembling a watchman's rattle, and a fellow who, striking every part of our irons with a kind of hammer, and examining them lest they should be cut, broke in upon that kind restorative, and awoke our souls to fresh horrors.

As it must be much more naturally matter of astonishment that any bodily strength could support itself under such complicated calamities, than that infirmity should sink beneath them, you will be rather grieved than surprised to hear that poor Mr. HALL was now approaching to his end with hourly accelerated steps. Every application that I made in his favour was refused, or rather treated with cruel neglect and contemptuous silence; and I foresaw, with inexpressible anguish and indignation, that the barbarians would not abate him in his last minutes one jot of misery, and that my most amiable friend was fated to expire under every attendant horror that mere sublunary circumstances could create. But that pity which the mighty, the powerful and enlightened denied, natural benevolence operating upon an uninformed mind, and scanty means, afforded us. HYAT SAHIB, the powerful, the wealthy, the governor of a great opulent province, refused to an expiring fellow-creature a little cheap relief—while a poor sepoy taxed his little means to supply it: one who guarded us, of his own accord, at hazard of imminent punishment, purched us a lamp and a little oil, which we burned for the last few nights.

Philosophers and divines have declaimed upon the advantages of a well-spent life, as felt *in articulo mortis;* and their efforts have had, I hope, some effect upon the lives of many. To witness one example such as Mr. HALL held forth, would be worth volumes of precepts on this subject. The unfeigned resignation with which he met his dissolution, and the majestic fortitude with which he looked in the face the various circumstances of horror that surrounded him, rendered him the most dignified object I ever beheld or conceived, and the most glorious instance of conscious virtue triumphing over the terrors of death, and the cunning barbarity of mankind. Were the progress of virtue attended with pain, and the practice of vice with pleasure, the adoption of the former would be amply repaid by its soothings in the dreadful moment, even if it were to accompany us no further. About a quarter of an hour before he died, Mr. HALL broached a most tender subject of conversation, which he followed up with a series of observations, so truly refined, so exquisitely turned, so delicate and so pathetic, that it seemed almost the language of inspiration, as if, in proportion to the decay of the body, intellect increased, and the dying man had become all mind. Such a conversation I never remembered to have heard, or heard of. Its effects upon me were wonderful; for, though the combination of melancholy circumstances attending my now critical situation had almost raised my mind to frenzy, the salutary influence of his words and example controuled the excesses of my sensations; and I met the afflicting moment of his departure with a degree of tranquility, which, though not to be compared to his, has on reflection appeared to me astonishing. This conversation continued to the very instant of his death; during which time he held my hand clasped in his, frequently enforcing his kind expressions to me with a squeeze—while my sorrow, taking its most easy channel, bedewed my face with tears. As he proceeded, my voice was choaked with my feelings; and I attempted once or twice in vain to speak. His hand grew cold: he said his lower limbs were all lifeless, and that he felt death coming over him with slow creeping steps—He again moralized, thanking GOD with pathetic fervour for his great mercy in leaving him his intellects unclouded, and the organ of communication (the tongue) unenfeebled, that, to the last, he might solace his friend and fellow-sufferer—" Ah! CAMPBELL!" continued he, " to what a series of miseries am I now leaving you! death in such circumstances is a blessing—I view mine as such; and should think it more so, if it contributed, by awakening those people to a sense of their cruelty, to soften their rigour to you: but cruelty like their's is systematic, and stoops not to the controul of the feelings. Could I hope that you would yet escape from their clutches, and that you would once more press your family to your bosom, the thought would brighten still the moment of our separation: and, oh! my friend! could I still further hope that you would one day see my most beloved and honoured parents, and tell them of my death without wringing their hearts with its horrid circumstances, offer them my last duties, and tell how I revered them—If, too, you could see my ———, and tell her how far, far more dear than———!" Here he turned his eyes toward the lamp, then faintly on me—made a convulsive effort to squeeze my hand—cried out, " CAMPBELL! oh, CAMPBELL! the lamp is going out!" and expired without a groan.

 The recital of this afflicting event has called up to my fancy so lively a picture of the scene as it passed with all its horrors—horrors which outstrip all efforts of description, and baffle all power of language—that my feelings are in part renewed, and I find myself incapable of proceeding further at present.

LETTER LIV.

FOR some time I was lost in grief for the death of Mr. HALL. Though I had long expected it, and might consequently be supposed to have wasted great part of my sorrow in anticipation; yet, having only considered and felt the point before his death merely as it respected him and his misfortunes, a great portion of the calamity yet remained unconceived: and, now that he was dead, I began for the first time to consider and feel the subject as it concerned myself. Reflection told me, that he was happily relieved from woe, and in a state of bliss—

> " After life's fitful fever, he sleeps well;
> " ——————— Nor steel nor poison,
> " Malice domestic, foreign levy—nothing
> " Can touch him further!"

But I still remained a prey to perhaps new barbarities, without hope of relief from the old. No partner to share, no social converse to alleviate, no friend to console me under my afflictions, I looked at the body of my friend with envy, and lamented that death had not afforded me, too, a shelter from the cruelties which fate seemed determined to heap upon me.

It is impossible for me to express to you the agonies of mind I underwent during the rest of the night. In the morning a report was made to the commandant, of the death of Mr. HALL; and in about an hour after, he passed me by, but kept his face purposely turned away from me to the other side. I patiently waited for the removal of the dead body till the evening, when I desired the Sepoys who guarded me to apply for its being removed. They returned, and told me that they could get no answer respecting it. Night came on, but there was no appearance of an intention to unfetter me from the corpse. The commandant was sitting in his court, administering, in the manner I have before described, *justice!* I called out to him myself with all my might, but could get no answer from him. Nothing could equal my rage and consternation; for, exclusive of the painful idea of being shackled to the dead body of a friend I loved, another circumstance contributed to make it a serious subject of horror. In those climates the weather is so intensely hot, that putrefaction almost instantly succeeds death, and meat that is killed in the morning, and kept in the shade, will be unfit for dressing at night. In a subject, then, on which putrefaction had made advances even before death, and which remained exposed to the open air, the process must have been much more rapid. So far, however, from compassionating my situation, or indulging me by a removal of the body, their barbarity suggested to them to make it an instrument of punishment; and they pertinaciously adhered to the most mortifying silence and disregard of my complaints. For several days and nights it remained attached to me by the irons. I grew almost distracted—wished for the means of putting an end to my miseries by death, and could not move without witnessing some new stage of putrescence it attained, or breathe without inhaling the putrid effluvia that arose from it—while myriads of flies and loathsome insects rested on it, the former of which every now and then visited me, crawling over my face and hands, and lighting in hundreds on my victuals. I never look back at this crisis without confusion, horror, and even astonishment; and, were it not connected with a chain of events preceding and subsequent to it, too well known by respectable people to be doubted, and too much interwoven with a part of the history of the last war in India to admit of a doubt, I should not only be afraid to tell, but absolutely doubt myself whether the whole was not the illusion of a dream, rather than credit the possibility of my enduring such unheard of hardships without loss of life or deprivation of senses.

At last, when the body had reached that shocking loathsome state of putrefaction which threatened that further delay would render removal abominable, if not impossible, the monsters agreed to take it away from me—and I was so far relieved: but the mortification and injury I underwent from it, joined to the agitation of the preceding week, made a visible inroad on my health. I totally lost my spirits; my appetite entirely forsook me: my long-nourished hopes fled; and I looked forward to death as the only desirable event that was within the verge of likelihood or possibility.

One day, my opposite friend (the native prisoner) gave me a look of the most interesting and encouraging kind; and I perceived a more than usual bustle in the citadel, while the sepoys informed me that they were ordered on immediate service, and that some events of great importance had taken place. From this feeble gleam, my mind, naturally active, though depressed by circumstances of unusual weight, again took fire, and hope brightened with a kind of gloomy light the prospect before me: I revolved a thousand things, and drew from them a thousand surmises; but all as yet was only conjecture with me. In a day or two, the bustle increased to a high pitch, accompanied with marks of consternation: the whole of the troops in the citadel were ordered to march; and the commandant, and a man with a hammar and instruments, came to take off my irons.

While they were at work taking off my irons, I perceived they were taking off those of the native prisoner opposite to me also. He went away under a guard: we looked at each other complacently, nodded and smiled, as who should say, "we hope to see one another in happier times not far distant." But, alas! vain are human hopes, and short and dark is the extent of our utmost foresight! This unhappy man, without committing any sort of offense to merit it, but in conformity to the damnable, barbarous polity of those countries, was, by the Jemadar's orders, taken forth, and his throat cut! This the Jemadar himself afterwards acknowledged to me—and, what was still more abominable if possible, undertook to justify the proceeding upon the principles of reason, sound sense, and precedent of Asiatic policy.

In order to elucidate the whole of this business, it is necessary for me to recur to events which happened antecedent to this time, but of which, by reason of my situation, I was then entirely ignorant; and as they involve, not only the grounds of my subsequent escape and proceedings, but a considerable portion of historical fact, and some of the material interests of the East India Company,

I will be the more particularly careful in relating them, and desire from you a proportionate share of attention—But their importance entitle them to a separate letter: therefore conclude with assuring you, &c. &c.

LETTER LV.

HYDER ALLI KHAWN, late Nabob of Mysore, and father to the present TIPPO SAHIB SULTAIN, was as extraordinary a man, and perhaps possessed as great natural talents, as any recorded in the page of history. Born and bred up in the lowest ranks of an unenlightened and ignorant people, and to the last day of his life perfectly illiterate, he not only emerged from his native obscurity by the vigor of his mind and body, but became an object of terror and admiration to surrounding potentates. Early initiated in the habits and inured to the toils of a military life, he rose, by the gradual steps of promotion, to a rank which afforded an opportunity of displaying his capacity and prowess: he soon obtained the command of that army in which he had once served as a common soldier, and immediately demonstrated that the sublimity of his mind was formed to keep pace with his extraordinary elevation.

The Marhattas, the most formidable people in Hither India, bordered on the Mysorean dominions, and kept their neighbours, by frequent hostilities, in a continual state of awe—making incursions on their territories, and taking possession, by force of arms, of large portions of their country: but no sooner had HYDER got the command of the armies of his country, than he drove back the Marhattas from the Myforean dominions, which he extended by confiderable acquifitions from the Marhatta frontiers; and followed up his conquefts with fuch fuccefsful ardour, that he compelled that warlike nation to refpect his countrymen as their equals, if not fuperiors, in military achievement. Thus, while he ingratiated himfelf with his fovereign and fellow-citizens by his wifdom, he acquired the admiration of the foldiery by his perfonal addrefs and valour; and at the fame time, by the feverity of his decipline, and the occafional aufterity of his deportmet, maintained an awe over them, which ftrengthened his authority with diminifhing their affection.

HYDER was therefore now arrived at that point of elevation, beyond which no exertion of mental capacity, if governed by virtue or integrity, could raife him—So far he owed all to guenius: but his towering ambition looked higher; and, unreftrained by any principle of religion or morality, he determined to accomplifh, at any rate, that which he knew nothing but crime could accomplifh. With wicked deliberation he looked forward into the womb of time, and with unparalleled policy arranged the whole fyftem upon which he was to act, when that order of things his penetrating and intuitive genius enabled him to fee would naturally arife from each other, fhould afford him a proper opportunity. Although he was utterly ignorant of books, and of courfe could derive little benefit from the examples of the great and ambitious men recorded in hiftory, yet, drawing upon the infinite refources of his own mind for information, he adopted the very fame means of furthering his views; and forefeeing, that, with an immenfe army devoted to his interefts, few things would be unattainable, he applied himfelf diligently to model and form that of the KING of MYSORE to the greateft perfection in difcipline, and to render it attached to his person, and subservient to his views, by a skilful mixture of severity and relaxation, toil and reward, danger and applause, which none but a master-hand like his was capable of exactly compounding.

The death of his sovereign the KING of MYSORE at length afforded him the opportunity to which he had so long, and with so prophetic an eye, looked forward—and gave him ample room for self-gratulation on the score of his sagacity and prudence.

The heir in succession to the throne being then an infant, the politic HYDER, setting aside all claims of the kindred of the young prince, took upon himself the guardianship—under the title of Regent assumed the supreme authority—and, though too well aware of the inviolable attachment of the people to their lawful monarch to put him directly to death, usurped the throne, and consigned him to imprisonment in Seringapatam, the capital of the Mysorean dominions.

Having thus, by his talents, acquired the possession of the throne, he gave a large range to the sublimity of his views, and soon displayed the exhaustless resources of his mind in the new office of Governor and Legislator—forming such vast well-ordered military establishments, and such judicious and salutary civil institutions, as made him blaze forth at once the terror of his neighbours, and rendered him, in the sequel, the most powerful and formidable potentate in the Hither Peninsula. In carrying on those, his deficiency in letters was supplied by his vigilance and sagacity, sharpened by suspicion: three secretaries executed all his orders in separate apartments: and if, on comparison, they were found to differ, he who committed the error received sentence of death. His natural cruelty made him take the execution of their sentence upon himself not unfrequently: to slice off a head with his own hand, or see it done by others, was a luxurious recreation to the sanguinary HYDER.

The natural sagacity of this great man suggested, that in order to accomplish the extensive objects which his active and ambitious temper held up to his imagination, the introduction of the most perfect military discipline was above all other things necessary; and his judgment informed him that the European was the best. He therefore held out the most tempting allurements to military adventures, and particularly to those, whether black or white, who had been trained in the service of the English East India company: he sent emissaries, for the purpose, to all parts of India, with instructions to offer great rewards; and carried this design so far, that whenever accident or war threw persons of that description into his hands, he never failed to detain them, and, if they refused to enter into his service, treat them with the most unpardonable rigour and barbarity; and by these means brought his army to a state of perfection till then unknown to a black power. He did not stop there, but determined to establish a navy—by large offers allured many ship-carpenters and artizans from Bombay—made no inconsiderable progress in constructing dock-yards, and had actually equiped some ships of the line, besides frigates, fitted to encounter European seas. Indeed, he seemed to have carried his views of conquest even to the Polar regions; for it is a fact, that he directed his people, in constructing those vessels, to fit them for encountering seas of ice, or, as he called it, the thick water.

To a man of such ardent ambition and deep penetration, the vast power which the English East India company had acquired, and were daily acquiring, in the East, could not fail to be an object of jealousy. He conceived a deadly and implacable animosity to the British Nation, which influenced his whole succeeding life, ended only with his death, and was then transmitted to his son Tippoo Sahib, with the exaction of a solemn oath, ever to retain those sentiments.

A coincidence of circumstances, which has seldom occured in the fortunes of men, tended, at a lucky crisis, to further the bold projects of Hyder; and neither fortune, though extremely propitious to him, nor his own unbounded talents and energetic spirit, favoured the execution of them, more than the bungling politics, the ludicrous ambition, and the consequent unjustifiable proceedings, of one of our Presidencies in India—I mean Bombay. Fortunately, the wisdom and moderation of our East India councils at this day, vindicate the wounded character of the British nation, and justify me in the remarks I make.

An ambitious and profligate chief of the Marhatta Tribes—his name Raganaut Row—had been deposed by the wise men of his country, for having murdered his nephew, in order to usurp the throne of Setterah. He fled to Bombay, and, by specious promises and other means, prevailed on that Presidency to afford him an asylum, and finally to take up arms in his defence against the united Marhatta States, who at the very time were able to raise an army of three hundred thousand fighting men. Hostilities were first commenced by the English; and by them peace was first proposed. The treaty of Poonah was made, by which it was provided that Raganaut Row would quit Bombay; and by the English the provisions of that treaty were broken—for, in direct violation of it Raganaut was kept at Bombay. This breach of the treaty led to another; for this crafty and unprincipled chief made use of it with such address as to persuade that Presidency to attack the Marhattas again:—by magnifying the power of his party among his countrymen, he prevailed upon them once more to affert his rights; and the Prefidency of Calcutta, I am afraid, were induced to join that of Bombay in the plan.

It happened unfortunately, that at this time the Prefidency of Bombay was compofed of perfons the moft unqualified, probably, that could be found in any community for offices of fuch importance. One, particularly, was allowed, by the almoft unanimous confent of thofe who knew his private or public character, to be ignorant, not only of the firft principles of government, but of the ordinary knowledge requifite for a gentleman; and for fituations of moment he was peculiarly difqualified by a fondnefs for minutiæ, to which he paid more attention than to matters of greater confequence. A temper and intellect of this kind were rendered ftill more incapable of the enlarged views any Reprefentative of a great Nation in a diftant colony fhould poffefs, by a mercantile education and habits, which narrowed even his circumfcribed mind, and left him not a fentiment, not an idea, that was not merely commercial. The adminiftration of fuch men was exactly what might have been expected; and, inftead of afferting the dignity of Great Britain, or promoting the advantage of their employers—narrow policy, felfifh views, and efforts arifing from miftaken notions of conqueft, made the whole tiffue of their conduct in India.

Blinded by the plaufible infinuations of RAGANAUT, and ftimulated, as I have already obferved, by a luft for conqueft, which would have been unjuftifiable even in an hereditary defpot, but which were peculiarly vicious and ridiculous in a body of merchants who were themfelves fubjects, the Eaft India company's fervants again determined to fupport, by force of arms, that moft atrocious murderer: and with the contemptibly inadequate force of four thoufand men, encumbered with an unwieldy train of baggage and fervants for the accommodation of finikin voluptuous officers, and led by two doughty compting-houfe champions (CARNAC and MOSTYN), with colonel EGERTON as *military affiftant* rather than commander, they fet out, to encounter the whole torrent of the Marhatta force, and conduct RAGANAUT to Poonah.

Had RAGANAUT advanced at the head of his own partizans only, the chiefs of the Marhatta Nation might poffibly have taken different fides of the queftion, and left between them a breach for his arms or intrigues to make an entrance fatal to the general caufe of the country: but the affaults of a foreign army—an army of interefted peculating ftrangers, as the company's troops then were—an army of avowed natural enemies, profeffing a different religion, entertaining different political principles, and formed by nature of a different complexion—roufed and united them in one common caufe, and compreffed difcordant interefts, which had been for time immemorial at irreconcilable variance, into one compact body of refiftance, which, as it became more firm from the ftrokes of hoftility, could not, in the nature of things, be fubdued; in the fame manner as the unjuftifiable confederacy of kings againft France lately united all the conflicting parties of that country—converted twenty-feven millions of people, male and female, into one compact armed force—rendered them not only invincible at home, but terrible abroad—and finally, has enabled them to beftride, Coloffus like, the univerfe.

LETTER LVI.

THE approach of the British troops with RAGANAUT caused great alarm at Poonah; and the ministers there sent to offer terms, which were contemptuously rejected. They then determined to save, by prowess, those rights which they could not preserve by justice or negociation—and took the field with such great force, that their menacing enemies found it expedient to consider of a retreat. The *faithful* RAGANAUT, finding his plans baffled, sent privately to SCINDIAH, the Marhatta chief, proposing to him to attack the English, and promising in that case to join him with his part of the army: his perfidy, however, being discovered, the English commanders began to retreat, carrying him along with them. They were, however, surrounded, and reduced to make the most abject concessions—offering a *carte-blanche* to SCINDIAH as the price of a retreat: but that august chief nobly disdained to take advantage of their situation, and contented himself with terms which justice should have exacted from them, even if necessity had not compelled their acceptance. The restoration of Salsette; and of the other conquests made by the company's troops during the preceding hostilities, and the delivery of RAGANAUT's person into the hands of the Marhattas, were among the provisions. RAGANAUT was delivered up: two hostages were taken for the remaining part of the treaty; and the harrassed remains of the English army were permitted to return to Bombay.

RAGANAUT having found means to escape, reached Surat; and the company's chiefs refused to comply with the provisions of the treaty: notwithstanding which, the noble Marhatta dismissed the hostages, and prepared for a more manly revenge than that which could be wreaked on two defenceless individuals. General GODDART, who had been sent with an army from Bengal, was commissioned to negociate for a pacification: but SCINDIAH making the delivery of RAGANAUT into his hands an indispensable preliminary, the negociation was broken off, and both parties determined to refer the controversy to the decision of the sword.

Every thing seemed to conspire to chastise the rashness and folly of our Indian councils. The difficulties in which our American contest had involved the nation, were reported with exaggeration in India, and gave additional firmness to our enemies in that quarter. The restless and intriguing spirit of the court of Versailles found its way with Monsieur ST. LUBIN to the shores of Indostan, and so powerfully worked upon the mind of HYDER, that he entered into a treaty with France against England, and brought the strength of both into the most formidable combination that ever was made in that country, to root out the power of Great Britain from the East.

Thus, by the depraved politics of the councils of a petty settlement, were the important interests of Great Britain in India, and the lives and properties of all its servants in that quarter, at once exposed to the fury of three formidable hostile powers—the Marhattas, HYDER and the French.

I will not entangle my narrative with a detail of the various military operations which arose from this confederacy: they were in general disastrous to the English, whose power there was preserved from utter annihilation by the energetic councils of Mr. HASTINGS, the unexampled courage of our troops, and the unparalleled abilities and gallantry of the veteran Sir EYRE COOTE. That part which applies to my present narrative, is the only part I think it necessary to detail; but I wish you to inform yourself of all of them fully, by an attentive perusal of the different histories of that war.

In order to relieve the Carnatic, which was suffering under the ravages of a formidable victorious army, who had not only cut off a great part of our forces on that coast, but affronted our army even at the walls of Fort St. George, descents upon the coasts of Malabar were planned, in order to make a diversion: and General MATHEWS, in January 1783, landed with a small army under his command, at a place called Rajamondroog—took Onore, and several forts: and being joined by other troops, which, under the command of Colonel HUMBERTSON, had done considerable service to the southward, and were now commanded by Colonel MACLEOD, marched from Cundapore, with an army consisting of twelve hundred Europeans and eight battalions of Sepoys, towards Hussaingurry Ghaut, a pass that leads over these immense mountains which divide the peninsula, running north and south from Persia to Cape Comorin. After surmounting obstacles that would have discouraged a less enterprising commander, and for which I refer you to his own letter, inclosed herewith,* he mounted the Ghaut, carrying every thing before him with the fixed bayonet; and reached within a short march of Hydernagur, the place where I was confined. Those operations were undoubtedly much facilitated by the death of HYDER ALLI, which happened while I was in prison, and which drew the attention of TIPPOO SAHIB to affairs of more immediate importance than the defence of the Malabar forts.

I have thus digressed from the straight path of my narrative, in order to explain to you the occa-

* See Appendix.

fion of the extraordinary revolution that fo fuddenly took place in the fort, which I ſtated to you in my laſt letter but one—You will therefore look back to the conclufion of that letter, from whence I again take up my narrative.

I was utterly at a lofs to conjecture what this fo fudden refolution to releafe me and my oppofite fellow-prifoner meant. I endeavoured to get fome explanation of it from the perfons about me ; but all I could at the time collect was, that the Jemadar had directed me to be taken out of irons, and ordered me to appear before him. I walked out of the citadel with two or three men who had got charge of me : it was a delightful afternoon ; and my fenfations on once more vifiting the open air—at again viewing the vaſt expanſe of the firmament above, and the profufion of beauties with which nature embelliſhed the earth beneath—were too blifsful, too fublime for defcription. My heart beat with involuntary tranfports of gratitude to that Being from which all fprung ; and I felt that man is, in his nature, even without the intervention of his reafon, a being of devotion. For an hour of fuch delight as I then experienced, a year of imprifonment was, I thought, hardly too dear a price. Thofe exquifite fenfations infenfibly led my heart to the moſt flattering prefages ; the animal fpirit appeared to have, in correfpondence with the body, fhaken off a load of chains ; and as I walked along, I feemed to tread on air.

As we proceeded forward, we found, at fome diſtance from the fort, an open dooly, into which the guards forcibly crammed me ; and I was carried off, ſtill attended by the fame men. As we went along, they gave me to underſtand that HYAT SAHIB, the Jemadar, was at a place ten or a dozen miles diſtant from Bidanore. I thought it within myfelf a moſt extraordinary circumſtance, and was at a lofs to conjecture for what purpofe he required my presence there. Perhaps, thought I, it is to deliver me personally into the hands of TIPPOO—perhaps to send me to Seringapatam. Suspence whetted my curiosity; and impatience to know my fate, set my mind afloat upon a wide sea of conjecture. Still, however, my senses acknowledged a degree of pleasure indescribable—I inhaled the fresh air with greediness, and, as I snuffed it in, said to myself, " Well, well—at the worst, this will enliven my spirits, and lay up a new stock of health and vigour, to enable me to endure with manhood whatever other sufferings the barbarians, into whose hands I have fallen, may have in store for me."

When we had got about a mile from the fort, we met a person attended by three others, all on horseback. He was a man of considerable rank in that country, and I recollected to have seen him at the Jemadar's Durbar, where he had manifested a favourable disposition towards me, looking always graciously, and nodding to me, which, considering my circumstances and his, was not a little extraordinary. The moment he recognized me, he leaped from his horse, apparently in great agitation: then turning to the guards, ordered them to leave me immediately—saying at the same time that he would be answerable for the consequences. They seemed at first to hesitate whether they would obey him or not; but on his shaking at them his sword, which was all along drawn in his hand, and smeared with blood, and repeating his orders a second time in a firm and decisive tone of voice and manner, they all ran off.

As soon as we were alone, he revealed to me, that he had all along known who I was—had most heartily pitied my sufferings, and privately entertained the most anxious wishes to serve me, but could not venture to interfere—the least jealousy, when once awakened, being there always followed up by summary vengeance. He then mentioned his name, informing me th'athe was the son of a Nabob near Vellore, whose dominions had been wrested from him by force, and united to the Carnatic; that his family had received great favours from my father, in return for which he felt himself bound to do me every service in his power; but that, having been, after the misfortunes which befel his family, taken into the service of HYDER, and holding then a place of consequence under him, he was disqualified from demonstrating his gratitude and esteem in the way he wished; he added, he had just come from the summit of the Ghauts, where he left the English army posted, after their having beat the Circar troops, and carried all the strong works which had been erected for the defence of the passes, and were deemed from their situation impregnable; that the Jemadar, HYAT SAHIB, had gone there to encourage the troops, and animate them to one grand effort of resistance, and would remain there till the succeeding day—Here he stopped, and seemed much agitated; but recovering himself soon, said, in a solemn and alarming manner, "This day I heard HYAT SAHIB give orders to bring you before him, in order that he might satiate his revenge by your death! How happy am I in having an opportunity to rescue you! I will carry you back with me, therefore, to Bidanore, and place you in a state of security with my family."

LETTER LVII.

SUCH unprecedented generosity affected me sensibly. To run such a hazard as he must have incurred, merely from a principle of gratitude for services so remote in both time and person, was more than we could hope to find even among Englishmen, who boast of their superior justice and generosity—but in a native of Indostan, where the tide of human feeling runs rather low, was astonishing. As well as my limitted knowledge of the language of the country enabled me, I endeavoured to make him a suitable acknowledgement: in such a cause, dullness must have become eloquent: and I lamented that my deficiency in the language prevented my giving vent to the extreme fullness of my heart. He seemed, however, to be satisfied with my meaning; and I was just on the point of returning with him to Hydernagur, when we were suddenly startled by the Jemadar's music, which was soon afterwards succeeded by the appearance of his guards advancing towards us at some distance. He seemed confounded and alarmed—lamented, in warm terms, his incapacity to serve me—and, pointed to a path which wound through a wood that lay on either side of the road, directed me to strike into it immediately, saying, that by following that route, I should certainly fall in with the British army. He then rode away, and I followed his advice, and proceeded for some time through the wood without interruption; for, though I did not implicitly believe the assertion that Hyat Sahib meant to have cut me off, I deemed it prudent to avail myself of the opportunity which offered to effect my escape, apprehending a worse fate than death, namely, being sent prisoner to Seringapatam.

Finding myself fairly extricated, I began to examine my situation, and to reflect on the different conversations which had passed between Hyat Sahib and me, and on his conduct previous to my being put in irons. I recollected the information I had from time to time received, touching the

Jemadar's disposition, HYDER's death, TIPPOO SAHIB's character and avowed hatred of HYAT, and the nature of the inhabitants. I moreover took into consideration, that my strength was impaired, and my constitution undermined; and that my prospects in India, in point of fame or emolument, could only be promoted by some extraordinary exertion, or some hazardous enterprise. The result of the whole was a determination on my part to return back to the fort, and venture an attempt to persuade the Jemadar to offer proposals for an accomodation to General MATHEWS, and to make me the instrument of his negociation.

In pursuance of this determination, I returned; and about six o'clock in the evening re-entered the fort, and proceeded to the palace of the Jemadar, where, desiring an audience, I was admitted. At the very first sight of him, I could perceive in his appearance all the mortification of falling power. He received me with a gloomy countenance, in which there was more of thoughtful sadness than of vindictive fury. After a minute's silence, however, he said to me, " Well, Sir! you have heard, I suppose, that the English army are in possession of the Ghauts, and doubtless know that the customs of this country authorise my proceeding against you with the utmost rigor." Here he paused for a few moments—then proceeded thus: " Nevertheless, in consideration of your family—in consideration of the regard I have for a long time conceived for you, from observing your conduct, and strict adherence to truth in answering all my questions, and still more on account of the suffering which you have sustained with fortitude, I will allow you to escape: haste you, then, away—fly from this fort directly—Begone!" Then waving his hand as a signal for me to depart, averted his face from me, and looked another way.

I thought that this was a very favourable opportunity for my intended purpose, and entreated him to hear me while I said a few words of perhaps more moment to him than to myself. He again turned towards me; and, nodding affent, while his eye befpoke impatient curiofity, I proceeded—And, firft, I expreffed in the ftrongeft terms I was able, the high fenfe I entertained of the favourable reception I met with when I firft came to the fort; affuring him, that I fhould never forget the kindnefs he fhewed me on that occafion, and that in my confcience I imputed all the fufferings I had undergone wholly to orders which he had been obliged to execute, and not to any want of humanity in himfelf. Here I perceived the clouds which had overfpread his countenance begin gradually to difperfe, and with the greater confidence proceeded to fay, that if he would condefcend to give me a patient hearing, and not take my boldnefs amifs, I would venture to intrude upon him with my advice. At this he ftared at me with a look of furprife—paufed—then faid, that he authorifed me to fpeak whatever I pleafed—continuing, in a tone of gentle melancholy, " But of what ufe can your advice be to me now?"

Having thus obtained his permiffion, I began by complimenting him on his great talents and temper in governing—on his fidelity, zeal and attachment to HYDER—and on the mild and beneficial ufe which he was acknowledged to have made of the unbounded power vefted in him by that great Prince, which was the more extraordinary, confidering how many examples he had to juftify him in a contrary practice. I reminded him, however, that circumftances were at prefent widely different from what they were—that he had now got a very different fovereign to ferve—that he had no longer the tender father (for fo HYDER might have been confidered to him), but TIPPOO SULTAN, now the master, once the rival, whose measures he had always opposed, against whom he had once laid a most serious charge, and who, considering the firmness of his nature, could not be reasonably supposed to have forgiven him; and I hinted, that whatever external appearance of regard TIPPOO might from the political necessity of the moment assume, his temper, and the spirit of Asiatic policy, were too well known to have a doubt remaining, that so far from continuing him (HYAT) in the same power and authority which he enjoyed during the life of his father HYDER, he would, on the contrary, proceed against him with rigor and cruelty.

Here I perceived the Jemadar involuntary nodding his head in a manner which, though not intended for my observation, denoted internal assent; and was convinced that I had exactly fallen in with the current of his own thoughts. No wonder, indeed, they should be his sentiments; for they had long been the sentiments of all persons who had known the circumstances of the Nabob's family.

Having, therefore, gone as far on that point as I conceived to be necessary to awaken the mind of HYAT to the precariousness, or rather danger of his situation with TIPPOO, I painted to him, in the strongest colours I was master of, the humanity, the fidelity, the bravery and generosity of the English, which, I said, were so universally acknowledged, that even their worst enemies bore testimony to them: and I assured him, that if, instead of making an unavailing opposition to them, he would throw himself with confidence upon their protection, and become their friend, he would not only be continued in his station, power and authority, and supported as heretofore, but be made a much greater man, with still greater security, than ever he had been before.

This was the general scope of my argument with him; but there were many more which suggested themselves at the time, though I cannot now remember them. I enforced them with all the power I had: they were supported by the acknowledged character for generosity of the English, and still more by Hyat's apprehensions of Tippoo; and they had their effect. That very night he authorised me to go to the British General; and, though he would not commit himself by sending proposals in writing, he consented to receive them from the General, and promised to wait for my return till day-light the next morning—adding, that if I did not appear by that time, he would go off with his family and treasure to some other place, and set the town, powder-magazine and store-houses on fire, leaving a person of distinguished character to defend the citadel or inner fort, which was strong, with a deep ditch, and mounted with many pieces of cannon, and send immediate intelligence to an army of six thousand horse and ten thousand infantry, who were at that time on their road from Seringapatam, to hasten their progress, and make them advance with all possible rapidity; and he further observed, that as Tippoo himself would come to the immediate protection of his country, and, if once come while the English army remained in the open field, would give them cause to repent their temerity, there was no time to be lost.

Accompanied by a person who had officiated as interpreter between the Jemadar and me, and whose good offices and influence with Hyat, which was very great, I had been previously lucky enough to secure, I set off at ten o'clock at night, on horseback to the British army. My companion was in high spirits when we first set out from the fort; but as we proceeded, he expressed great apprehension of being shot in approaching the camp, and earnestly entreated me to sleep at a choreltry, which lay in our way, till morning. His terror must have been great indeed, to induce him to make such a proposal, as he knew very well that we had pledged ourselves to be back before dawn next day. I rallied him upon his fears, and endeavoured to persuade him there was not the smallest danger, as I knew how to answer the outposts, when they should challenge us, in such a manner as to prevent their firing. As we advanced to the camp, however, his trepidation increased; and when we approached the sentries, I was obliged to drag him along by force. Then his fears had very nearly produced the danger he dreaded, (the almost invariable effect of cowardice); for the sentry next to us, hearing the rustling noise, let off his piece, and was retreating when I had the good fortune to make him hear me. My companion, alarmed at the noise of the musquet, fell down in a paroxysm of terror, from which it was some time before he was completely recovered. The sentry who had fired, coming up, conducted us to a place where other sentries were posted, one of whom accompanied us to a guard, from whence we were brought to the grand guard, and by them conducted to the General.

LETTER LVIII.

I WAS no less pleased than surprised to find, that the commander of this gallant and successful little army was General MATHEWS—an old friend of my father's, and a person with whom I had served in the cavalry soon after I entered the service. When I arrived he was fast asleep upon the bare ground in a choreltry. His dubash, whose name was SNAKE, recollected me immediately, and was almost as much frightened at my appearance at first, as my interpreter companion was at the shot of the sentry; for it was full five months since my hair and beard were both shaved at the same time, during which period a comb had never touched my head: I had no hat—no stockings—was clad in a pair of very ragged breeches, a shirt which was so full of holes that it resembled rather a net than a web of cloth, and a waistcoat which had been made for a man twice my size—while my feet were defended from the stones only by a pair of Indian slippers. SNAKE, as soon as he was able to conquer his terror, and stop the loquacious effusions of astonishment, brought me to the General, whom I found fast asleep. We awoke him with great difficulty, and, on his discovering me, expressed great pleasure and surprise at so unexpected a meeting; for, though he had heard of my imprisonment at Bidanore, he did not expect to have had the pleasure of my company so soon.

Having stated to the General the nature and object of my mission, and related to him what had happened in the fort, he instantly saw the great advantages that must accrue from such an arrangement—entered into a full but short discussion of the business—settled with me the plan to be pursued in either case of HYAT SAHIB's acceding to or dissenting from the terms he proposed to offer; and in less than an hour after my arrival, I was dispatched back to the fort in the General's palanquin, with a cowl from him, signifying that the Jemadar HYAT SAHIB's power and influence should not be lessened, if he should quietly surrender up the fort. Before my departure, the General expressed, in the warmest terms, his approbation of my conduct; and added that considering the importance of the fort, the extensive influence of H‍yat Sahib, and the advantages that might be derived from his experience and abilities, coupled with the enfeebled state of his army, the benefits of such a negociation scarcely admitted of calculation.

Notwithstanding the very flattering circumstances with which my present pursuit was attended, I could not help, as I returned to Hydernagur, finding some uneasy sensations, arising from the immediate nature of the business, and from my knowledge of the faithless disposition of Asiatics, and the little difficulty they find in violating any moral principle, if it happens to clash with their interest, or if a breach of it promises any advantage. I considered that it was by no means impossible, that some resolution adverse to my project might have been adopted in my absence, and that the Jemadar's policy might lead him to make my destruction a sort of propitiation for his former offences, and to send me and the cowl together to Tippoo, to be sacrificed to his resentment. These thoughts, I own, made a very deep impression on my mind—but were again effaced by the reflection, that a laudable measure, once begun, ought to be persevered in, and that the accomplishing a plan of such importance and incalculable public utility, might operate still further by example, and produce consequences of which it was impossible at present to form a conception. Those, and a variety of such suggestions, entirely overcame the scruples and fears of the danger; and I once more entered the fort of Hydernagur. At this time the British troops were, by detaching a part with Colonel Macleod, to get round the fort, and attack it in the rear, and, by death and sickness, reduced to less than four hundred Europeans and seven hundred Sepoys, without ordnance.

When I delivered the cowl to the Jemadar, he read it, and seemed pleased, but talked of four or five days to consider of an answer, and seemed to be wavering in his mind, and labouring under the alternate impulses of opposite motives and contradictory passions. I saw that it was a crisis of more importance than any other of my life—a crisis in which delay, irresolution, or yielding to the protractive expedients of Hyat, might be fatal. To prevent, therefore, the effects of either treachery or repentance, I took advantage of the general confusion and trepidation which prevailed in the fort—collected the Arcot Sepoys, who, to the number of four hundred, were prisoners at large—posted them at the gates, powder-magazines, and other critical situations; and, having taken these and other precautions, went out to the General, who, according to the plan concerted between us, had pushed on with the advanced guard; and, conducting him into the fort with hardly an attendant, brought him straight to the Jemadar's presence while he yet remained in a state of indecision and terror. General Mathews, in his first interview with the Jemadar, did every thing to re-assure him, and confirmed with the most solemn asseverations the terms of the cowl; in consequence of which the latter acceded to the propositions contained in it, and the British colours for the first time waved upon the walls of the chief fort of the country of Bidanore.

Having thus contributed to put this important garrison, with all its treasures, which certainly were immense, into the hands of the Company, without the loss of a single man, or even the striking of a single blow, my exultation was inconceivable; and, much though I wanted money, I can with truth aver, that avarice had not even for an instant the least share in my sensations. 'Tis true, the consciousness of my services assured me of a reward; but how that reward was to accrue to me, never once was the subject of my contemplation—much less did I think of availing myself of the instant occasion to obtain it. How far my delicacy on the occasion may be censured or approved, I cannot tell; but if I got nothing by it, I have at least the consolation to reflect that I escaped calumny, which was with a most unjustifiable and unsparing hand lavished on others. The General, it is true, promised that I should remain with him till he made some arrangements; and HYAT SAHIB offered, on his part, to make me, through the General, a handsome present. The General, however, suddenly became dissatisfied with me; and I neither got HYAT SAHIB's present, nor ever received even a rupee of the vast spoil found there.

Here I think it a duty incumbent on me to say something of General MATHEWS, and, while I deplore the unfortunate turn in his temper, which injured me, and tarnished in some measure his good qualities, to rescue him from that unremitted obloquy which the ignorant, the interested and the envious have thrown upon his fame. Light lie the ashes of the dead, and hallowed be the turf that pillows the head of a soldier.! General MATHEWS was indeed a soldier—was calumniated too; and although he did not use me as I had reason to hope he would, I will, as far as I can, rescue his fame from gross misrepresentation.

An extravagant love of fame was the ruling passion of General MATHEWS: it was the great end of all his pursuits; and while, in his military profession, he walked with a firm pace towards it, he lost his time, distorted his progress, and palsied his own efforts, by a jealous vigilance and envious opposition of those whom he found taking the same road, whether they walked beside him, or panted in feeble effort behind. This was his fault; it was doubtless a great alloy to his good qualities: but it has been punished with rigour disproportionate to the offence. Those who personally felt his jealousy, took advantage of his melancholy end to traduce him, and magnify every mole-hill of error into a mountain of crime. It is unmanly in any one—indeed it is—to traduce the soldier who has fallen in the service of his country; but it is heresy in a soldier to do so. No sooner did the buzz of calumny get abroad, than thousands of hornets, who had neither interest nor concern in the affair, joined in it. The malignant, who wished to sting merely to get rid of so much of their venom—and the vain, who wished to acquire a reputation for knowledge of Asiatic affairs at the expence of truth —united together, and raised a hum which reached Europe, where the hornets (I mean authors), under the less unjustifiable impulse of necessity, took it up, and buzzed through the medium of *quartos* and *octavos* so loud, that public opinion was poisoned; and the gallant soldier who, for the advantage of England, stood the hardest tugs of war, and at last drank the poisoned cup from the tyrant hands of her enemy, was generally understood to be a peculator, and to have clandestinely and dishonestly obtained three hundred thousand pounds.

On this assertion I put my direct negative. It may be said, however, that this is only assertion against assertion—True! Sorry should I be to rest it there: my assertions are grounded on such proofs as are not to be shaken—proofs on record in the office of the Presidency of Bombay.

As soon as Hydernagur was taken possession of, HYAT SAHIB immediately issued orders to the forts of Mangalore, Deokull, Ananpore, and some others in that country, to surrender to the British arms. Some obeyed the mandate; but those three resisted, and were reduced by General MATHEWS. Rendered incautious by success, our army became less vigilant, and TIPPOO retook Hydernagur; and, in direct breach of the capitulation, made the garsion prisoners, treated them with a degree of inhumanity which chills the blood even to think of, and forced General MATHEWS to take poison in prison!

Mean-time HYAT SAHIB, with whom the General had got into disputes, arrived at Bombay, and laid a charge against him, which he, being in the hands of TIPPOO, could not controvert, or even know. And what was the charge? The whole extent of it was his (MATHEWS's) having got two lacks of rupees, and a pearl necklace, as a present—a sum, considering the country and circumstances, not at all extraordinary, but which is completely vindicated by the General's letter to the Court of Directors, dated at Mangalore, the 15th of March, 1783; in which he states the present, and requests permission to accept it. This, as I said before, is on record, and was translated by Mr. SYBBALD, who was then Persian interpreter at Bombay. The letter I allude to, you will see in the APPENDIX. In short, General MATHEWS had his faults, but an unjust avarice was not amongst them.

LETTER LIX.

HAVING, in my last letter, said as much as I thought justice demanded in defence of General MATHEWS, against the charge of peculation, I am now to speak of him as his conduct touched me. He was, as I have already mentioned, an old friend of my father's, and an intimate of my own: I had reason, therefore, to expect from him, according to the usual dispositions and manners of men, if not partiality, at least friendship; and in such a case as

I have related, where my services gave me a claim to notice, it was not unreasonable to suppose that he would have been forward to promote my interest, by stating my services in such a manner as to call attention to them. He had, however, some disagreeable discussions with his officers; and seeing I was on a footing with Colonel HUMBERTSON, and still more with Major CAMPBELL (he who so ably and gallantly defenced Mangalore against TIPPOO'S whole army and six hundred French), and finding me extremely zealous and importunate to have his arrangement with HYAT SAHIB adhered to, he became displeased, and, though he himself had determined that I should remain with him, changed his mind, and ordered me away at an hour's notice—many days sooner than he had originally intended to send off any dispatches. He moreover occasioned my losing a sum of money, and on the whole paid less attention to my interest than the circumstances of the case demanded.

In the evening of the day on which he determined on my departure, I set off with his dispatches to the governments of Madras and Bengal, and reached the most distant of our posts that night. From thence I had thirty miles to Cundapore, a seaport town upon the Malabar coast, taken by us from the enemy. During this journey, which was through the country of TIPPOO SAHIB, I had only six Sepoys to conduct me: yet, such was the universal panic that had seized all classes and distinctions of people at the progress of the British arms in that quarter, I met only a few scattered Sepoys, who were so badly wounded I presume they were unable to travel—the villages throughout being completely abandoned by all their inhabitants.

The sudden change of diet, which physicians tell us, and I experienced, is dangerous, from bad to good, as well as the reverse, conspiring with the mortification I felt at seeing things going on so very contrary to what I wished, and what I had reason to expect, had a most sudden and alarming effect upon my constitution; and I was seized on the road with the most excrutiating, internal pains, which were succeeded by a violent vomiting of blood. At length, with great difficulty, I reached Cundapore, where the commanding officer, and all about him did every thing in their power to afford me assistance and comfort under my miseries, which increased every hour rapidly. I felt as if my inside was utterly decayed, and all its functions lost in debility: at the same time my head seemed deranged—I could scarcely comprehend the meaning of what was said; lifting up my head was attended with agonizing pain; and if I had any power of thought, it was to consider myself as approaching fast to dissolution. I had the sense, however, to send to General MATHEWS, to acquaint him with my indisposition, and utter inability to pro-proceed with his dispatches. To this I received the following letter:

"*Bidanore, Feb.* 3, 1783.

"DEAR CAMPBELL,

" I am sorry to hear that you have been unwell.
" Should your indisposition increase, or continue,
" so as to render you unable to pursue your jour-
" ney with the necessary expedition, I beg that
" you will forward the letters to Anjengo by a
" boat, with directions to Mr. HUTCHINSON to
" send them per tappy* to Palamcotah, and so on
" to Madras.

" I shall hope to hear of your recovery, and that
" you'll have gone to sea.

"Your's very truly,
"RICHARD MATHEWS."

* Post, or express.

The receipt of this letter induced me, bad as I was, to make one other exertion; and I resolved, though I should die on the way, not to leave any thing which, even by malicious construction, could be made a set-off against my claims: I therefore hired an open boat to carry me along the coast to Anjengo, and set out with every prospect of having the virulence of my disorder increased, by being exposed in an uncovered vessel to the damp of the night air, and the raging heat of the sun in the day, and of being arrested by the hand of death in my way. By the time I had got down the coast as far as Mangalore, my complaints increased to an alarming height; and I became speechless, and unable to stand. Fortunately there happened to be a Company's vessel then lying at anchor off that place, the captain of which had the goodness to invite me to remain on board with him, strenuously advising that I should give up the thoughts of proceeding immediately on my voyage to Anjengo, which I could not possibly survive, and to forward my dispatches by another hand. The surgeon of the ship joining the captain in opinion that I could not survive if I attempted it, and my own judgment coinciding with their's, I at length consented, and remained there.

Tranquility, kind treatment, and good medical assistance, produced, in the space of two or three weeks, so material a change in my health, I was in a condition to avail myself, at the expiration of that time, of a ship bound to Anjengo, and which offering the additional inducement of touching at Tellicherry, determined me to take my passage in her. When I arrived at Tellicherry, and during my stay there, the great attention shewn me by Mr. FREEMAN, the chief of that place, and the comforts of his house, restored me to a great share of health and spirits—And here a very singular circumstance occurred.

One day a vessel arrived; and perceiving a boat coming on shore from her, Mr. FREEMAN and I walked down to the beach, to make the usual inquiries—such as, where she came from? what news she brought? &c. &c. As soon as the boat touched the shore, a gentleman leaped out of it, whose person seemed familiar to me: upon his nearer approach, I discovered that it was Mr. BRODEY, a gentleman who had been kind enough to take upon him the office of my attorney, upon my leaving India some years before---not my *attorney* in the ordinary acceptation of that word, but a liberal and disinterested friend, who obligingly undertook the management of my affairs in my absence, without the smallest hope of advantage, or rather under circumstances which served as preludes to further obligations. I was certainly pleased and surprised to see him; but his astonishment to see me amounted almost to a distrust of his eye-sight: he had received such indubitable proofs of my death, that my sudden appearance on his landing, at the first rush of thought, impressed him with the notion of a *deceptio visus*. My identity, however, was too positive for resistance; and his wonder melted down into cordial satisfaction, and congratulations on my safety. He then took out a pocket account-book, in which, for security against accidents, he kept accounts-current, written in a brief manner—and shewed me mine, settled almost to the very day, upon which was transcribed a copy of a letter he had received, and which he thought was a testimony of my death. So, cutting out the account, and presenting it to me, he expressed, in the most cordial and handsome manner, his joy that it was into my own hands he had at last had an opportunity to deliver it. This gentleman is now in this Kingdom, and too well known for me to describe him. Suffice it to say, that in England, as well as in India, he has always enjoyed the esteem and respect of all his acquaintances, to as great an extent as any other person I know.

I again embarked to proceed on my voyage, and had hardly got on board when a ship dropped anchor along side of us, in which captain CAMPBELL of Comby, a very near connection of mine, was passenger. On hailing one another, he heard that I was on board, and immeditely was with me. Those who sincerely love each other, and whose hearts confess the fond ties of consanguinity, can alone conceive what our mutual pleasure was at meeting so unexpectedly in so remote a corner of the world. He was then on his way to join the army. This amiable young man, now reposes in the bed of honour at Mangalore! He fell, after having distinguished himself in the very gallant defence made by that place against the whole force of TIPPOO. With regret we parted: and in due time I arrived at Anjengo without any accident befalling me, which was rather extraordinary.

Leaving Anjengo, I set out for Madras, designing to go all the way by land—a journey of near eight hundred miles. I accordingly struck through the Kingdom of Travancore, whose sovereign is in alliance with the English; and had not long entered the territories of the Nabob of Arcot, before Major MACNEAL, an old friend of mine, and commandant of a fort in that district, met me preceded by a troop of dancing girls, who encircled my palanquin, dancing around me until I entered the Major's house.

It would be difficult to give you an adequate notion of those dancing girls. Trained up from their infancy to the practice of the most graceful motions, the most artful display of personal symmetry, and the most wanton allurements, they dance in such a style, and twine their limbs and bodies into such postures, as bewitch the senses, and extort applause and admiration where in strictness disapprobation is due : nor is their agility inferior to the grace of their movements—though they do not exert it in the same skipping way that our stage dancers do, but make it subservient to the elegance, and, I may say, grandeur, of their air. They are generally found in troops of six or eight, attended by musicians, whose aspect and dress are as uncouth and squalid, as the sounds they produce under the name of music, are inelegant, harsh and dissonant. To this music, from which measure as much as harmony is excluded, they dance, most wonderfully adapting their step to the perpetual change of the time, accompanying it with amorous songs, while the correspondent action of their body and limbs, the wanton palpitation and heaving of their exquisitely formed bosoms, and the amorous, or rather lascivious expression of their countenance, excite in the spectators emotions not very favourable to chastity. Thus they continue to act, till, by the warmth of exercise and imagination, they become seemingly frantic with ecstacy, and, sinking down motionless with fatigue, throw themselves into the most alluring attitudes that ingenious vice and voluptuousness can possibly devise.

That such incitements to vice should make a part of the system of any society, is to be lamented : yet, at all ceremonies and great occasions, whether of religious worship or domestic enjoyment, they make a part of the entertainment ; and the altar of their gods, and the purity of the marriage rites, are alike polluted by the introduction of the dancing girls. The impurity of this custom, however, vanishes in India, when compared with the hideous practice of introducing dancing *boys*.

The Major, after having entertained me in the most hospitable manner, accompanied me to Palamcotah, to the house of Doctor DOTT, who lived in a generous and hospitable style. I had once had an opportunity of evincing my good difpofition to this gentleman, when he was moft ctitically fituated; and the reception he gave me demonftrated, that he than retained a lively fenfe of my conduct to him.

Leaving Palamcotah, I continued my route thro' Madura. This country is rendered remarkable by the revolt of the famous ISIF CAWN, who made a bold and well-conducted attempt to erect himfelf into the fovereignty of that province, independent of the Nabob of the Carnatic, in whofe fervice he was: and as the affair occurs to my thoughts, I will, for your information, notwithftanding its being unconnected with my ftory, digrefs into an account of it. As foon as the revolt of ISIF CAWN was known, General MONSON, an officer of great military fkill and perfonal merit, went againft him at the head of the King's and company's troops, and invefted the fort of Madura, in which that rebellious chief was pofted. The general made a practicable breach, and, in ftorming, was beat back with great flaughter by ISIF; and the fetting in of the monfoons immediately after, retarded the further operations of our army againft the place; and in the interim, peace having been concluded between the courts of St. James's and Verfailles, the King's troops were withdrawn.

On the recall of the King's troops, an army of company's troops was formed, to proceed againft Madura, in order to reduce this gallant turbulent rebel to fubjection; and the renowned general LAWRENCE being rendered incapable of actual fervice, and obliged to remain at the prefidency by extreme age and infirmity, the chief command devolved upon my father by feniority: he headed the expedition; and, after overcoming innumerable difficulties thrown in his way by the inventive genius and enterprifing fpirit of ISIF CAWN, again made a breach, which was deemed practicable by the chief engineer, now Sir JOHN CALL. An assault was made with no better success than the former; for our army was again repulsed with incredible slaughter: more than two thirds, I believe, of our European officers, were among the killed or wounded; and the death o Major PRESTON, second in command, a man endeared to the army by the possession of every advantage of person, heart and talents—an active, intrepid and able officer—aggravated the calamities of the day.

If, impelled by my feelings, or tempted by remembrance of the past, I sometimes digress from the direct path of my narrative, my FREDERICK will accompany me, not only with patience, but I dare say with pleasure: I cannot refrain, therefore, from mentioning a memorable occurrence during that siege, not only as it is somewhat extraordinary in itself, but as it relates to a very near and dear connection. Colonel DONALD CAMPBELL, who then commanded the cavalry, received no less than fourteen sword-wounds and a musquet-ball in his body—yet continued doing his duty with such cool intrepidity, that brave soldiers who were witnesses to it, expressed the utmost astonishment: upon being requested to quit the field, he replied, that as his family were provided for, he had nothing to fear; and as it was very unlikely his life could be saved, he would not deprive his country of any advantage that might be derived from his exertions for the short residue of it, but continue to the last moment at his duty. With all this firmness and magnanimity, he was gentle, good-humoured, modest and unassuming; and was admired for his great personal beauty, as well as military talents, particularly by the Duke of CUMBERLAND, under whom he served in the war in Germany as a subaltern officer, in so much that his Royal Highness had his picture drawn. It was to him the company were first indebted for the introduction of perfect military discipline into their army in India. In the various relations in which he stood, whether domestic or public, as the subject, the citizen, the father, or the friend, he was so uniformly excellent, that the shafts of malevolence, which the best and wisest of men have but too often felt, seldom reached him; and he may justly be reckoned amongst that very small number of created beings, of whom scarcely any one had the audacity to speak ill. Upon my first arrival in India, I was put under his command, and lived in his family—when, instead of deporting himself towards me with that reserve and austerity which rank and reputation like his, coupled with the circumstance of his being my uncle, might in some sort have justified, he took me into his confidence, treated me with the greatest affection, and acted rather as the brother and the equal, than as the parent and superior; and thus his gentle admonitions had more effect in restraining the sallies of youth, and impetuosity of my temper, than the sour, unpalatable documents of a supercilious preceptor could possibly have had.

The wonderful effects of this happy temper in swaying the stubborn disposition of headstrong youth, was exemplified in another instance—of which, since I am on the subject, I will inform you. Mr. Dupres, then governor of Madras, wrote to him about a young gentleman, in the following words:

"My dear Colonel,
"In the list of officers appointed to your garri-
"son, you will see the name of ————. This
"young man (nephew to Mrs. Dupres), with
"abilities that might render him conspicuous, I
"am sorry to say, stands in need of a strict hand.
"All the favour I have to request of you is to

"shew him no favour: keep him rigidly to his
"duty; and, if he requires it, rule him with a
"rod of iron. Should his future conduct meet
"your approbation, it is unnecessary for me to ask
"it, as you are always ready to shew kindness to
"those who merit it."

The peculiar style of this letter made such an impression on my memory, that I am able to give the exact words. Colonel CAMPBELL, however, took his own unalterable method, mildness—treated the young gentleman in such a manner as to raise in him a consciousness of his dignity as a man, the first and best guard against misconduct—and appointed him to the grenadier company. The result was answerable to his expectations; for the young man's conduct, both as an officer and a gentleman, was such in the sequel as to reflect credit on himself and his family; and his very honourable and hopeful career was at last terminated by a cannonball at the siege of Tanjore.

If the veneration in which I shall ever hold this most dear and respected relative admitted of increase, it would certainly receive it from the contrast I am every day obliged to draw between him and the wretched *butterflies* who sometimes flutter round us under the name of men: for, how can I help contrasting his inflexible courage, united to angelic mildness, with the insolence of lilly-livered Hectors, who, conscious of the most abject cowardice, dare to give an insult, and basely skulk from honest resentment beneath the arm of the law!—fellows who, like *Bobadil* in the play, can kill a whole army with the tongue, but dare not face a pigmy in the field!—and, while they want the prudence to restrain the torrent of effeminate invective, have patience enough to bear a kicking, or a box in the ear!—who bluster and vapour to hide the trembling limb and poltroon aspect, as children whistle in the dark to brave the ghosts they dread! Beware of all such wretches as you would shun plague or pestilence. I hope you do not imagine that I have so little common sense or philanthropy as to censure those who, from physical causes or constitutional delicacy, are averse to contest: No, no—I do assure you, on the contrary, that my observation leads me to think such men, though slow to quarrel, and inoffensive in conduct, are very gallant when honour or duty demand from them a conquest over their weakness. I have, in my time, seen such men at first the sport, and at last the terror of your blustering bullies; and I have always thought, that in such a triumph over their feelings, they had more true merit than men constitutionally courageous: the latter has his valour in common with the mere animal; the other possesses the valour of sentiment. I mean that most ignominious of all beings, who, prodigal in offence, yet reluctant in reparation—who, hoping to find some person passive as themselves over whom to triumph, hazard the giving of an insult, with the malignant view to gasconade over him if he submits—and, if he resents, to wreak the whole vengeance of law upon him. In society with such men, there is no safety; for they leave you only the casual alternative to choose between shame and ruin. Him who submits, they call poltroon; and him who resents, they fleece in form of law. There are others who, to bring their fellow-creatures down to their own level, brave the execrations of mankind, and the vengeance of Heaven: such harpies do exist, who, though bold enough to insult, are tame enough to receive chastisement without resistance; and, though tame enough to submit to chastisement, are so furiously vindictive as to proclaim their shame, their cowardice, perhaps in the face of an open court, in order to glut their revenge by the pillage of their adversary's purse.

Let such men enjoy the fruits of their machinations, if they can—To their own feelings I consign them; for I can wish a villain no greater curse than the company of his own conscience, nor a poltroon a more poignant sting than that which the contempt of mankind inflicts upon him.

LETTER LX.

PASSING through Madura, I arrived at Trichinopoly, where I met Mr. SULLIVAN, the resident of Tanjore, who very politely furnished me with a letter to Mr. HIPPESLEY, his deputy at Tanjore, from whom I received many marks of civility. At that place I had the pleasure of meeting a gentleman with whom I had been at college, and for whom I had always entertained a great esteem: this was Colonel FULLARTON. It is an old maxim, that we should say nothing but good of the dead—" De mortuis nil nisi bonum." It is not a new maxim, I believe, to avoid praising the living: I am aware of the indelicacy of it; and therefore purposely avoid in this, as I shall in other instances, speaking the full opinion I entertain. To the general esteem in which he was held by all ranks of people in India, I refer you to Colonel FULLARTON's character: it is of such a sort, that I wish to hold it up for your imitation. At a time of life when others have arrived to some perfection in their profession, he made choice of his, and entered for the first time into the arduous military department, with a command for which the training of many years is no more than sufficient to prepare other men. The Minister of that day gave him this important charge, underwent the clamours of

Opposition for it, and was justified in the event. When the Colonel came to act, so far from being deficient, his whole conduct was distinguished, not less for military talent than courage—while the most fortunate command and temper and captivating address subdued the spirit of prejudice, reconciled the most discordant, and gained him, though a King's Officer, the esteem as much of the Company's as King's troops. In short, all ranks of people, civil as well as military, whether belonging to King or Company, united in approbation of his conduct—a thing not before, nor since, but in the person of LORD CORNWALLIS.

Too much cannot be said of the advantages resulting from a proper command of temper. To promote that in my FEDERICK, will be attended with little difficulty: on the contrary, my only doubt is, that the placability and mildness of his disposition will too often subject him to imposition. JOHN is, however, of a different temper; there is something in it which requires both admonition and good example to repress within proper bounds: to shew him the beauty as well as use of a mild, cool temper, such instances as Colonel FULLARTON may be of weight, and I wish him to reflect upon it. And here I am reminded of a person and a circumstance so exactly in point, that I cannot refrain from noticing them: they convey no inadequate idea of the happiness resulting from a gentleness of nature, and dominion over the mind; and as the person I allude to is dead, I may speak of him with the greater freedom in that full strain of praise of which his shining virtues deserve.

Of all the men I have ever had the good fortune to know, Sir ARCHIBALD CAMPBELL possessed, in the highest degree, that heavenly turn of mind, which not only is at peace with itself, but diffuses harmony and cheerfulness around it. No business, however urgent in occasion, restricted in point of time, or embarrassed with difficulty—no accident, however unexpected, or event, however sinister—none of those innumerable minutiæ which fret and chafe the tempers of other men, ever suspended the cool tenor of his thought even for a moment: nothing shook the serenity of his temper—nothing deranged the presence of his mind: uniform and placid, he in all situations had the full dominion of himself, and in the field it gave him a decided superiority; nor was this felicity of nature confined to his public conduct; it attended him at the domestic enjoyments of the fire-side—at the social board—in the private recesses of his closet; and the very same habit of soul which, in his great public duties, rendered him valuable to his Country, and formidable to her enemies, gained him the admiration and esteem of his friends, the unbounded affection of his family, and the blessing of all his dependants.

An incident that occured in my presence may serve in some measure to decipher the mind of this admirable man—I shall never forget it. Previously to his going to India, he had exerted his interest to obtain from the East India Company some reward for my services; and, a few days before his departure, promised to speak again to Mr. DEVAYNES, Chairman of the East India Company. I waited on him on the day he was setting off: he was just about to depart, and surrounded by a numerous circle. In the midst of this bustle, and the confusion, one would suppose, inseparable from such a crisis, he recollected his promise—told me Mr. DEVAYNES had that minute taken leave of him, and he had forgot to mention me, but said that he would write to him on the subject: and, though he was at the instant on the point of moving to the carriage that was to carry him off, sat down, and with that amiable sweetness of manners and happily collected mind so peculiarly his own, wrote a letter for me to Mr. DEVAYNES—holding conversation, the while, in the most lively, engaging manner, with the persons around him. The conciseness and perspicuity of language in which this letter was couched, will serve to elucidate what I have said---I therefore transcribe it for you:

"*St. James's Hotel, Sept.* 30, 1785.

"DEAR SIR,

"I forgot to mention to you this forenoon, and
"again, to repeat my earnest wishes, you would
"take the case of Mr. CAMPBELL speedily into
"your consideration. His sufferings were of such
"a nature, and his services so meritorious, that I
"am persuaded, upon a fair investigation of both,
"you will give him your firmest support. I have
"looked into all his papers; and the testimonies
"of essential services rendered to the Company by
"him, do him, in my opinion, the highest ho-
"nour. Unless such merits are recompensed, few
"will risk every thing, as Mr. CAMPBELL did, to
"promote the success of the Company's arms in
"India: but I trust you will see it in its proper
"light; and in that hope I shall only add, that
"whatever acts of kindness you shew to him, will
"be considered as an obligation conferred on,

"DEAR SIR,
"Your faithful and most obedient humble servant,
"ARCHIBALD CAMPBELL."
"*To William Devaynes, Esq.*"

Be assured, my dear boys, (for now I speak to JOHN as well as FREDERICK), that one act of triumph over the temper is worth a million of triumphs over our fellow-creatures, and that the perfect dominion of our mind is more advantageous and laudable than the dominion over Provinces or Nations. The one attaches merely to our corporeal part, and is buried with our dust in the grave: the other follows our immortal part, and passes with it into eternity.

On my leaving Tanjore, Colonel FULLARTON honoured me with the care of a letter to Lord MACARTNEY, then Governor of Madras—an extract of which I give you, as it applied to my business particularly:

"*Tanjore, March* 20, 1783.

"MY LORD,

"I had the honour to write to your lordship on "the 8th by Captain HALLAM, who carried from "hence very large packets to you. The opportu- "nity of Captain CAMPBELL tempts me to trou- "ble your lordship, merely to inform you, that "all my letters from Bidanore ascribe in a great "degree the success of our arms in that quarter, "and the *romantic* Revolution effected there, to "the influence he had with HYAT SAHIB, and "to the proposals of surrender which he suggest- "ed, and transacted with the General and Jema- "dar. I think it necessary that you, my lord, "may know how much the Public is indebted to "Captain CAMPBELL, whose good fortune in this "affair has only been equalled by his good conduct. "He is perfectly acquainted with the state of af- "fairs on the other coast, and has seen and heard "much of our transactions here; so that no person "can give a more clear or unbiassed view of "events."

I had also the good luck to meet, at Tanjore, Mr. BUCHANAN, a very near connection of mine, for whom I had long entertained a sincere and warm regard. It has been my misfortune to have been obliged frequently to censure some of my relatives for ill-nature and ingratitude: I never did so without the most painful sensations. When, on the contrary, I am enabled to speak to their honour, I feel a proportionate share of pleasure: I am therefore happy in mentioning Mr. BUCHANAN as a man as amiable in his private as respectable in his public character; but the satisfaction I felt at this meeting was much alloyed by finding him in a very bad state of health.

Before I left Tanjore, I had an opportunity of being eye-witness to that extraordinary and horrid ceremony, the burning of a Gentoo woman with the body of her husband. As this is a point which has occasioned much speculation and some doubt among Europeans, I inclose you an accurate account of the ceremony, as minuted down at the time it happened.

Description of the Ceremony of the Gentoo Women burning themselves with the bodies of their Husbands.

"This day, ————, I went to see a Gentoo woman resign herself to be burned along with the corpse of her deceased husband.

"The place fixed upon for this tragic scene, was a small islet on the bank of one of the branches of the river Cavery, about a mile to the Northward of the fort of Tanjore.

"When I came to the spot, I found the victim, who appeared to be not above sixteen, sitting on the ground, dressed in the Gentoo manner, with a white cloth wrapped round her, some white flowers like jessamins hanging round her neck, and some of them hanging from her hair. There were about twenty women sitting on their hams round her, holding a white handkerchief, extended horizontally over her head, to shade her from the sun, which was excessively hot, it being then about noon.

"At about twenty yards from where she was sitting, and facing her, there were several Bramins busy in constructing a pile with billets of firewood: the pile was about eight feet long, and four broad. They first began by driving some upright stakes into the ground, and then built up the middle to about the height of three feet and a half with billets of wood.

"The dead husband, who, from his appearance, seemed to be about sixty years of age, was lying close by, stretched out on a bier, made of Bamboo canes. Four Bramins walked in procession three times round the dead body, first in a direction contrary to the sun, and afterwards other three times in a direction with the sun, all the while muttering incantations; and at each round or circuit they made, they untwisted, and immediately again twisted up the small long lock of hair which is left unshaven at the back of their heads.

"Some other Bramins were in the mean time employed in sprinkling water out of a green leaf, rolled up like a cup, upon a small heap of cakes of dry cow-dung, with which the pile was afterwards to be set on fire.

"An old Bramin sat at the North-east corner of the pile upon his hams, with a pair of spectacles on, reading, I suppose, the Shafter, or their Scriptures, from a book composed of Cajan leaves.

"Having been present now nearly an hour, I inquired when they meant to set the pile on fire: they answered, in about two hours. As this spectacle was most melancholy, and naturally struck me with horror, and as I had only gone there to assure myself of the *truth of such sacrifices being made*, I went away towards the fort. After I was gone about five hundred yards, they sent some one to tell me they would burn immediately; on which I returned, and found the woman had been moved from where she was sitting to the river, where the

Bramins were bathing her. On taking her out of the water, they put some money in her hand, which she dipped in the river, and divided among the Bramins: she had then a yellow cloth rolled partially round her. They put some red colour, about the size of a sixpence, on the centre of her forehead, and rubbed something that appeared to me to be clay. She was then led to the pile, round which she walked three times as the sun goes: she then mounted it at the North-east corner, without any assistance; and sat herself down on the right side of her husband, who had been previously laid upon the pile. She then unscrewed the pins which fastened the jewels or silver rings on her arms: after she had taken them off, she shut them, and screwed in the pins again, and gave one to each of two women who were standing: she unscrewed the ear-rings, and other toys, with great composure, and divided them among the women who were with her. There seemed to be some little squabble about the distribution of her jewels, which she settled with great precision; and then, falling gently backwards, pulled a fold of the yellow cloth over her face, turned her breast towards her husbands side, and laid her right arm over his breast; and in this posture she remained without moving.

" Just before she lay down, the Bramins put some rice in her lap, and also some in the mouth and on the long grey beard of her husband: they then sprinkled some water on the head, breast and feet of both, and tied them gently together round the middle with a slender bit of rope: they then raised, as it were, a little wall of wood lengthways on two sides of the pile, so as to raise it above the level of the bodies; and then put cross pieces, so as to prevent the billets of wood from pressing on them: they then poured on the pile, above where the woman lay, a potful of something that appeared to me to be oil; after this they heaped on more wood, to the height of about four feet above where the bodies were built in; so that all I now saw was a stack of fire-wood.

"One of the Bramins, I observed, stood at the end of the pile next the woman's head—was calling to her through the interstices of the wood, and laughed several times during the conversation. Lastly, they overspread the pile with wet straw, and tied it on with ropes.

"A Bramin then took a handful of straw, which he set on fire at the little heap of burning cakes of cow-dung; and, standing to windward of the pile, he let the wind drive the flame from the straw till it catched the pile. Fortunately, at this instant, the wind rose much higher than it had been any part of the day; and in an instant the flames pervaded the whole pile, and it burnt with great fury. I listened a few seconds, but could not distinguish any shrieks, which might perhaps be owing to my being then to windward. In a very few minutes, the pile became a heap of ashes.

"During the whole time of this process, which lasted from first to last above two hours before we lost sight of the woman by her being built up in the middle of the pile, I kept my eyes almost constantly upon her; and I declare to GOD that I could not perceive, either in her countenance or limbs, the least trace of either horror, fear, or even hesitation: her countenance was perfectly composed and placid; and she was not, I am positive, either intoxicated or stupified. From several circumstances, I thought the Bramins exulted in this hellish sacrifice, and did not seem at all displeased that Europeans should be witnesses of it."

From Tanjore I proceeded to Negapatnam, which had been taken from the Dutch by the Company's troops, and where Mr. COCHRAN, an old friend of mine, was Chief.

The communication by land between Negapatnam and Madras being interrupted by the enemy's troops, I embarked in a veſſel, and proceeded thither by ſea—Major JOHNSTON, of the Engineers, being alſo a paſſenger.

LETTER LXI.

HITHERTO every ſtep of my journey has been marked by occurrences ſo unexpected, and accidents ſo extraordinary, that I ſhould feel ſome repugnance to relate them, leſt my veracity ſhould be called in queſtion, were they not atteſted by ſo many living perſons of reſpectability, and by written documents of authority on record. Were one to conſider them merely as the offspring of fiction, they would perhaps have intereſt enough to catch the attention; but, viewing them as facts, they borrow, from their number and rapid ſucceſſion, as well as from their ſingularity, ſo much of the complexion of imaginary adventure, that the combination cannot, I think, fail to intereſt your mind as well as your feelings.

Arrived at Negapatnam, within a ſhort run of Madras, it is natural for you to ſuppoſe that adventure was at an end, and that fortune, fatigued by the inceſſant exertion of her caprice, might have left me to proceed the ſhort reſidue of my way without further moleſtation. It fell out otherwiſe: ſhe had marked me as her game, and reſolved to worry me to the laſt moment; for, as we approached Madras, we were chaſed by a French frigate, and taken near Fort St. George.

This appeared to me the greateſt misfortune I had yet met with, and likely to be the moſt fatal in its confequences. In order to explain this, I muft recur to certain circumftances, which though I was informed of them fince my releafe from Hydernagur, I did not relate to you, becaufe they were no way connected with my narrative till now.

Monfieur SUFFREIN, the French Admiral, having a number of Britifh prifoners in his poffeffion, whom he found it extremely inconvenient to fupport, made a propofal for an exchange—which, from fome failure in the conveyance, or ambiguity in the terms of the correfpondence, was neglected.

The motives or accidents which gave rife to this neglect have never been completely developed; and perhaps the Admiral himfelf, Sir EDWARD HUGHES, and Lord MACARTNEY, were the only perfons who knew the bottom of that tranfaction. In fuch cafes, however, the ignorance of fact is generally fupplied by conjecture; and men have prefumed to cenfure unequivocally on the mere hypothetical fuggeftions of their own imaginations. Candour, however, in fuch a cafe, where it could not fpeak with certainty, would fpeak with caution. An Hiftorian, particularly, fhould fteer clear of party rancour, and not fuffer the prejudice or malignity which mifled himfelf, to go down to and miflead pofterity. Where pofitive proof is wanting, if we are obliged to decide, we muft judge by analogy and inference; and in the cafe now before us, we have little but the characters of the perfons concerned to guide us in our decifion.

Of the horrid cataftrophe which fucceeded the neglect of exchanging prifoners, it is hardly poffible that any one but Monfieur SUFFREIN himfelf could have had a conception. To fuppofe, that, under fuch an impreffion, our leading men would have hefitated to prevent it, would be to fuppofe their intellects weak, and their hearts corrupt and inhuman. I fancy it will be difficult to faften on

Lord MACARTNEY either the one or the other; for he was wise and humane: those whom the disappointment of unreasonable expectations, or the malevolence of party, have induced to suspect his Lordship's heart, have been forced by his conduct to revere his talents; and the breath of calumny has never touched the humanity of Sir EDWARD HUGHES. Whatever their motives, therefore, may have been—reason, conscience, and candour, must acquit them of the consequences. It should be recollected, too, that Monsieur SUFFREIN's character was a very probable security, in the mind of men of sense and honour, against any act of horrid inhumanity: his conduct as an officer had made a new æra in the Naval History of France: his talents and courage might be compared, without disadvantage, to those of the best of our British Admirals; and he had exhibited marks of uncommon generosity to those whom the chance of war had thrown into his hands. It would therefore have been something more than prescience to have presupposed what actually happened; and I declare most solemnly, that the inference I draw from the whole information I have had on the subject is, that, calamitous though the event was, it attaches no positive guilt on any of the parties concerned. The fact is plainly this: The French Admiral having no place on the coast where he could secure his prisoners, and grieving, as he himself subsequently wrote to Mr. HASTINGS, to see the unhappy men, who had been six or seven months at sea, dying of the scurvy, delivered over the prisoners, to the number of above three hundred, to HYDER. Their fate afterwards was such as it would harrow up your soul to hear related.

Take the whole of the circumstances into one glance, and see what my feelings must have been on finding myself once more a prisoner. HYDER ALLI, who was, when compared with the worst set-

pots of the European world, a monster, must yet be considered, when put in comparison, with his successor Tippoo, mild and merciful. Hyder, from policy and hypocrisy, shewed some lenity to the prisoners who fell into his hands. Instances are known where British captives have broke through the crowd that surrounded him into his presence for protection—when he has hypocritically feigned anger, threatened the persons who had treated them ill, reprobated severity, and sent them off satisfied for the present. Tippoo, on the contrary, was so perfectly savage, that cruelty seemed to be, not only the internal habit of his soul, but the guide of all his actions, the moving principle of his policy, the rule of his public conduct, and the source of his private gratification. Like the tyger which, Buffon tells us, kills the whole flock before he begins to feed, every appetite of his yielded to the more urgent calls of barbarity; and while one drop blood of remained unspilled, one agony uninflicted, one tear unshed, the natural appetites of Tippoo stood suspended, and the luxuries of life courted his enjoyment in vain. Like the hyena which Thompson calls the fellest of the fell, the fury of his nature was neither to be controuled by resistance, nor assuaged by blandishments. Aloof from the general order of the workings of Providence, he stands a single instance, in which the Omnipotent has presented a glowing living picture, ALL SHADE: not one ray breaks in, to relieve the gloomy aspect of the piece; but, distinct from the whole human race, of him alone it may be said, that he never yet disclosed, even for a moment, one spark of virtue.

From barbarity so inflexible to those taken in the ordinary chance of war, what could I expect if I fell again into his hands—I who had been the instrument of one of his chief Governor's defection —who had, by my negociations, contributed to deprive him of a Province, and, what perhaps might have had greater weight with him, robbed him of the gratification of a long harboured revenge, by putting his enemy HYAT SAHIB under the protection of the Company? Diabolical vengeance never perhaps met with a subject of such sublime enjoyment, as the torturing of me would have been to this monster. Couple this then, my FREDERICK, with the fears of SUFFREIN's doing by me as he had already done by the other English prisoners—and guess what my terror and consternation must have been at falling into the hands of the French!

Having struck our colours to the French frigate, the Captain ordered us to follow her, and steered to the northward. We obeyed him for some time: at length night fell; and, a fresh and favourable breeze fortunately aiding the attempt, we put about, ran for Madras, and luckily dropt anchor safely in the roads. In the escapes I had hitherto had, there was always some disagreeable circumstance to alloy the pleasure arising from them—In this instance, my joy was pure and unqualified; and I looked forward with a reasonable hope that the worst was all over.

Here I found Lord MACARTNEY governor, struggling to support the credit of the Company, and directing their affairs through such embarrassments and difficulties as made the most wise and temperate despair of success. So arduous an undertaking as the government of Madras then was, has rarely occurred: and a more successful final accomplishment is not to be instanced. In the incessant conflicts to which he was exposed, he maintained his post with inflexible firmness and unabated energy of mind—and, in the most trying circumstances, discharged his important duty with zeal, integrity and wisdom. The strict discharge of the duty he owed to his country, raised clamours against him among an interested few in India; but the united applauses of all parties, on his return to England, stamped currency on his fame, and has broken the shafts of detraction.

LETTER LXII.

AFTER so many hazards and hardships as I had undergone, it was a most pleasing reflection to find myself in a society composed of my oldest professional connections, and warmest and sincerest friends: but this was a happiness I could not long enjoy; for, being charged with a mission from HYAT SAHIB to the Governor-General and Supreme Council, I was constrained to proceed to Bengal, and accordingly set sail, for Calcutta, which I reached in little more than a week, without encountering any accident, or meeting a single occurence, worth the relation. Upon my arrival there, Sir JOHN MACPHERSON, who was in the Supreme Council, gave me a kind invitation to live at his house, and presented me to Mr. HASTINGS, with whom I entered into a negociation on behalf of HYAT SAHIB, which will appear by the following letters:

LETTER TO WARREN HASTINGS, ESQ.

"*Calcutta, May 3, 1782.*

"HONOURABLE SIR,

"Indisposition has put it out of my power, since "the first day after my arrival here, to have the "honour of paying you my respects, and of laying "before you, for the information of the board, the "objects of my mission to your superintending go- "vernment.

" As these objects are of public importance, and as ill health may prevent me, for some time longer from having the honour of waiting upon you, I take the liberty to beg your attention to this address.

" The great revolution in favour of the India Company upon the west side of India, and to which I had the happiness of being in some little degree instrumental, has been certainly brought about by the zeal and spirit of General MATTHEWS: but that officer ascribes to the orders and supplies of your government the principal merit of the undertaking: he looks to the same government for support in the arrangement which he has made, and may make, for the security of the conquered province.

" The hurry in which I left him, and his anxiety for my speedy communication of his successes, gave no time for a formal communication to the Governor-General and council, of the particulars of his successes, and of the arrangements which he wished to be adopted. He wrote a short account of the first to the Presidency of Fort St. George; and gave me a public letter to the Commander in Chief of the Military Establishment of that Presidency to which I particularly belong, in attestation of the services I rendered in the negociation between him and the Governor of Bidanore, for the surrender of that capital and province. A copy of that letter I have the pleasure to lay before you.

" As I was charged with a particular commission from HYAT SAHIB, the manager of the Bidanore province, to the Governor-General and council, as appears by his letter, which I had the honour of presenting to you, General MATHEWS gave me, in verbal instructions, and memorandums written in his own hand, the particulars of what he wished me to represent to your Government:

"he gave me, besides, short notes of introduction to two of the members of Government, whom he knew personally—referring them to me for an account of his situation, and allowing me, I believe, more credit than I deserve, for the share I had in contributing to his final acquisition of Bidanore without drawing a sword.

"It would be tedious, and more fit for the detail of conversation than of a public address, to inform you of the various steps that led to the surrender of the capital and province of Bidanore. I had had several conferences with Hyat Sahib before Hyder's death, and endeavoured to suggest to him the advantage which would arise to him from a revolt in favour of the Company. My efforts in these conversations ended ultimately in the most rigorous distress to myself: I was put in irons, and remained so for four months, in a situation only of existence without any hopes of ever escaping. When General Mathews had stormed the Ghauts, Hyat Sahib sent for me, and, after various struggles, and much indecision, agreed to my proceeding to the English camp; and I conducted General Mathews, almost unattended, into Bidanore. Hyat Sahib at length agreed to submit: but as, in his various conversations with me before and after that event, he made a very particular distinction between the government of Bombay and the chief government of the English in Indostan, so he proposed that I should immediately depart, after he had given up the place and all the forts of the Province, with a letter to you, to obtain your sanction to me to his arrangements with the English General.

"These arrangements were not even clearly defined before my departure; and so anxious was he for my speedy arrival at Calcutta, that he only "gave me the general propositions that are contained in his letter.

"Permit me here to observe, that it is by the treatment which Hyat Sahib meets with, that the other chiefs of Hyder's country will estimate the advantage of abandoning the interests of Tippoo Sahib, or will confirm their dependence upon him. Tippoo was prevented by his father from all intercourse with the Governors of his provinces, or any interference in country affairs; so that those left in charge at his father's death are stranger's to him, and are men to whom he has little attachment. He is, besides, considered to be of a cruel disposition. His father was cruel upon a political principle: he is thought to be so from nature.

"The unfortunate differences about money which arose in General Mathews's camp, and of which you will probably hear from the Presidency of Bombay, took up much of the General's time, and may have retarded his operations: however, his success in the reduction of Mangalore gives a security to his conquests. The revenues of the Bidanore Province are about twenty lacks of pagodas per annum.

"The particular situation of the capital merits attention. It is placed in a valley of considerable extent in circumference: according to the best observation I could make, there is an ascent to it, from all sides, of near seven miles: it can only be approached by four roads, which are cut among the hills, and which were judiciously fortified with great pains by Hyder: woods, to the depth of many miles, are a frontier round its skirts; and where these admitted a passage, Hyder took the precaution to plant bamboos and thorns—so that I have little fear but that General Mathews will be able to defend these passes; and as for provisions, and military stores

"of all kinds, that were found in Bidanore, of
" the latter particularly, what, according to Gene-
" ral MATHEWS's own declaration, would equip
" nine such armies as his.

" Cundapore is the next sea-port to Bidanore,
" and is distant about fifty miles : Mangalore is
" distant about a hundred miles. The road lead-
" ing from Mangalore joins with that from Cunda-
" pore, where the ascent of the hills commence:
" another road from Bidanore leads to Seringapatam,
" and a fourth into the Marhatta country.

" It was from the lower country, along the sea-
" coast, between Onore and Mangalore, which is
" watered by many rivers, and is the best cultivated
" country I ever saw, that HYDER got the greatest
" part of his provisions for his army in the Carna-
" tic; and, independent of the advantages which
" the Company have gained by the acquisition of
" these countries, the consequent losses of the
" Mysoreans are immense, and such as will disable
" them from assisting the French in the Carnatic.

" It becomes not an officer of my rank to make
" any observations that relate to the conduct of the
" different governments of my employers; but I
" am obliged to observe, in justice to HYAT SA-
" HIB's declaration to me, that he will not rely
" upon any arrangement made in his favour by the
" Governor and council of Bombay, unless he has
" a speedy answer to his letter from this govern-
" ment. He has requested me to return with that
" answer, and with the sanction of the Governor-
" General to the cowl given to him by General
" MATHEWS. Though I am worn down by my
" sufferings in prison, and my health can scarcely
" enable me to be carried by land, I am ready to
" undertake this service; for I know it is the
" greatest I may ever have it in my power to ren-
" der to the company and to my country.

" My return to the other coast with a favoura-
" ble answer to HYAT SAHIB, will be the signal to

"other Chiefs to throw off the yoke of TIPPOO; and if Colonel LONG has made any progress in the Coimbatore country, or that General MATHEWS has not been too severely pressed by TIPPOO, I may arrive upon the other coast in time to be of real use to the company.

"I know, Honourable Sir, the liberal and great system of your administration: I will not, therefore, point out any little circumstances about the footing upon which I should return to HYAT SAHIB, or remain upon the other coast. I wish only to be rewarded by my employers as I am successful; and I shall leave it to your goodness, and to your distinguished zeal for the public propriety, to give me any instructions for my conduct, or to charge me with any advices to General MATHEWS, as you may think proper.

"I hope you will pardon this long and irregular address, and honour me by communicating any part of it that you may think worthy of communication to the gentlemen of the council.

"I have the honour to be, &c. &c.

"DONALD CAMPBELL."

"P. S. When you are at leisure, and I am able to have the honour of attending you, I would wish to communicate to you a more particular detail of my conversation with HYAT SAHIB—what General MATHEWS's hopes of support from this government were, and the future plans he then meditated—and my ideas of the measures that should be pursued by the Presidency of Fort St. George, to support General MATHEWS, and improve the advantages he has gained.

"To *Warren Hastings, Esq.*
Governor-General of Bengal."

LETTER FROM HYAT SAHIB, ALLUDED TO
IN THE FOREGOING.

(Usual Introduction.)

"I have directed the affairs of the Soobeh of Hydernagur for some years past, on the part of the NAVVAUB HYDER. When lately attacked by the victorious forces of the English under the command of General MATHEWS, I opposed him, and fulfilled my duty in every respect: but seeing the superior fortune and force of the English, and receiving proposals for peace from General MATHEWS, by these circumstances, but more especially by the persuasions of Captain CAMPBELL, the son of Colonel CAMPBELL, who was formerly at Chinaputtan, I was induced to come to terms, and delivered up to General MATHEWS the treasury, property, stores and keys of the forts of this country. If I had been disposed, I had it in my power to have appropriated this collected wealth to other purposes; but, from a regard to the high fortune of the KING of ENGLAND, and the uprightness and integrity of the English people, I have included myself in the number of your servants, and have determined, with the utmost sincerity and purity of heart, to serve you well and faithfully. By the blessing of GOD, under your auspices, my endeavours towards the well and full performance of my duty shall be ten-fold greater than heretofore; and as General MATHEWS intends to proceed to Seringputtam, your loyal servant will assist, to the utmost of his ability and power. You will be fully informed on this subject by Captain CAMPBELL. Honour, and favour, and reward, must flow from you.

"From the time of your first establishment in this country to the present period, the engagements of

"the English have been sacredly performed and ad-
"hered to; nor have they been wanting in their
"protection of the honor and dignity of the Sur-
"dars of Bengal, and other places. I hope, from
"your favour and benevolence, that you will issue
"your commands to General MATHEWS, to favour
"me with all due kindness and attention. I have
"taken shelter under the shadow of your benevo-
"lence. Captain CAMPBELL has shewn me great
"kindness in this respect, and, by encouraging me
"to hope for your favour, has led me to become
"your servant. You will be fully informed of the
"state of affairs in this quarter by Captain CAMB-
"BELL's letters.

"Written on the 25th of Suffur, A. H. 1197."
"A true copy,
"J. P. AURIOL, Sec."

LETTER TO WARREN HASTINGS, ESQ.

"*Calcutta*, May 25, 1783.

"HONOURABLE SIR,
"Some time ago, I did myself the honour of
"writing to you, on the subject of my mission
"from HYAT SAHIB to this government.
"It is with pleasure I now understand that you
"have come to the resolution of sending an answer
"to his letter. I cannot help delivering it as my
"opinion, that a decided and avowed protection
"granted to him from this government, will be
"productive of great public utility: but should
"you, and the other gentlemen of the council,
"think proper to decline this, from motives best
"known to yourselves, and of which I shall not
"pretend to judge, I beg leave humbly to repre-
"sent, that the sooner HYAT SAHIB's letter is
"acknowledged, the more satisfactory it will be to

"him, and the more efficacious in its probable
"good consequences.
"I am ready and anxious to proceed immediate-
"ly to the other coast with the answer to HYAT
"SAHIB, and shall take the liberty of hoping that
"you will give me instructions to remain some
"time with him, that he may have an opportunity
"of transmitting, through me, any communication
"that he may wish to establish with this govern-
"ment. I have the pleasure to inform you, that
"that Presidency to which I particularly belong,
"have granted me their consent to be employed in
"the final arrangement of the Bidanore treaty,
"should your board think proper to choose me as
"a fit person; and they have further unanimously
"done me the honour to approve of my conduct
"in the commencement of this business.

"With respect to the appointments you may
"judge right to allow me, I trust entirely to your
"own ideas of propriety. I wish for nothing more
"than what is sufficient to defray the expences of
"such a journey, and to enable me to maintain
"that character in a situation of this kind which is
"requisite to promote the public good.
"I have the honour to be, with the greatest respect,
"HONOURABLE SIR,
"Your most faithful and most obedient servant,
"DONALD CAMPBELL."

After some delay, I received instructions, together with a letter from Mr. HASTINGS for HYAT,
with which I set off in order to deliver it into his
own hands, as follows:

LETTER TO CAPTAIN DONALD CAMPBELL.

"SIR,
"I have it in command from the Honourable
"the Governor-General and council, to transmit

" you the inclosed answer from the Governor-
" General to the letter which you brought from
" Hyat Sahib, the Fousdar of Bidanore, to this
" government, upon the occasion of his surrender-
" ing that country to the company. As you pro-
" pose to return to Bidanore, the Board request
" that you will deliver this answer in person to
" Hyat Sahib, with the assurances from them of
" every protection and support which the eminent
" services rendered by him to the company give
" him so good a right to expect, and which they
" have it in their power to grant; and you will
" acquaint him, that they have further agreed to
" recommend him in such terms to the Honoura-
" ble the Court of Directors, as may encourage
" him to hope for every attention from their
" justice.

" Considering the great importance of the ac-
" quisition of Bidanore to the company, its propor-
" tionable disadvantage to the enemy, and the
" magnitude of the object to be obtained by hold-
" ing out every possible incitement and encourage-
" ment to the Managers of the Mysore country, to
" throw off a new and unsettled dependence on
" the enemy's government, in order to obtain a
" more secure and beneficial tenure from the com-
" pany's possession, the Board are the more readi-
" ly inclined to afford this early return to the ad-
" vances of Hyat Sahib, in the hope that it will
" inspire him with fresh confidence in the English
" government, and rivet his attachment to it.

" It will be at your option, either to return im-
" mediately with Hyat Sahib's answer to the
" Governor-General's letter, if you shall deem it
" of sufficient consequence to require it, or to re-
" main with him, if you conceive that your resi-
" dence there for any time will be more conducive
" to the public interests; but, in either case, you
" are desired to report the particulars of your re-

"ception and proceedings to this government,
with any other information which you may think
it useful for them to know.

   "I am, Sir,
 "Your most obedient, humble servant,
      "J. P. Auriol, Sec."
"Fort William, May 29, 1783."

It would be unpardonable in me to let this occasion pass, without expressing the high sense I entertain of Mr. HASTINGS's politeness, and Sir JOHN MACPHERSON's kindness and hospitality, during my stay at Calcutta. As to Mr. HASTINGS, in his public capacity, it would be presumptuous and injudicious to say much, as he now stands for the judgment of the highest tribunal in this country. My own observation leads me to consider him as a man of sound, acute and brilliant talents, and of a vast and comprehensive mind—of manners sociable, amiable, meek and unaffected—and of a disposition truly benevolent. His superior knowledge of the political interests of Indostan, and particularly of the affairs of the East India company, has never been questioned; and, if the suffrage of the people of India may be allowed to decide, his conduct as Governor-General, though, like every thing human, intermixed with error, was, on the whole, great and laudable—for I declare I scarcely ever heard a man in India, Native or European, censure him, although he was often the subject of conversation with all persons and in all companies in the East.

The social virtues of Sir JOHN MACPHERSON are so well known, that it would be superfluous to notice them. The same friendship and hospitality I experienced in his house, has been shared by many, who are not backward in doing him ample justice on that head. But his conduct during his short administration can be known only by those who make the political concerns of India a subject of studious attention. To enter into a detail of his various wise regulations for the restoration of the company's affairs, would be destructive of the end I propose, which is, by a concise and simple summary of the whole, to render a fair picture of his administration so clear as to be understood by any person, however ignorant he may be of the politics of that country, and so brief as not to discourage the reading of it.

Sir JOHN MACPHERSON took the reins of government into his hands on the first of February, 1785. He found the company's revenues diminished, and their expenditure increased, by the continual claims of Proprietors, Directors, and Ministers, to a share in the patronage of Mr. HASTINGS—and a public debt accumulating to an enormous amount. He therefore saw the necessity of putting in practice every expedient possible, and trying every experiment that the state of the country suggested, as likely to promote an increase of the revenue, a diminution of the public expenditure, and a liquidation of the debt. He, therefore, on the fourteenth day of his administration, commenced a reform, which he continued with indefatigable zeal and industry to introduce through the various departments of government—and, beginning with himself, discharged his body-guards. While he was thus employed in India, the Company and Parliament in England were unremittingly engaged in considering and molding into shape a system of reform also; and, extraordinary as it may appear, the fact is, that the sagacity of Mr. MACPHERSON had adopted by anticipation, and actually reduced to practice, the identical speculative reforms which the Parliament and Company were proceeding upon in England; and the general plan of reform which passed the court of directors on the eleventh of April, 1785, had been actually carried into execution by Sir JOHN MACPHERSON in Bengal, in the months of February, March and April, 1785. He made arrangements for the diffusion of knowledge—established the settlement of Pulo Penang, or Prince of Wales's Island—settled the bank of Calcutta on a firm basis —regulated the markets—and, by a plan of his own conception, secured the Company from the accustomed fraudulent compositions with Zemindars, by bonding their balances, and making the bonds cancelable only by the Court of Directors. In fine, he introduced and carried into effect a system of reform which had a most sudden and salutary effect on the British affairs in India; and in an administration of only eighteen months, he had the felicity to perceive the fruits of his wisdom and industry maturing—to receive that best of earthly rewards, the esteem and applause of his fellow-citizens—and to be honoured by the best of Sovereigns with the dignity of a Baronet.

While I was at Sir JOHN MACPHERSON's house, I happened, in conversation one day with Mr. MACAULY, Sir JOHN's Secretary, to be talking over some part of my adventures; and found to my astonishment, that he had, in his route to India, accidentally hired the very servant whom I had lost at Trieste by sending him for letters to Venice; and Mr. MACAULY assured me, that he found him possessed of all the good qualities I had expected to meet in him: but the poor fellow had died before my arrival at Calcutta, to my great mortification and disappointment.

As the season in which I was to leave Calcutta was very unfavourable for a voyage by sea, and the coast thereabouts is one of the most inhospitable in the world, I set off by land for Madras, and in my way had an opportunity of surveying that curious and grotesque monument of superstitious folly, called the Jagranaut Pagoda. It is an immense, barbarous structure, of a kind of pyramidal form, embellished with devices cut in stone-work, not more singular than disgusting. Christian idolators, in forming types and figures of divine beings, always endeavour to represent them with personal beauty, as proportionate to their divine nature as human skill can make it. Those Pagans, on the contrary, in forming their idols, cast out every vestige of beauty—every thing that, by the consent of mankind, is supposed to convey pleasing sensations; and, in their place, substitute the most extravagant, unnatural deformity, the most loathsome nastiness, the most disgusting obscenity. It is not in language to convey an adequate idea of their temples and idols; and if it was, no purpose could be answered by it, only the excitement of painful and abominable sensations. To keep pace with the figures of their idols, a chief Bramin, by some accursed artificial means, (by herbs, I believe), has brought to a most unnatural form, and enormous dimensions, that which decency forbids me to mention; and the pure and spotless women, who from infancy have been shut up from the sight of men, even of their brothers, are brought to kiss this disgusting and misshapen monster, under the preposterous belief that it promotes fecundity.

In this Pagoda stands the figure of Jagranaut, (their god under Brama); and a sightly figure it is truly!—nothing more than a black stone, in an irregular pyramidal form, having two rich diamonds in the top by way of eyes, and a nose and mouth painted red. For this god, five hundred priests are daily employed in boiling food, which, as he seldom eats it, they doubtless convert to their own use in the evening.

I stopped at Vizagapatnam for a few days with Mr. RUSSEL, who was chief of that place. His style of living was so exactly similar to that of an elegant family residing at their country-house in England, that I felt myself more happy and comfortable than I had been since my arrival in India; and that happiness was much increased by meeting Mr. MAXTON, who was married to Mr. RUSSEL's daughter. This gentleman and I had, when mere boys, been shipmates on our first going out to India: a warm friendship took place between us, which has met with no interruption, but rather increased from lapse of time, and greater habits of intimacy. To see a man whom I so entirely esteemed, in possession of the most perfect domestic felicity, and surrounded by a number of amiable connections and friends, was to me a subject of the most pleasing contemplation.

LETTER LXIII.

LEAVING Vizagapatam, I took my route along the coast, and arrived at Masulipatam, where I heard rumours of the unfortunate fate of General MATHEWS. This threw such a damp upon my spirits, that all the hospitality and kindness of Mr. DANIEL, the chief, could scarcely raise me from despondence; and on my arrival at Madras, I found the whole amply confirmed.

As HYAT SAHIB's affair yet remaining unsettled, and I considered myself in a degree pledged to obtain him some satisfaction for his services in surrendering the province of Bidanore, and to fulfil my engagements with him and the Supreme Council, I determined to proceed to Bombay, notwithstanding the disaster of General MATHEWS, which had entirely crushed all my private prospects in that quarter, and to co-operate with HYAT SA‑

him in such measures as might yet remain to us for promoting the public good. I left Madras, therefore, and prosecuted my journey without any material interruption until I reached Palamcotah, where the chagrin arising from my various disappointments, co-operating with fatigue and climate, threw me into a fit of sickness, which confined me to my bed for five or six weeks. Upon recovering a little, I crawled on to Anjengo, where, at the house of Mr. HUTCHINSON, the Resident, (who treated me with cordial kindness), I waited for an opportunity of getting to Bombay, and during that time laid in a stock of strength and spirits: at length a Europe ship touched at Anjengo on her way to Bombay, I obtained a passage and proceeded.

At Bombay I found HYAT SAHIB, it having been deemed expedient to send him away from Bidanore on the approach of TIPPOO with his army, where I received from him a confirmation of what I have stated respecting General MATHEWS receiving only two lacks of rupees and a necklace. And now, as peace was negociating between us and TIPPOO, and my remaining on the Malabar coast could be of little use, I determined to return to the Carnatic. And here I have an incident to add to the many disagreeable occurrences of my life, in which, with intentions the most innocent, I was made the subject of obloquy and unmerited scandal.

Just at the time I was leaving Bombay, a young lady, the daughter of a person formerly of high rank in India, and now a member of Parliament, but whose name it would be useless to mention, wished to return to the Carnatic; and I, at the request of herself, and another lady with whom she lived, unguardedly took charge of her during the journey. Before our departure, I reflected upon the difficulties and impropriety of this step, and communicated my ideas to the ladies, who, instead of listening to the objections I started, pressed me to fulfil my promise: I consented, purely from principles of politeness and good-nature. During the course of our journey, she unfolded to me, of her own accord, certain acts of cruelty and injustice she had suffered from her father, at the instigation of her *mother-in-law*, with a story of her innocence having fallen, and her reputation having been destroyed, by a connection of the lady under whose charge she was, and who for that reason had pressed her departure with me; and added, she was so disgusted with India, that she determined to quit it; and entreated me to assist her in the accomplishment of her wishes. I disapproved, in the most unqualified terms, of her project—gave her the best and most disinterested advice—and, through the whole disagreeable business which was imposed upon me, acted merely with a view to her honour and happiness; and several of the most respectable people in Palamcotah, where she passed some time, and at Madras, where she afterwards resided, could attest the delicacy of my conduct towards her, as well as the concern and interest I took in every thing that was likely to be of advantage to her.

This is a fair statement of the matter; and yet, on account of it, I was most infamously scandalized; and the scandal reached even the ears of my father, whom, however, I soon satisfied on that head. But that which stung me to the quick was the conduct of some of my own relations, (who, if they even could not justify or approve, ought at least to have been silent), in becoming the most virulent of my detractors—though, when the character of those very relations had on former occasions been reflected upon, I stood up and defended them at the imminent hazard of my life. Such conduct appeared to me most atrocious; for, whether from affection, selfishness, or pride, I always strenuously supported my relations, if I heard them traduced in their absence—and, when I was not able to justify their proceedings, at least suppressed the conversation. To a man who had uniformly acted so, were there even no reciprocation of family affection, mutual justice demanded different treatment from that I experienced, which could have sprung only from depravity of heart, poverty of intellect, and the most abject meanness of spirit. And what is remarkable on this, as well as on other occasions, those who had been under the greatest obligation to my father and myself, were the most inveterate.

On the death of my father, looking over his papers in the presence of the Deputy Sheriff of Argyll, and three other gentlemen, we met with a letter on the subject from the young lady's father to mine, reflecting in a gross manner on my character. I directly wrote to that gentleman, explaining the whole affair, and demanding justice to be done to my reputation. Upon an ecclairecissement of the matter, he wrote to me a complete apology, acknowledging that he had acted on that occasion through misrepresentation, and had too easily given credit to ill-founded reports; and saying, that as the letter in question had, by the perusal of the Deputy Sheriff and other gentlemen, in some measure become a matter of public notoriety, he thought it incumbent on him to make that apology, and to express his sincere regret for any detriment I might have sustained, by his yielding unguardedly to a sudden impulse of passion, caused, as he was then perfectly convinced, by misinformation.

Thus was my character at once cleared of a calumny which the industrious villany of a few had contrived to propagate through every spot of the earth where I was known.

CONCLUSION.

This story may serve as an instructive lesson to you, my FREDERICK, to avoid, in the very first instance, any connection with women that in the probable course of things can lead to private acts of confidence: they are at best indiscreet—tend, as in this case, to make a man a dupe—and never fail to lead to scandal and reproach. You will also, from the letter of the lady's father, found eight or ten years after it was written among my father's papers, see the impropriety and hazard of committing your thoughts incautiously to paper. I have known it frequently, as in this instance, end in mortification and regret.

Before quitting entirely the Malabar coast, I took a trip to Surat, which amply repaid me for my trouble. It surpasses any part of India for extent and variety of commerce, for populous streets and suburbs, and for a continually moving scene of opulence. For a more minute account of it, I refer you to the Abbé RAYNAL, who, though not generally accurate, is so elegant, that you will be able, from his description, to form a lively conception of the place, and its singular customs.

Here I was received in a very friendly manner by Mr. SETON. And indeed I may now once for all declare, that at every place where I stopped, and every post I passed, from my leaving England till my return, I experienced the most kind and liberal reception, and the most assiduous attention: my wants of every kind, whether of vessels, boats, guards of Sepoys, letters of introduction, &c. being supplied by anticipation, I had scarcely occasion to make a request, or express a wish; nor was the attention shewn to the public service less than that which was manifested for my private convenience. To kindness so truly consolatory as it then was to me, I never look back without sentiments of unbounded gratitude and unfeigned acknowledgment.

My journeys by land in India after my shipwreck, independent of long voyages by sea, amounted to more than three thousand miles. After getting back to Madras, my health being materially injured, I resolved to return to England: but, having seen almost all the Company's possessions, I felt a curiosity to see China, and determined to make that my way. To render this route more agreeable to me, Lord MACARTNEY, in addition to his other favours, gave me the following handsome letter of introduction to Mr. PIGOU, the Company's chief supercargo at Canton:

"*Fort St. George, July* 23, 1784.

" SIR,

" This letter will be delivered to you by Captain
" DONALD CAMPBELL, of this Establishment—a
" gentleman who has signalized himself on many
" occasions, but more particularly by his ability
" and address in accomplishing the surrender of the
" fort of Bidanore, at which place he had been
" long a prisoner. His ill state of health contract-
" ed there, renders a voyage to China, perhaps to
" Europe, absolutely necessary. Should he remain
" any time at your Settlement, I shall be much
" obliged to you for any attention and civility
" shewn to him; and I shall be happy, on any oc-
" casion you may afford me, of returning your po-
" lite attention to an officer of so much merit
" as Captain CAMPBELL, and of proving how
" much I am,
" SIR,
" Your most obedient and most humble servant,
MACARTNEY,

" *To William Henry Pigou, Esq.*"

I had also a letter to Mr. FREEMAN, another Supercargo there; by whom, as well as by Mr.

CONCLUSION. 403

Pigou, I was treated with great politeneſs; and Mr. Freeman being obliged to leave Canton, and go to Macao, for the recovery of his health, invited me to accompany him there. I availed myſelf of the opportunity: and, as we went all along through the rivers, had an opportunity of ſeeing more of the country than many of the Europeans who viſit that country. With the obſervations which I made in the courſe of this excurſion and my reſidence at Canton, I would furniſh you, but that Lord Macartney's embaſſy is juſt returned from that country; and there is every reaſon to hope that he, or ſome of the gentlemen who attended him, and who poſſeſs ſuperior abilities and more ample materials, will favour the public with a much more perfect account than mine could poſſibly be.

While I remained at Canton, a very diſagreeable rupture took place between the Factory and the Chineſe. An Engliſh ſhip lying at Wampoa, in ſaluting, ſhattered a Chineſe boat; by which accident, two men in it were much hurt with the ſplinters, and one of them died of his wounds ſoon after. The matter was clearly explained to the Mandarins; and they ſeemed to be ſatisfied that it was merely an accident. A few days after, the Supercorgo of the ſhip was forcibly ſeized, and carried into the city: the Council met, and determined to ſend for the ſailors from the ſhips; and in the evening after dark, fifteen or ſixteen, boats, with four or five hundred men attempted, in an irregular manner, to come up to Canton—were fired upon by the Chineſe boats and forts in paſſing, and, with a few men wounded, were compelled to retreat. Nothing could ſurpaſs the conſternation and indeciſion of the Council; and after the moſt humiliating language, they were obliged to appeaſe the Chineſe, and ſettle the affair by giving up the gunner of the ſhip to their reſentment.

CONCLUSION.

On the 29th December, 1784, I embarked in the Ponſborne Eaſt-Indiaman, Captain HAMMET, in which I had come from Madras to China; and, after a tolerable voyage of five months and two days, got on board a fiſhing boat off Falmouth, and was put on ſhore there, having been exactly four years and five days from England.

Such was my impatience to ſee you, that I wrote from Falmouth for you to meet me at Bath. We arrived there the ſame day: and never in my life did I experience ſuch tranſports as in firſt preſſing you to my boſom: I found you all that my heart could wiſh; and I muſt, in juſtice to my opinion, aver, that not one action of your life has tended ſince to give me a moment's pain: on the contrary, I have every reaſon to be ſatisfied that my ſanguine hopes of you will be realized. The turn of your thoughts and actions have been vigilantly watched and cloſely examined by me; and from your affection to myſelf and your mother, your gentle deportment to my domeſtics, your frankneſs and candour with your brother and ſchool-fellows—even from your fondneſs for your favourite dog *Pompey*, and frequent ſilent contemplations of the etchings of his countenance, I have drawn the moſt pleaſing preſages of purity and innocence of heart, ſweetneſs, of temper, and refined honour and generoſity. If it pleaſes GOD to ſpare your life, and ſtrengthen your conſtitution, I ſhall ſtill be the happieſt of men, notwithſtanding the inroad made upon my feelings by the hardſhips and afflictions I had undergone, of which many aroſe from unavoidable accident, and ſome from malignant and unnatural perſecution, ariſing from baſe envy, dictated by cowardly revenge. I do not wiſh you to know who the wretches are: I only wiſh you to know that ſuch deteſtable paſſions do exiſt in human nature—that, warned by their wickedneſs to me, you may, in your progress through life, be cautious, temperate and guarded.

Another thing I am anxious to impress upon the mind, particularly, of your brother JOHN, is the danger of a warm, impetuous temper. Many of the hazards and difficulties of my life arose from the predominance of a fiery spirit, and an ungovernable, mistaken ambition. A single instance will serve to shew it. When I was under the command of Captain, afterwards General MATHEWS, in his regiment of cavalry, being cantoned at a place called Tuckolam, in the neighbourhood of extensive woods, information was brought us that wild bulls infested the neighbouring villages, and had killed some people: we prepared to enter the wood, and destroy, if possible, these ferocious animals, which had become the terror and destruction of the contiguous country. The origin of those wild herds was this—From time immemorial, a religious custom had prevailed among the Pagan inhabitants, of offering a calf to the wood upon the accomplishment of any favourite purpose, such as the safe delivery of his wife, or the obtaining an employment, &c. In process of time, those calves bred, and became numerous and incredibly fierce. Independent of protecting the defenceless natives, it was in itself a most interesting kind of hunting. The mode of doing it was this—A large party, well mounted, galloping in a body up to a great flock, and marking out the fiercest champion of the whole, attacked him with swords and pistols. One day, a bull which was wounded, and thereby rendered more fierce, though not less vigorous, got posted in some thick bushes, in such a manner as to be approached only in front: a whim of the most extravagant kind came into my head, suggested by vain-glory and youthful fire—I thought it ungenerous for so many to attack him at once; and, wishing to have the credit of subduing him, I dismounted from my horse, and attacked him with a pike: I soon, however, had cause to repent this rash and unwarrantable step; it had nearly been fatal to me—for the bull soon threw the pike into the air, and, had it not been for the very gallant exertions of my brother officers, who rode in upon him, and rescued me at the moment that the brute's horns had touched my coat, I must have been killed. An Indian officer, who was in my troop, particularly distinguished himself, at the imminent hazard of his life, the bull having tossed his horse and himself to a distance from his horns. At this time I was but eighteen years of age, and had not the judgment to reflect, that if I had been killed, my fate would be attended with only pity or scorn for my folly; whereas, had I succeeded, the whole reward of my danger would have been the useless applause of some youngsters, idle and inconsiderate as myself—while my rashness would have been reprobated by every man whose good opinion was worth enjoying. One or two people who were present at the time, are now living in great repute in England. We succeeded, however, in driving those wild cattle into the interior recesses of the wood, dividing the flesh of those we killed among such of the poor Sepoys as would eat it, and thereby rendered essential service to the contiguous villages.

Often when I have heard, in coffee-houses and play-houses, some of our sporting sparks boasting of their prowess over a timid hare or a feeble fox, I could not help recollecting with respect the hunters of India, who chase the destructive monsters of the forest—the boar, the tyger, the hyena, the bull, or the buffalo; and, while they steel the nerves, animate the courage, and, by habitual deeds of pith, fit themselves for war, render essential service to their fellow creatures, and save the lives and property of thousands. Such greatness of spirit, under the controul of good sense, and the direction of prudence, must render a man respectable—but, if not managed with discretion, leaves a man no other praise than that of a magnanimous madman. Take every opportunity, my dear FREDERICK, of inculcating these precepts in the mind of your brother: the natural warmth of his temper often makes me fearful of the mischievous consequences which I have myself too often experienced—though, I thank GOD, it never stimulated me to revenge, or to a premeditated intention of injuring any one.

I have already said more than once, that I have a most perfect conviction your amiable disposition will ensure to you the love of mankind; but it will at the same time subject you to many impositions—to gaurd against which, a great share of sternness is sometimes necessary: there is, besides, a certain degree of fortitude absolutely requisite to give lustre to a gentle disposition; without it, meekness is thought timidity—modesty, weakness—and the charming mildness of the forgiving heart, abused as the pitiful resource of abject apprehension and a mean spirit. There are times, therefore, when the wickedness of men, and the customs of the world, make it necessary to lay aside the lamb, and assume the lion. EUROPE at this moment presents an awful and alarming crisis. In a neighbouring country, the conduct of the higher classes of society has produced a dreadful convulsion: social order has been subverted, and the stability of property annihilated: all reasoning from the history of former times is found inapplicable to the present: the system of warfare itself has undergone a revolution; and no man is able to say from positive inference, " Thus will it be to-morrow." Our insular situation, thank GOD! protects us: and the precarious footing upon which civil order and property stand in most countries on the continent, make our state in England enviable. The time is nevertheless pregnant with extraordinary event; and you are now approaching that age at which men should be ready to act at the call of their country. It is therefore fitting for you to make such things the subject of frequent contemplation—to habituate your mind to the meeting of danger, so as to be ready, at a moment's warning, to lay down your life, if necessary, for the good of your country; for, after all, my FREDERICK, what avails it whether we die in this way or in that?—to die with honour and a good conscience, is all. Let prejudice be laid aside—and who, possessed of common sense, could hesitate a moment to prefer death in the field, to death with the loathsome aggravation of sickness, the crocodile tears of pretended friends, and the painful emotions and lamentations of those who really love us?

Finally, I must observe, that at the time I left India, the affairs of the British Nation wore so very lowering an aspect, all persons acquainted with our concerns there, allowed nothing but a long series of wise measures, with the best efficient servants to execute them, could rescue the company from ruin. I am happy in being able now to state, without the possibility of contradiction, that the clouds which menaced us in that quarter have since been gradually dissipating beneath the measures of the BOARD of CONTROUL, under the direction of Mr. DUNDAS; and are at last entirely dispersed by the glorious administration of Lord CORNWALLIS, whose wisdom in the cabinet tended no less to the security, than his military talents, justice and moderation, to the honour, of GREAT BRITAIN in the East. The choice of such a person for the government of India, reflects credit on HIS MAJESTY's Councils, and evinces that the paternal care and solicitude of our amiable SOVEREIGN extend to the most remote part of the Empire.

END OF PART III.

APPENDIX.

LETTER FROM GENERAL MATHEWS,

TO

THE COURT OF DIRECTORS OF THE EAST INDIA COMPANY.

(REFERRED TO IN THE FOREGOING LETTERS.)

HONOURABLE SIRS,

I HAVE the honour of informing you of the success of your arms on the Malabar coast. You will have received advices of the outset of the expedition from Bombay, and the general purport of it. On the 12th of December, I sailed with a small party; and thought proper, of my own accord, to land at Rajamundroog, in preference to any other place—because, on this part of the coast I had the double advantage of being able to secure myself until reinforced, and to procure provisions, which I could not have done at Cundapore, or any place to the southward, by reason of the numerous garrisons, and the vicinity of them to the capital. The measures and dispositions of the gentlemen at Bombay were such, that I could not place any dependence upon being timely reinforced from thence, or of having any supply of provisions. Rajamundroog is on the top of a high hill, and commands the entrance of the best river on the coast. We took it by storm. The moment we landed, a short time was taken up in preparing to move towards Onore; for we had not a cooly, carriage, or bullock, to convey any stores. The battering cannon, ammunition, provisions, &c. were sent by sea; and the great additions that HYDER had made to the fortifications of Onore and fortified Island, prevented my entering the river with the small craft, and obliged me to land every thing through a heavy surf on the beach, and then to cross the river to the northward of the fort. These impediments were got over; and a practicable breach being effected, the assault was made—and the garrison, consisting of two thousand five hundred men, were either killed, drowned, or made prisoners.—Shortly after this event, the troops from the southward, under Lieutenant Colonel MACLEOD, were landed at Rajamundroog. To wait for a junction, would take up much time: so, that not a moment should be lost, I embarked, and landed near Cundapore, under the fire of the Bombay Grab and the Intrepid, and immediately seized a small fort that served to secure our stores. The enemy were in sight, and seemed numerous: some prisoners that we took, reckoned them at twelve hundred horse, one thousand Sepoys, and five hundred Peons. My party was composed of three hundred and fifty Europeans, six hundred Sepoys, and four in all field-pieces—with which I marched, first towards the enemy, who drew back, and then I proceeded to Cundapore. They incommoded my rear very much; but being determined to attack the fort, I only acted on the defensive, and at seven in the evening got possession of the fort, and the several redoubts that commanded the river. The grand object of the expedition, an attack upon Bidanore, remained to be undertaken; and much serious reflection it required before the

hazardous enterprize should be determined on.—
Your Honours will now take a view of the state
of my army: No carriage-bullock, and the few
draft not able to draw eight light field-pieces—not
a cooly to carry musquet, ammunition or provisions
—not a tent—and many officers, HIS MAJESTY's
in particular, had not a single servant—neither bullock
or sheep to be had, the enemy having drove
them off. The army, at this time, consisted of
about eleven hundred effective Europeans, and
three thousand Sepoys. The distance from Cundapore
to the foot of the Ghaut is thirty miles,
through a woody country: the enemy's army had
been reinforced, and lay in the way. The reports
of the strength of the various works that defended
the pass up the mountains, was such as gave me
but very faint hope of success; and the difficulty
of supplying my troops with rice, was almost of
itself sufficient to deter a person from the attempt.
However, having positive orders to take possession
of Bidanore, I resolved to make a trial, and issued
directions for the march. We had not gone six
miles, before the enemy opposed us in force. We
pushed forwards; and, by the effect of well served
artillery, and the steadiness of the men, the enemy
retired as we advanced. The skirmish continued
about three hours—after which we were left to
pursue our route unmolested; nor did the enemy
make any stand till we were on the fourth day's
march, within three miles of the pass—where, the
ground being favourable, they attempted opposition,
and were roughly treated, losing, by the bayonet
and shot, above three hundred men. They
were pursued to a small fort, which was immediately
abandoned; and then fled to the first barrier
or entrance of the pass. This was a line of masonry
that covered all the open ground, and was
closed by woods to the right and left. Upon six
bastions were mounted fifteen pieces of cannon;

and on the left was a work on a steep mountain, with two twelve pounders. This altogether had too formidable an appearance to attack in front; but having reconnoitred the right, I imagined that the flank might be turned by ascending the hill through the wood. Early in the morning, two parties were formed—one to attempt the flank, the other to escalade the wall; but the enemy saved us that trouble by evacuating the place. This was a happy moment to try the pass; for the enemy, by felling trees, &c. would have thrown so many obstacles in the way, that the want of provision would have compelled me to relinquish the design. A party was instantly ordered to follow the enemy up the hill, which, with little loss, gained the second barrier, on which were mounted eleven guns. Fifty of the enemy were killed or taken at this work. Having this success, I relieved the exhausted by fresh detachments, which excited emulation, and encouraged the ardour of the Sepoys; for, to the unremitting exertions of this branch of your troops is due the honour of this day. Battery after battery was taken; and the possession of the fort on the top of the Ghaut, about five in the afternoon, called Hyderghur, crowned the whole. At this fort we found mounted thirty pieces of cannon, from twenty-four to four pounders; and at the different works in the pass, forty others, from four to twelve.

When we contemplated the numerous redoubts and the height of the Ghaut, and were told by prisoners that we had drove off seventeen thousand men, including dismounted cavalry, regular Sepoys, and match-lock Peons, we could not consider the victory we had gained as due to us—our weak efforts would have been in vain. The progress of your arms is to be ascribed to the Divine will. In the course of this war, Providence has been peculiarly bountiful—When we were in want of rice, we were sure to find a supply left for our use by the enemy—when our musquet-ammunition was expended, the enemy's magazines furnished us abundantly—cannon we found in every fort, and such quantities of warlike stores, that we are apt to suppose that HYDER supplied all his garrisons from this coast and from Bidanore. Hyderghur is about fourteen miles from Hydernagur, *alias* Bidanore, the capital of the Province.

In the night of the day that we gained the Ghaut, I was visited by Captain DONALD CAMPBELL, the son of Colonel CHARLES CAMPBELL. He had been wrecked off the coast, was seized, and kept in irons, until the approach of this army caused the Jemadar to release him, to employ him as an Ambassador. His message was, that the Jemadar having lost his Master (HYDER), and being upon bad terms with TIPPOO SAHIB, would willingly put himself under the protection of the Company, provided that the management of the country was continued to him. The idea of getting possession of the capital and the forts of the kingdom towards Seringapatam, as well as the very great advantage I might expect from his experience, abilities and influence, with the weak state of my army, induced me to close with the proposal; and I lent him a cowl, signifying that his power and influence should not be lessened. This, tho' not drawn with a pen of a lawyer, was equal in value to the capital of Bidanore. Captain CAMPBELL returned with it, and was to tell the Jemadar that I should march in the morning.

Not expecting the great success that we had met with by forcing the pass on the main road, I had detached Lieutenant-Colonel MACLEOD to the left to ascend the Ghaut through a narrow path, in order to attack Hyderghur in the rear. The absence of this detachment, and the fatigue of the former day, reduced my party to about four hund.ed Eu ropeans and seven hundred Sepoys; and all my guns were at the bottom of the Ghaut. With this detachment I moved towards Bidanore, and was within a mile of the walls before any message came from Captain CAMPBELL or the Jemadar: but having nothing to apprehend in the field from the panic-struck enemy, we continued our march until the welcome approach of Captain CAMPBELL assured me the place was our own. On entering it, I was pleased to see about four hundred of your Sepoys that had been taken in the Carnatic, who offered me their service. Upon visiting the Jemadar, I repeated my assurances, that while he behaved faithfully to the Company, the management of the country should be continued to him; and, although the sword must be in your hands, that he should have as much power and influence as his station required and that you would not refuse settling upon him very ample allowances. The enemy being in force, and my army much weakened, with other disagreeable matters that occured, prevented my further advance than to take possession of two forts to the Eastward; for, being apprehensive that the Killidar of Mangalore would not deliver up that place to the order of HYAT SAHIB, and considering that famous seaport of more consequence to your affairs than acquiring territory beyond the mountains, I held myself in readiness to march that way, and was forced to lay siege to it. A practicable breach being made, the Killidar thought proper to surrender it. Upon this happy event give me leave to congratulate you; for it partly secures our conquests from Carwar to Cananore. There are two or three places that I have not been able to summons; but as these garrisons cannot expect any succour, they will fall of course.

Thus have I given your honours a short recital, from the first landing of your arms on the 12th of December, to the reduction of Mangalore on the 9th;

of March; in which short time a series of success
has attended us that can hardly be paralleled. All
the enemy's marine has fallen in our hands, among
which are eight ships of the line, either built or
on the stocks; and five of them might be sent to
sea in a short time. After informing you of the
happy and glorious success of your arms, it is painful for me to tell you, that dissention in the army, on account of plunder and booty, has arisen
to such a height as to threaten open mutiny. I
have informed your Honours of the terms that the
Jemadar required, and that I in your name granted;
and you know in how peaceable a manner this capital
was resigned to you. I am sorry to say, that His
Majesty's officers have been foremost in the clamours; and that the agents appointed by them have
occasioned me much trouble and anxiety, and a
great deal of discontent throughout the army. I
shall send you copies of the several letters that have
passed, for your determination. They may suppose that I have appropriated treasure to my own
use, or bargained to restore the private property of
the Jemadar to him; or that I should agree that he
should call all treasure and jewels his private property, to the exclusion of what of right should belong to the Honourable Company or the captors.
I have only to assure your Honours, that I have
made no bargain whatever, either public or private,
but what was expressed in the cowl sent from Hyderghur, to which Captain CAMPBELL was witness: and as I have frequently mentioned to my
friends, that I would not receive a present of consequence without the consent of the Honourable
Company, I shall inform you, that on my first visit
the Jemadar insisted on making me a present of a
lack of rupees; and when he pleased to give a do-
nation to the army of two lacks and thirty thousand
of rupees, which sum waits your pleasure, he requested I would accept of another lack of rupees.

To both of these requests respecting myself, I replied, that provided your Honours would give me leave, I should certainly embrace that fortunate moment to gain an independence, and shall wait your orders as to the disposal of two lacks of rupees. How far my former and the present services may entitle me to your good opinion, and to your acquiescence in thus rewarding me, is left to the generosity of your Honours: but I beg that you will believe, that during the course of my services, every thing of a similiar nature shall be laid before you.

If it were possible to satisfy the avidity of a body of men, this little army would have a sufficency of honour and profit to fill the most greedy; but the infirmities of nature are not to be controuled by reason. Avarice of the most pernicious tendency has pervaded the limits of sense, and stepped beyond the bounds of duty. The army, not content with acquiring, at the different places, that has been taken on the coast in ships of war, naval stores, merchandize, &c. &c. and in goods of various kinds at Bidanore, which altogether the Jemadar says may be valued at thirty lacks of pagodas; they seek to deprive the Jemadar of his private property, under pretence of the lawful rights of war; and assume a style and manner in their clamours and united addresses, that appears intended to force from me what I think ought to be preserved for the public service, and for the benefit of the Honourable Company. The manner that the fort and city was delivered to the company, does not authorise me to touch private property; and the cowl implies a perfect securtiy for all such. Would your honours be pleased, that by any rapacious action of your Commander in Chief, that he or the troops should forfeit the good opinion that may be entertained of them from their rapid success, or that the public service should be considered as a secondary object? Our name has fallen almost to contempt, but, as far as lays in my power, it shall be recovered, if not raised to its former eminence.

Mangalore, March 16, 1783.

www.ingramcontent.com/pod-product-compliance
Lightning Source LLC
Chambersburg PA
CBHW030604300426
44111CB00009B/1091